OLE 2

Programmer's Reference

VOLUME TWO

Creating
Programmable
Applications with
OLE Automation

Microsoft
PRESS

PUBLISHED BY
Microsoft Press
A Division of Microsoft Corporation
One Microsoft Way
Redmond, Washington 98052-6399

Library of Congress Cataloging-in-Publication Data
Microsoft OLE 2 programmer's reference.
         p.   cm.
    Includes index.
    Contents: Contents: v. 1. Introduction and API reference -- v.
2. Creating programmable applications with OLE automation.
    ISBN 1-55615-628-6 (v. 1). -- ISBN 1-55615-629-4 (v. 2)
    1. Windows (Computer programs)   2. Microsoft Windows (Computer
file)   I. Microsoft Corporation.   II. Title: OLE 2 programmer's
reference.
QA76.76.W56M52325   1993
005.4'3--dc20   93-36458
                                                        CIP

Printed and bound in the United States of America.

 2 3 4 5 6 7 8 9 AG-M 9 8 7 6 5

Distributed to the book trade in Canada by Macmillan of Canada, a division of Canada Publishing Corporation.

Distributed to the book trade outside the United States and Canada by Penguin Books Ltd.

Penguin Books Ltd., Harmondsworth, Middlesex, England
Penguin Books Australia Ltd., Ringwood, Victoria, Australia
Penguin Books N.Z. Ltd., 182-190 Wairau Road, Auckland 10, New Zealand

British Cataloging-in-Publication Data available.

Printed in the United States of America.

Contents

Introduction

This document provides procedural and reference information for OLE
Automation. While OLE Automation runs on other platforms, such as the
Windows NT™ operating system and the Apple® Macintosh® system, the focus of
this book is applications that use the Microsoft® Windows™ operating system,
version 3.1.

To get the most out of this book, you should be familiar with:

- The C++ programming language concepts.
- The Microsoft Windows programming environment, version 3.1 or later. The
  OLE protocols are implemented through dynamic-link libraries (DLLs) that
  are used in conjunction with other Microsoft Windows programs.
- The OLE 2 component object model. This model is the foundation of OLE. It
  is explained in depth by the books described in the following section.

Other Books and Technical Support

OLE Automation is part of OLE 2, which provides mechanisms for in-place
activation, visual editing, structured file storage, and many other application
features. These other parts of OLE 2 are fully described by two books:

- *OLE 2 Programmer's Reference, Volume 1* describes the component object
  model, in-place activation, visual editing, structured file storage, and
  application registration in terms of the APIs and interfaces provided by OLE 2.
- *Inside OLE 2* by Kraig Brockschmidt provides an introduction and how-to
  information about implementing OLE 2 objects and containers.

If you are interested in OLE 2 features other than OLE Automation, you should
consider reading these two books, particularly *Inside OLE 2*. If you are only
interested in OLE Automation, this book and the OLE 2 SDK should answer all
your questions.

Technical support for OLE Automation is provided through a forum on
Compuserve. To access this forum, type **GO WINOBJ** at any Compuserve
prompt. Once you are in the forum, ask your question in Section 8.

Document Conventions

The following conventions are used throughout this book:

Typographical Convention	Meaning
Bold	Indicates a word that is a function name or other fixed part of the Microsoft Windows and OLE Application Programming Interface. For example, **OleSave** is an OLE-specific function. These words must always be typed exactly as they are printed.
italic	Indicates a word that is a placeholder or variable. For example, *ClassName* would be a placeholder for any OLE object class name. Function parameters in API reference material are italic to indicate that any variable name can be used. In addition, first time use of OLE terms are italicized to highlight their definition.
UPPERCASE	Indicates MS-DOS® file names and paths as well as constants. For example, C:\WINDOWS\SYSTEM\OLE2.H is an MS-DOS path and filename. WM_DESTROY is a Windows constant.
monospace	Indicates source code and syntax spacing. For example:

```
typedef struct _APPSTREAM
{
   OLESTREAM    olestream;
   int          fh;
} APPSTREAM;
```

Note The interface syntax in this book follows the variable-naming convention known as Hungarian notation, invented by programmer Charles Simonyi. Variables are prefixed with lower-case letters indicating their data type. For example, *lpszNewDocname* would be a long pointer to a zero-terminated string named *NewDocname*. See *Programming Windows* by Charles Petzold for more information about Hungarian notation.

CHAPTER 1

Overview of OLE Automation

OLE Automation is a way to manipulate an application's objects from outside that application. OLE Automation uses OLE's component object model, but may be implemented independently from the rest of OLE. Using OLE Automation, you can:

- Create applications that expose objects to programming tools and macro languages.
- Create and manipulate objects exposed in one application from another application.
- Create tools that access and manipulate objects. These tools can include embedded macro languages, external programming tools, object browsers, and compilers.

The objects an application exposes are called *OLE Automation objects*. Applications and programming tools that access those objects are called *OLE Automation controllers*. OLE Automation objects and controllers interact like this:

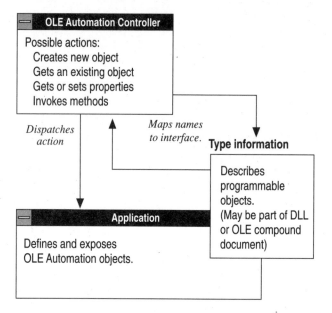

Why Expose Objects?

Exposing objects provides a way to operate your application's tools programmatically. This allows your customers to use a programming tool to automate repetitive tasks that you could not anticipate.

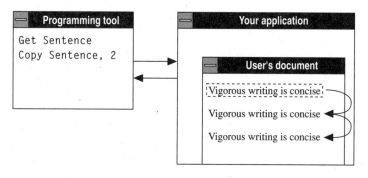

OLE Automation offers advantages over implementations of macro languages included within some applications:

- Exposed objects from many applications are available in a single programming environment. In this way, systems integrators can bring together the best pieces from different applications and can create completely new, specialized applications out of existing pieces.

- Exposed objects are accessible from any macro language or programming tool that implements OLE Automation. Customers may choose a programming tool based on their current knowledge, rather than learning a new language for each application.

- Object names can remain consistent across versions of an application.

- Object names can automatically conform to the user's national language.

What Is an OLE Automation Object?

An *OLE Automation object* is an instance of a class within your application that you wish to manipulate programmatically, such as with a macro language. These may be new classes whose sole purpose is to collect and expose data and functions in a way that makes sense to your customers. In an application that manages documents, the OLE Automation objects might look like this diagram:

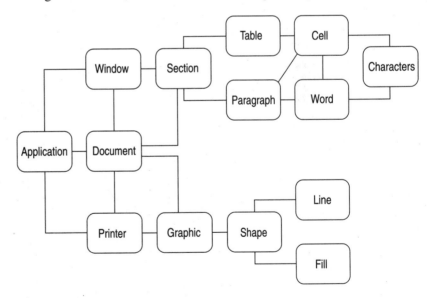

Each of the objects in the illustration has member functions that uniquely apply to that object. The object becomes programmable when you expose those member functions. OLE Automation defines two types of members that you may expose for an object:

- *Methods* are member functions that perform an action on an object. For example, a Document object might provide a Print method.

- *Properties* are member function pairs that set or return information about the state of an object. For example, a Drawing object might have a Color property.

For example, the following objects could be exposed by implementing the listed methods and properties for each object:

OLE Automation object	Methods	Properties
Application	Help Quit Save Repeat Undo	ActiveDocument Application Caption DefaultFilePath Documents Height Name Parent Path Printers StatusBar Top Value Visible Width
Document	Activate Close NewWindow Print PrintPreview RevertToSaved Save SaveAs	Application Author Comments FullName Keywords Name Parent Path ReadOnly Saved Subject Title Value

To provide access to more than one instance of an object, expose a collection object. A *collection object* manages other objects. All collection objects support iteration over the objects they manage. For example, an application with a multiple document interface (MDI) might expose a Documents collection object with the following methods and properties:

Collection object	Methods	Properties
Documents	Add	Application
	Close	Count
	Item	Parent
	Open	

Guidelines for organizing and naming the OLE Automation objects your applications exposes are described in Chapter 4, "Standards and Guidelines."

Components of OLE Automation

OLE Automation includes components used to create applications that expose objects and components used to create programming tools that access those objects.

The following table describes the interfaces, functions, and tools used to create applications that expose OLE Automation objects.

Item	Description	Reference material
Dispatch interfaces	**IDispatch**, **IEnumVariant**, dispatch functions and data manipulation functions (OLE2DISP.DLL).	Chapter 5
Data manipulation functions	Functions for creating and manipulating variants, arrays, and strings (OLE2DISP.DLL).	Chapter 6
Object Description Language	Language read by MkTypLib to compile type libraries.	Chapter 7
Type library functions	Functions for loading and registering type libraries.	Chapter 8
National language support	String comparison functions for objects, properties, and methods provided in more than one language (OLE2NLS.DLL).	Chapter 10

Item	Description	Reference material
OLE testing tools	DispTest OLE Automation controller and the OLE 2 custom control.	Chapter 11

The following table describes the interfaces used to create programming tools that access OLE Automation objects.

Item	Description	Reference material
Type description interfaces	**IITypeLib**, **ITypeInfo**, and type information functions (TYPELIB.DLL).	Chapter 8
Type information building interfaces	**ICreateTypeLib** and **ICreateTypeInfo** interfaces (TYPELIB.DLL).	Chapter 9

Components for Creating OLE Automation Objects

Dispatch interfaces and functions are used by the widest audience. They let you expose OLE Automation objects and provide a standard implementation of functions to access exposed objects:

Interface	Implemented by	Purpose
IDispatch	Applications that expose objects.	Accesses objects exposed within an application.
Dispatch functions	OLE2DISP.DLL	Create and retrieve type information on objects and invoke methods and properties.
IEnumVARIANT	Applications that expose collection objects.	Iterate over collection objects exposed within an application.
Type library functions	TYPELIB.DLL	Accesses type libraries.

Data manipulation functions create and manipulate strings, arrays, and variant data types. Data manipulation functions are provided by OLE2DISP.DLL.

National language support functions provide a way to evaluate and act on language differences. This allows programmers to provide localized object, method, property, and argument names for their applications that expose objects. National language support functions are provided by OLE2NLS.DLL.

Automation tools are used when developing applications that expose objects:

Automation tool	Purpose
DISPTEST.EXE	Tests objects exposed in an application by manipulating them with Visual Basic language constructs.
MKTYPLIB.EXE	Builds type libraries from interface descriptions.

Components for Creating OLE Automation Controllers

Type description interfaces are used by OLE Automation controllers that read compiler or object browser type libraries:

Interface	Implemented by	Purpose
ITypeInfo	TYPELIB.DLL	Gets information about the members of an object described in an object library.
ITypeLib	TYPELIB.DLL	Gets information about the set of objects contained in an object library.

The type building interfaces are used to write programming tools that create type libraries:

Interface	Implemented by	Purpose
ICreateTypeInfo	TYPELIB.DLL	Creates type information within a type library.
ICreateTypeLib	TYPELIB.DLL	Creates a type library.
ITypeComp	TYPELIB.DLL	Provides a fast way to access information compilers need when binding to and instantiating data types and interfaces.

Creating OLE Automation Objects

The following figure shows the interfaces and member functions you need to implement in order to expose OLE Automation objects:

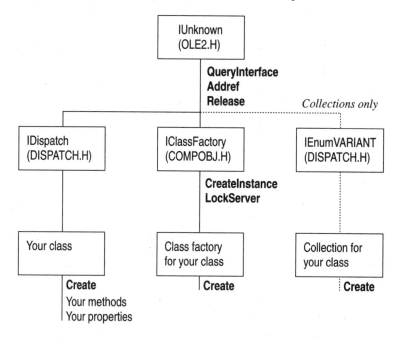

The member functions you must implement are shown in **bold**. The interfaces (**IUnknown**, **IDispatch**, **IClassFactory**, and **IEnumVARIANT**) are defined in the indicated header files. The following table describes the purpose of each interface.

Interface	Purpose
IUnknown	Defines a set of member functions that identify and keep track of exposed objects. All OLE objects derive from **IUnknown**.
IClassFactory	Defines a set of member functions to allow OLE to create objects.
IDispatch	Defines a set of member functions to allow OLE Automation to get information about your application's objects and to invoke methods and get or set properties.
IEnumVARIANT	Defines a set of member functions you must implement to expose collections of objects.

For more information about these interfaces and the services they provide, see Chapter 2, "Exposing OLE Automation Objects."

Files You Need

To expose OLE Automation objects, you need the following files which are provided with OLE. The file names shown in **bold** are required by your application at run time.

File names	Purpose
OLE2DISP.DLL, OLE2DISP.LIB, DISPATCH.H	Accesses OLE Automation objects by invoking methods and properties.
TYPELIB.DLL	Accesses type libraries.
OLE2NLS.DLL, OLE2NLS.LIB, OLENLS.H	Facilitates string comparisons based on the user's national language. These files are only required if you support multiple national languages.
MKTYPLIB.EXE	Builds type libraries from interface descriptions.
OLE2.REG	Registers OLE and OLE Automation.
OLE2.DLL, OLE2.LIB, OLE2.H	Provides OLE functions which may be used by OLE component objects or containers.
COMPOBJ.DLL, COMPOBJ.LIB, COMPOBJ.H	Supports component object creation and access.
OLE2PROX.DLL	Coordinates object access across processes.

Steps to Exposing Objects

When you implement OLE Automation in your application, you must write code to initialize your objects, implement the objects, and reset OLE when your application terminates.

▶ **To initialize your exposed objects**

1. Initialize OLE.

2. Register the classes of your exposed objects.

3. Initializes the active object.

▶ **To implement your exposed objects**

1. Write the classes for your exposed objects.

2. Create your type information.

3. Create a registration file (.REG) for your application.

▶ **To reset OLE when your application terminates**

1. Release the class objects and revoke the active object.

2. Reset OLE.

These tasks are described in greater detail in Chapter 2, "Exposing OLE Automation Objects."

Creating OLE Automation Controllers

There are several strategies for accessing OLE Automation objects:

- Use existing OLE Automation controllers, such as Microsoft Visual Basic or DispTest, to create packaged scripts.

- Write code within an application that accesses another application's objects through OLE Automation.

- Create new OLE Automation controllers, such as compilers or type information browsers, that support OLE Automation.

- Revise existing programming tools, such as an embedded macro language, to become OLE Automation controllers.

The following figure shows the interfaces you use when accessing exposed objects through DispTest.

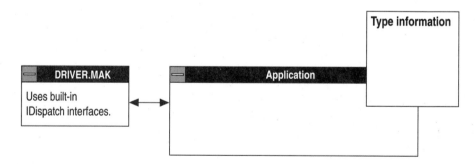

The following figure shows the interfaces you use when you create compilers or browsers that access type libraries.

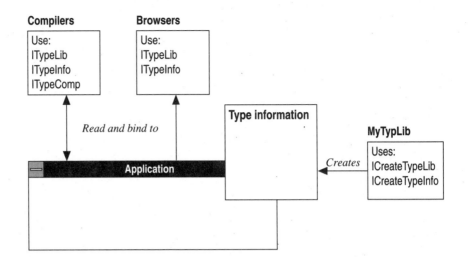

Files You Need

To access OLE Automation objects, you need the following files which are provided with OLE. The file names shown in **bold** are required by your programming tool at run time.

File names	Purpose
DISPTEST.EXE DISP200.DLL MSOLE2.VBX MSOLE2.BAS VB.HLP AUTOLOAD.MAK	Accesses exposed objects using Visual Basic language constructs. Use these files when testing applications that expose objects as described in the next section, "Packaging Scripts Using DISPTEST.EXE."
TYPELIB.DLL	Accesses type libraries.
OLE2.REG	Registers OLE and OLE Automation.
OLE2DISP.DLL	Provides functions for creating objects and retrieving active objects at run time.
OLE2.DLL OLE2.LIB OLE2.H	Provides OLE functions which may be used by OLE objects or containers.
OLE2PROX.DLL	Coordinates object access across processes.
COMPOBJ.DLL COMPOBJ.LIB COMPOBJ.H	Supports object creation and access.
STORAGE.DLL STORAGE.LIB STORAGE.H	Supports access to subfiles, such as type libraries, within compound documents.

Packaging Scripts Using DISPTEST.EXE

To help you get a feel for manipulating your objects programmatically, OLE Automation provides DispTest (DISPTEST.EXE). DispTest lets you create programs that access and manipulate your application's OLE Automation objects.

You can call programs written with DispTest directly from an application that exposes its objects. This figure shows how this was done for the sample program DISPCALC.EXE:

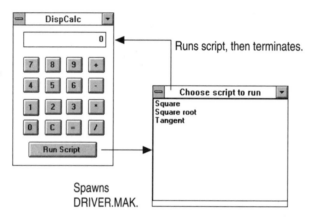

▶ **To access an exposed object from DispTest**

1. Start DispTest.

2. Add code to declare a variable of the type **Object**. For example:

   ```
   Dim Calculator As Object
   ```

3. Add code in an event procedure to create an instance of the object and to manipulate the object using its properties and methods. For example:

   ```
   Sub Form_Click ( )
       Set Calculator = CreateObject("Dispcalc.CCalc")
       For x = 1 to 9
           Calculator  = x              ' Set object's default property
           Calculator.Op OP_MULTIPLY    ' Invoke Op method.
       Next x
   End Sub
   ```

4. From the Run menu, choose Start and trigger the event. (In this case, click the form.)

For more information on creating packaged scripts with DispTest, see Chapter 3, "Accessing OLE Automation Objects," and Chapter 7, "Object Description Language." For the syntax and semantics of the language used by DispTest, see the Help file VB.HLP.

Packaging Scripts Using Microsoft Visual Basic

Microsoft Visual Basic, version 3.0 or later, improves upon DispTest. DispTest is intended as a tool for testing programmable interfaces; Visual Basic provides a complete development environment for creating stand-alone applications.

Visual Basic supports all of the language constructs used by DispTest and includes the following improvements over DispTest:

- Lets you create and access databases.
- Lets you create stand-alone .EXE files.
- Provides superior run-time performance.
- Includes more complete documentation.

This document describes accessing OLE Automation objects using DispTest, however all of the procedures and code shown for DispTest also work with Visual Basic.

Creating Applications and Tools that Access Objects

OLE Automation provides interfaces for accessing exposed objects from an application or programming tool written in C or C++. When you access exposed objects using C or C++, initialize the object, manipulate methods and properties, and release OLE when your application or programming tool terminates.

▶ **To initialize your exposed objects**

1. Initialize OLE.
2. Create an instance of the exposed object.

▶ **To manipulate methods and properties**

1. Get the method and property IDs from the object's type information.
2. Invoke the methods and properties.

▶ **To release OLE when your application or programming tool terminates**

1. Release the object.
2. Release OLE.

These tasks are described in greater detail in Chapter 3, "Accessing OLE Automation Objects."

C H A P T E R 2

Exposing OLE Automation Objects

When you implement OLE Automation in your application, you must write code to do the following tasks:

- Initialize your exposed objects.
- Implement your exposed objects.
- Release OLE when the application terminates.

This chapter provides a quick overview of this procedure, then describes these tasks in detail using the Hello, DispCalc, and SPoly2 sample applications for demonstration. Throughout this chapter, the file name for the example precedes the example in parentheses.

1 Initialize

```
OleBuildVersion
OLEInitialize
CoRegisterClassObject
RegisterActiveObject
LoadTypeLib
```

2 Implement

```
ObjectCF :: IClassFactory
Object :: IDispatch
Object :: Member Functions
Type Information
Registration file
```

3 Release

```
RevokeActiveObject
CoRevokeClassObject
OLEUninitialize
```

"Hello World" Example

The fastest way to implement OLE Automation objects is to use the standard implementation of **IDispatch** that OLE Automation provides through the dispatch function **CreateStdDispatch**. The following sections demonstrate how you expose a simple class. The code shown is abridged to emphasize the essential parts; see the Hello sample in the OLE 2 SDK for a complete listing.

Initializing Class ID

In a header file, define and allocate the class IDs for the top-level OLE Automation objects and the application's type library. OLE provides the DEFINE_GUID macro to do this. For example (CLSID.H):

```
DEFINE_GUID(CLSID_CHelloTypeLib, 0x3F480E00, 0x83B9, 0x1067, 0x1E, 0xF1,
0x00, 0xDD, 0x01, 0x0E, 0xDF, 0x02););
DEFINE_GUID(CLSID_CHello, 0x3F490E00, 0x84A9, 0x1068, 0x9C, 0xF1, 0x00,
0xDD, 0x01, 0x0E, 0xDF, 0x05););
```

The class ID is the mechanism by which OLE identifies objects and type libraries within the system. Class IDs appear in the system registration database (.REG). You generate GUIDs by running GUIDGEN.EXE provided in the OLE 2 SDK.

Initializing OLE

When your application starts, verify the OLE version, initialize OLE, and initialize the class. For example (MAIN.CPP):

```
HRESULT hresult;
DWORD g_dwHelloCF = 0;
IClassFactory FAR* pcf;
DWORD g_dwRegistered = 0;

        DWORD dwVer = OleBuildVersion();

    // check to see if we are compatible with this version of the
    // libraries. Constants rmm and rup are defined in OLE2.H
    if (HIWORD(dwVer) != rmm || LOWORD(dwVer) < rup)
        OutputDebugString("*** WARNING: Not compatible with current
libraries ***\r\n");

hresult = OleInitialize(NULL)

pcf = CHelloCF::Create()

// Initialize the class.
hresult = CoRegisterClassObject( CLSID_CHello, pcf, CLSCTX_LOCAL_SERVER,
                                 REGCLS_MULTIPLEUSE, &g_dwHelloCF);

pcf->Release();
```

The preceding code checks the version of the OLE DLLs using the **OleBuildVersion** function. Then it initializes the OLE DLLs using **OleInitialize** and the default memory allocator (indicated by the parameter NULL). It then creates an instance of the object's class factory and then registers the class factory with OLE using the **CoRegisterClassObject** function.

CoRegisterClassObject tells OLE which classes OLE can create. You only need to create a class factory and call **CoRegisterClassObject** for OLE Automation objects that can be created from OLE Automation controllers. Most applications provide this ability for their Application and Document objects.

Initializing the Active Object

When your application creates its instance, initialize the active object. For example (MAIN.CPP):

```
BOOL InitInstance(HANDLE hinst, int nCmdShow)
{
    CHello FAR* phello;

    if((phello = CHello::Create()) == NULL)
    return FALSE;

// Omitted conditional code that parses command line.
    // Initialize this object as active object.
    hresult = RegisterActiveObject(phello, CLSID_CHello, NULL,
              g_dwRegister);

    // . . . code omitted here . . .
    return TRUE;
}
```

Registering an active object lets OLE Automation controllers retrieve an object that is already running, rather than creating a new instance.

Implementing IUnknown

As with all other OLE 2 objects, you must create the object's **IUnknown** interface. For example (HELLO.CPP):

```
STDMETHODIMP CHello::QueryInterface(REFIID riid, void FAR* FAR* ppv)
{
    if(riid == IID_IUnknown){
      *ppv = this;
    }else
    if(riid == IID_IDispatch){
      return m_punkStdDisp->QueryInterface(riid, ppv);
    }else
      return ResultFromScode(E_NOINTERFACE);
```

```
        AddRef();
        return NOERROR;
}

STDMETHODIMP_(ULONG) CHello::AddRef() { . . . }
STDMETHODIMP_(ULONG) CHello::Release() { . . . }
```

Implementing IClassFactory

Create the object's class factory. For example (HELLO.CPP):

```
IClassFactory FAR* CHelloCF::Create()
{
    return new FAR CHelloCF();
}


STDMETHODIMP CHelloCF::CreateInstance(IUnknown FAR* punkOuter,
    REFIID riid, void FAR* FAR* ppv)
{
extern CHello FAR* g_phello;
    return g_phello->QueryInterface(riid, ppv);
}


STDMETHODIMP CHelloCF::QueryInterface(. . .) {. . .}
STDMETHODIMP_(ULONG) CHelloCF::AddRef() { . . . }
STDMETHODIMP_(ULONG) CHelloCF::Release() { . . . }
STDMETHODIMP CHelloCF::LockServer(. . .) { . . . }
```

A class factory is a class which is capable of creating other instances of a class. In the preceding example, CHelloCF can create instances of CHello. The class factory is used earlier in this section with **CoRegisterClassObject**.

Implementing IDispatch

Load the object's type information and create the **IDispatch** interface. For example (HELLO.CPP):

```
CCalc FAR* CHello::Create()
{   // Note: error checking code omitted.
    HRESULT hresult;
    CHello FAR* phello;
    ITypeInfo FAR* ptinfo;
    IUnknown FAR* punkStdDisp;
extern DWORD g_dwRegister;

    phello = new FAR CHello()

// Load type information from the type library.
```

```
    hresult = LoadRegTypeLib(CLSID_CHelloTypeLib, wMajorVer, wMinorVer,
            LANG_ENGLISH, &ptlib);

// Get a pointer to the loaded type information.
    hresult = ptlib->GetTypeInfoOfGuid(CLSID_CHello, &ptinfo);

// Create a standard IDispatch interface from the type information.
    hresult = CreateStdDispatch(punkController, phello, ptinfo,
                                &punkStdDisp);

    ptinfo->Release();

    return punkStdDisp;
}
```

Creating the Type Information

Describe the object's type information using the object description language
(ODL) and compile the description to create a type library. This code shows the
description for CHello's properties and methods (HELLO.ODL). This
information is compiled using MkTypLib to create a type library
(HELLOTL.TLB) and a header file (HELLOTL.H).

```
// HELLOTL.ODL to compile, use the following command line:
// MKTYPLIB /tlb hellotl.tlb /h hellotl.h hellotl.odl
//
[  uuid(4561EB60-8D30-1068-9CF5-00DD010EDF05),
   helpstring("A simple OLE Automation sample.")]
library Hello
{
    importlib("c:\\ole2\\rel\\stdole.tlb");

    [     // The uuid for the interface IID_IHello.
     uuid(51BDC280-8BAA-1068-9CF4-00DD010EDF05),
     helpstring("Hello")    ]
    [odl]
    interface _IHello : IUnknown
    {      [propput]
          void HelloMsg([in] BSTR b);
       [propget, helpstring("The message to display.")]
          BSTR HelloMsg();
          BSTR SayHello(void);    }

    [ // The uuid for the class we expose.  Same as registry
      // entry for hello.hello
      uuid(3F490E00-84A9-1068-9CF1-00DD010EDF05),
      helpstring("An object that displays a message.")    ]
    coclass Hello
    {      interface _IHello;    }
};
```

Releasing Objects and OLE

When your application ends, release the class factory, active object, and OLE. For example (Hello sample, MAIN.CPP):

```
if(g_dwCHelloCF != 0)
    CoRevokeClassObject(g_dwCHelloCF);

hresult = RevokeActiveObject(gw_Register, NULL);

OleUninitialize();
```

CoRevokeClassObject tells OLE that the object is no longer available for creation. **OLEUninitialize** tells OLE that this application is no longer using the OLE DLLs. (If no other applications are using the DLLs, they are unloaded from memory.)

Creating a Registration File

Create an OLE registration file for your application. The system registration database contains a list of all the OLE objects contained in your system. OLE uses this database to locate objects and to determine their capabilities. For example (HELLO.REG):

```
REGEDIT
; registration info Hello.Application (defaults to Hello.Application.1)
HKEY_CLASSES_ROOT\Hello.Application = OLE Automation Hello Application
HKEY_CLASSES_ROOT\Hello.Application\Clsid = {D3CE6D43-F1AF-1068-9FBB-08002B32372A}


; registration info Hello.Application.1
HKEY_CLASSES_ROOT\Hello.Application.1 = OLE Automation Hello 1.0 Application
HKEY_CLASSES_ROOT\Hello.Application.1\Clsid = {D3CE6D43-F1AF-1068-9FBB-08002B32372A}


; registration info Hello 1.0
HKEY_CLASSES_ROOT\CLSID\{D3CE6D43-F1AF-1068-9FBB-08002B32372A} = IDispatch Hello Example
HKEY_CLASSES_ROOT\CLSID\{D3CE6D43-F1AF-1068-9FBB-08002B32372A}\ProgID = Hello.Application.1
HKEY_CLASSES_ROOT\CLSID\{D3CE6D43-F1AF-1068-9FBB-08002B32372A}\VersionIndependentProgID =
Hello.Application
HKEY_CLASSES_ROOT\CLSID\{D3CE6D43-F1AF-1068-9FBB-08002B32372A}\LocalServer = hello.exe
/Automation


; registration info Hello TypeLib
HKEY_CLASSES_ROOT\TypeLib\{D3CE6D44-F1AF-1068-9FBB-08002B32372A}
HKEY_CLASSES_ROOT\TypeLib\{D3CE6D44-F1AF-1068-9FBB-08002B32372A}\1.0 = OLE Automation Hello
1.0 Type Library
HKEY_CLASSES_ROOT\TypeLib\{D3CE6D44-F1AF-1068-9FBB-08002B32372A}\1.0\HELPDIR =
HKEY_CLASSES_ROOT\TypeLib\{D3CE6D44-F1AF-1068-9FBB-08002B32372A}\1.0\409\win32 = hello.tlb
HKEY_CLASSES_ROOT\TypeLib\{D3CE6D44-F1AF-1068-9FBB-08002B32372A}\1.0\409\win16 = hello.tlb
```

This registration entry should be merged with the system registration database when your customer installs your application. To merge the preceding file with the registration database, use the following command line:

```
regedit hello.reg
```

Note If you are developing your application in C, you must also initialize the VTBLs to the OLE interfaces your application supports. For information on how to do this, see the *OLE 2 Programmer's Reference, Volume 1*.

Limitations of the "Hello World" Example

The "Hello World" example was simplified for demonstration purposes. It has the following limitations:

- Uses only scalar argument types. OLE Automation also supports methods and properties that accept arguments of complex types including: arrays, references to objects, and formatted data.

- Does not raise user-defined exceptions on **Invoke**. The **CreateStdDispatch** function provides predefined exception codes.

- Does not expose a collection of objects. Collections are supported through the **IEnumVARIANT** interface.

- Supports one national language. **CreateStdDispatch** does not accommodate multiple localized member names.

The rest of this chapter explains the preceding steps and these more advanced features in greater detail.

Creating Class IDs

You need a unique class ID (CLSID) for each object you expose for creation. CLSIDs are universally unique identifiers (UUIDs, also called GUIDs). Run the UUIDGEN utility included in the OLE \TOOLS directory to generate UUIDs.

Exposing a class for creation means that an instance of the object may be created directly through OLE Automation. For example, an application may expose one top-level object for creation, but have many other programmable objects that can be created or destroyed by referencing the top-level object. In this case, only the top-level object needs a class factory.

The CLSID identifies the object to OLE and is included in your application and must be registered with the user's system when your application is installed. OLE provides the DEFINE_GUID macro to define a CLSID within your application.

For example:

```
DEFINE_GUID(CLSID_CHello, 0x3F490E00, 0x84A9, 0x1068, 0x9C, 0xF1, 0x00,
0xDD, 0x01, 0x0E, 0xDF, 0x05);
```

Initializing OLE

OLE2.DLL provides functions to initialize OLE for your application and to initialize your application's objects for creation using OLE Automation.

▶ **To initialize OLE**

1. Check the registration database to verify that your application is registered and, if it isn't, register your application.
2. Verify the OLE version by calling **OLEBuildVersion**.
3. Initialize the OLE DLLs by calling **OLEInitialize**.
4. Create an instance of each class factory you expose.
5. Call **CoRegisterClassObject** for each class your application exposes for creation.

The following example initializes OLE, then registers the CPoly class using its class factory (SPOLY.CPP):

```
HRESULT
InitOle() {
    HRESULT hresult;

    hresult = OleInitialize(NULL);
    if(hresult != NOERROR)
      goto LExit;

    // Register the CPoly Class Factory.
    g_ppolyCF = CPolyCF::Create();
    if(g_ppolyCF == NULL){
      hresult = ReportResult(0, E_OUTOFMEMORY, 0, 0);
      goto LReleaseCPointCF;
    }

    hresult = CoRegisterClassObject(
      CLSID_CPoly2,
      g_ppolyCF,
      CLSCTX_LOCAL_SERVER,
      REGCLS_MULTIPLEUSE,
```

```
            &g_dwPolyCF);
        if(hresult != NOERROR)
            goto LReleaseCPolyCF;

        g_ppolyCF->Release();

        return NOERROR;

LReleaseCPolyCF:;
        g_ppolyCF->Release();

LUninitOle:;
        UninitOle();

LExit:;
        return hresult;
}
```

The *OLE 2 Programmer's Reference, Volume 1* provides more information on the **OLEBuildVersion**, **OLEInitialize**, and **CoRegisterClassObject** functions. *Inside OLE 2* provides more information on checking the OLE build version and verifying your application's entries in the registration database.

Initializing the Active Object

OLE2DISP.DLL provides these functions to identify and retrieve the running instance of an object or application through OLE Automation:

- **RegisterActiveObject**—Sets the active object for an application. (Use when application starts.)

- **RevokeActiveObject**—Revokes the active object. (Use when application ends.)

- **GetActiveObject**—Retrieves a pointer to the object that is active. (In DispTest, this is implemented by the **GetObject** function.)

You use these functions to initialize your application's objects as they are created at run time. Applications can have more than one active object at a time. In order to be initialized as the active object, an object must:

- Have a class factory (that is, the object provides an interface for creating instances of itself).

- Identify its class factory by a ProgID in the system registry.

- Run **RegisterActiveObject** when the object is created or becomes active.

- Run **RevokeActiveObject** when they the object is deactivated or closed.

Every application should have one top-level object called the *Application object*. This allows tools that access the application's programmable interface to do several things:

- Bind to the application if it is already running, as with the DispTest **GetObject** function.

- Create a new instance of the application, as with the DispTest **CreateObject** function.

- Treat the application as an available prenamed object that exposes functionality.

- Navigate the objects provided by an application.

OLE defines two command-line switches that may be used when starting an application:

- /Embedding—indicates that an application was started by an OLE container application.

- /Automation—indicates that the application was started for programmatic access.

Only expose your Application object's class factory if the application is launched with the /Automation switch. Expose it using the REGCLS_SINGLEUSE attribute. OLE will launch your application with the /Automation switch if your registration entry contains the /Automation switch.

When a multiple document interface (MDI) application starts up, it will generally register the class factories for each of the objects it creates that can be linked or embedded so that when instances of those objects need to be created, the existing application instance will be used. Because each new Application object requires a new instance of the application to be launched, the rules are somewhat different here. If the application registered its class factory every time it was launched, the next **CreateObject** call that tried to create the application would get an existing copy.

The following chart shows how applications should expose their Application and document objects.

Command line	MDI application	SDI application
/Embedding	Expose class factories for document classes, but not for the application.	Expose class factories for document class, but not for the application.
	Call **RegisterActiveObject** for the Application object.	Call **RegisterActiveObject** for the active object.

Command line	MDI application	SDI application
/Embedding /Automation	Expose class factories for document classes.	Expose class factory for the Application object using **RegisterClassObject**.
	Expose class factory for the application using **RegisterClassObject**.	Do not expose class factory for document class.
	Call **RegisterActiveObject** for the Application object.	Call **RegisterActiveObject** for the active object.
No OLE switches	Expose class factories for document classes, but not for the application.	Call **RegisterActiveObject** for the active object.
	Call **RegisterActiveObject** for the Application object.	

Creating the IUnknown Interface

IUnknown defines three member functions you must implement for each object you expose. The prototypes for these functions reside in COMPOBJ.H:

- **QueryInterface**—identifies which OLE interfaces the object supports.
- **AddRef**—increments a member variable that tracks the number of references to an object.
- **Release**—decrements the member variable that tracks the instances of an object. If an object has zero references, **Release** frees the object.

These functions provide an interface by which OLE can access your objects. Implement these functions according to the requirements discussed in the *OLE 2 Programmer's Reference, Volume 1.*

The implementation for the CPoly object looks like this (CPOLY.CPP):

```
STDMETHODIMP CPoly::QueryInterface(REFIID riid, void FAR* FAR* ppv)
{
    if(riid == IID_IUnknown || riid == IID_IDispatch){
      *ppv = this;
      AddRef();
      return NOERROR;
    }
    *ppv = (void FAR*)NULL;
    return ResultFromScode(E_NOINTERFACE);
}

STDMETHODIMP_(ULONG) CPoly::AddRef()
{
    return ++m_refs;
}

STDMETHODIMP_(ULONG) CPoly::Release()
```

```
{
      POLYLINK FAR* FAR* pppolylink, FAR* ppolylinkDead;

    if(--m_refs == 0){
      Reset(); // release all CPoints

      for( pppolylink = &g_ppolylink;
      *pppolylink != NULL;
       pppolylink = &(*pppolylink)->next)
      {
    if((*pppolylink)->ppoly == this){
      ppolylinkDead = *pppolylink;
      *pppolylink = (*pppolylink)->next;
      delete ppolylinkDead;
      break;
    }
      }

      if(m_ptinfo != NULL){
        m_ptinfo->Release();
      }

      if(--g_cPoly == 0){
        if(g_fExitOnLastRelease)
      PostQuitMessage(0);
      }

      SBprintf(g_psb, "#poly = %d", g_cPoly);

      delete this;
      return 0;
    }
    return m_refs;
}
```

Exposing Objects for Creation with IClassFactory

Before OLE Automation can create an object, it must create the object's class.
IClassFactory creates an instance of an object's class, so that instances of the
object may be created.

You need to implement **IClassFactory** when an object may be created explicitly
using OLE Automation. For example, application should expose an Application
object for creation, but have many other programmable objects that can be created
or destroyed by referencing the Application object. In this case, only the
Application object needs a class factory.

You need to implement two member functions for each class factory. The prototypes for these functions reside in COMPOBJ.H.

- **CreateInstance**—creates an instance of the object's class.
- **LockServer**—prevents the object's class from being released, even if the last instance of an object is released. This can improve performance if an application creates and releases objects frequently.

These member functions provide services for OLE API functions. The implementation for the CPoly object looks like this (CFPOLY.CPP):

```
CPolyCF::CPolyCF()
{
    m_refs = 0;
}

CPolyCF::~CPolyCF()
{
}

IClassFactory FAR* CPolyCF::Create()
{
    CPolyCF FAR* pCF;

    if((pCF = new FAR CPolyCF()) == NULL)
      return NULL;
    pCF->AddRef();
    return pCF;
}

STDMETHODIMP CPolyCF::CreateInstance(
    IUnknown FAR* pUnkOuter,
    REFIID iid,
    void FAR* FAR* ppv)
{
    HRESULT hresult;
    CPoly FAR *ppoly;

    if((ppoly = CPoly::Create()) == NULL){
      *ppv = NULL;
      return ResultFromScode(E_OUTOFMEMORY);
    }
    hresult = ppoly->QueryInterface(iid, ppv);
    ppoly->Release();
    return hresult;
}

STDMETHODIMP CPolyCF::LockServer(BOOL fLock)
{
    return NOERROR;
}
```

The object's class factory must also implement an **IUnknown** interface. For example (CFPOLY.CPP):

```
STDMETHODIMP CPolyCF::QueryInterface(REFIID iid, void FAR* FAR* ppv)
{
    if(iid == IID_IUnknown || iid == IID_IClassFactory){
      *ppv = this;
      ++m_refs;
      return NOERROR;
    }
    *ppv = NULL;
    return ResultFromScode(E_NOINTERFACE);
}

STDMETHODIMP_(ULONG) CPolyCF::AddRef(void)
{
    return ++m_refs;
}

STDMETHODIMP_(ULONG) CPolyCF::Release(void)
{
    if(--m_refs == 0){
      delete this;
      return 0;
    }
    return m_refs;
}
```

The class factory implementation of **IUnknown** should always look very similar to the preceding example.

Note Class factories are described more extensively in the *OLE 2 Programmer's Reference, Volume 1* and in *Inside OLE 2*.

Creating the IDispatch Interface

IDispatch provides a mechanism to get information about an object's methods and properties. In addition to the member functions inherited from **IUnknown**, you need to implement the following member functions within the class definition of each object you expose through OLE Automation:

- **GetTypeInfoCount**— This function is reserved for future use. For objects that support **IDispatch**, the type information count is always 1.
- **GetTypeInfo**—retrieves a description of the object's programmable interface.
- **GetIDsOfNames**—maps the name of a method or property to a dispatch ID used when invoking the method or property.
- **Invoke**—accesses the object's methods and properties.

You may implement **IDispatch** at one of three levels:

- By calling the **CreateStdDispatch** function.
- By adding the member functions to your class and delegating to the **DispInvoke** and **DispGetIDsOfNames** functions.
- Or by implementing the member functions without delegating to the dispatch functions.

Implementing IDispatch by CreateStdDispatch

Using **CreateStdDispatch** is the fastest way to implement the IDispatch interface for an object. It is useful if your OLE Automation object uses only the standard dispatch exception codes and supports one national language.

The **CreateStdDispatch** function used in the DspCalc2 sample on the OLE 2 SDK implements these member functions for the CCalc object by calling **CreateStdDispatch** on the loaded type information (DSPCALC2.CPP):

```
if((hresult = LoadTypeLib(TLB_NAME, &ptlib)) != NOERROR){
    MessageBox(NULL, "error loading type library", "dspcalc2", MB_OK);
    goto LError0;
    }

if((hresult = ptlib->GetTypeInfoOfGuid(IID_ICalculator, &ptinfo)) !=
NOERROR){
    MessageBox(NULL, "error accessing type information", "dspcalc2",
MB_OK);
    goto LError0;
    }
```

```
hresult = CreateStdDispatch(
    pcalc,                // controlling unknown
    &pcalc->m_arith,      // vtable* to dispatch on
    ptinfo,
    &punkStdDisp);

hresult = CreateStdDispatch(pcalc, &pcalc->m_arith, ptinfo,
    &punkStdDisp);
```

Implementing IDispatch by Delegating

Delegating to the **DispInvoke** and **DispGetIDsOfNames** allows your object to handle special situations before or after calling the provided functions. Using **DispInvoke** and **DispGetIDsOfNames** allows you to support multiple national languages and to create application-specific exceptions that are passed back to OLE Automation controllers.

The SPoly2 sample application implements the **IDispatch** interface using the dispatch functions **DispInvoke** and **DispGetIDsOfNames** (CPOLY.CPP):

```
STDMETHODIMP CPoly::Invoke(
    DISPID dispidMember,
    REFIID riid,
    LCID lcid,
    unsigned short wFlags,
    DISPPARAMS FAR* pdispparams,
    VARIANT FAR* pvarResult,
    EXCEPINFO FAR* pexcepinfo,
    unsigned int FAR* puArgErr)
{
    if(riid != IID_NULL)
        return ResultFromScode(DISP_E_UNKNOWNINTERFACE);

    return DispInvoke(
        this, m_ptinfo,
        dispidMember, wFlags, pdispparams,
        pvarResult, pexcepinfo, puArgErr);
}

STDMETHODIMP CPoly::GetTypeInfoCount(UINT FAR* pctinfo)
{
    *pctinfo = 1;
    return NOERROR;
}

STDMETHODIMP CPoly::GetTypeInfo(UINT itinfo, LCID lcid,
    ITypeInfo FAR* FAR* pptinfo)
{
    if(itinfo != 0)
```

```
        return ResultFromScode(DISP_E_BADINDEX);

    m_ptinfo->AddRef();
    *pptinfo = m_ptinfo;

    return NOERROR;
}

STDMETHODIMP CPoly::GetIDsOfNames(
    REFIID riid,
    char FAR* FAR* rgszNames,
    UINT cNames,
    LCID lcid,
    DISPID FAR* rgdispid)
{
    if(riid != IID_NULL)
        return ResultFromScode(DISP_E_UNKNOWNINTERFACE);

    return DispGetIDsOfNames(m_ptinfo, rgszNames, cNames, rgdispid);
}
```

Implementing IDispatch Without the Dispatch Functions

Implementing **IDispatch** without using **CreateStdDispatch**, **DispInvoke**, or
DispGetIDsOfNames provides complete control. This approach allows you to
create an implementation that best suits the needs of your application. For
example, you may want to create your own implementations of the dispatch
functions to handle consistently recurring needs within your application.

The SPoly sample implements **GetIDsOfNames** and **Invoke** without using the
dispatch functions (CPOLY.CPP):

```
STDMETHODIMP CPoly::GetIDsOfNames(
    REFIID riid,
    char FAR* FAR* rgszNames,
    UINT cNames,
    LCID lcid,
    DISPID FAR* rgdispid)
{
static PARAMDESC rgpdAddPoint[] = {
    {"X",         IDPARAM_CPOLY_ADDPOINT_X},
    {"Y",         IDPARAM_CPOLY_ADDPOINT_Y}
};
static MEMBERDESC rgmdCPoly[] = {
    {"DRAW",        IDMEMBER_CPOLY_DRAW,     NULL,          0},
    {"RESET",        IDMEMBER_CPOLY_RESET,         NULL,        0},
    {"ADDPOINT", IDMEMBER_CPOLY_ADDPOINT, rgpdAddPoint,    2},
    {"ENUMPOINTS",  IDMEMBER_CPOLY_ENUMPOINTS,  NULL,      0},
    {"GETXORIGIN",  IDMEMBER_CPOLY_GETXORIGIN,  NULL,      0},
```

```
                     {"SETXORIGIN",   IDMEMBER_CPOLY_SETXORIGIN,   NULL,      0},
                     {"GETYORIGIN",   IDMEMBER_CPOLY_GETYORIGIN,   NULL,      0},
                     {"SETYORIGIN",   IDMEMBER_CPOLY_SETYORIGIN,   NULL,      0},
                     {"GETWIDTH",IDMEMBER_CPOLY_GETWIDTH, NULL,        0},
                     {"SETWIDTH",IDMEMBER_CPOLY_SETWIDTH, NULL,        0},
                     {"GETRGB",       IDMEMBER_CPOLY_GETRGB,        NULL,      0},
                     {"SETRGB",       IDMEMBER_CPOLY_SETRGB,        NULL,      0},
                     {"DUMP",     IDMEMBER_CPOLY_DUMP,      NULL,        0}
              };
          if(riid != IID_NULL)
              return ResultFromScode(DISP_E_UNKNOWNINTERFACE);


          return SPolyGetIDsOfNames(
              rgmdCPoly, DIM(rgmdCPoly), rgszNames, cNames, lcid, rgdispid);
      }
      STDMETHODIMP CPoly::Invoke(
          DISPID dispidMember,
          REFIID riid,
          LCID lcid,
          WORD wFlags,
          DISPPARAMS FAR* pdispparams,
          VARIANT FAR* pvarResult,
          EXCEPINFO FAR* pexcepinfo,
          UINT FAR* puArgErr)
      {
          HRESULT hresult;
          VARIANTARG varg0, varg1;
          VARIANT varResultDummy;

          if(riid != IID_NULL)
              return ResultFromScode(DISP_E_UNKNOWNINTERFACE);

          // This makes the following code a bit simpler if the caller
          // happens to be ignoring the return value.
          if(pvarResult == (VARIANTARG FAR*)NULL)
              pvarResult = &varResultDummy;

          VariantInit(&varg0);
          VariantInit(&varg1);

          // Assume the return type is void, unless we find otherwise.
          VariantInit(pvarResult);

          switch(dispidMember){
          case IDMEMBER_CPOLY_DRAW:
            Draw();
            break;

      // . . . case statements omitted here . . .

          case IDMEMBER_CPOLY_GETRGB:
            V_VT(pvarResult) = VT_I4;
```

```
      V_I4(pvarResult) = GetRGB();
      break;

  case IDMEMBER_CPOLY_SETRGB:
      hresult = DispGetParam(pdispparams, 0, VT_I4, &varg0);
      if(hresult != NOERROR)
        return hresult;
      SetRGB(V_I4(&varg0));
      break;

  default:
      return ResultFromScode(DISP_E_MEMBERNOTFOUND);
  }
  return NOERROR;
}
```

Creating the Programmable Interface

An object's programmable interface is its defined set of properties and methods. Organizing the objects, properties, and methods that an application exposes is akin to creating an object-oriented framework for an application. Chapter 4, "Standards and Guidelines" discusses some of the concepts behind naming and organizing the programmable elements your application may expose.

Creating Methods

A method performs an action on an object and may or may not return a value. Like C-language functions, methods can take any number of arguments, any of which may be optional. Arguments may be passed by value or by reference.

In the SPoly2 sample, the class for the CPoly object includes the Draw method shown below (CPOLY.CPP):

```
void PASCAL __export CPoly::Draw()
{
    HDC hdc;
    RECT rect;
    short xorg, yorg;
    HPEN hpen, hpenOld;
    POINTLINK FAR* ppointlinkFirst, FAR* ppointlink;

    if((ppointlinkFirst = m_ppointlink) == (POINTLINK FAR*)NULL)
      return;

    GetClientRect(g_hwndClient, &rect);
    xorg = m_xorg + rect.left;
    yorg = m_yorg + rect.top;

    hdc = GetDC(g_hwndClient);
    hpen = CreatePen(PS_SOLID, m_width, m_rgb);
```

```
hpenOld = SelectObject(hdc, hpen);
MoveTo(hdc,
   xorg + ppointlinkFirst->ppoint->m_x,
   yorg + ppointlinkFirst->ppoint->m_y);

for(ppointlink = ppointlinkFirst->next;
ppointlink != (POINTLINK FAR*)NULL;
ppointlink = ppointlink->next)
{
   LineTo(hdc,
xorg + ppointlink->ppoint->m_x,
yorg + ppointlink->ppoint->m_y);
}

LineTo(hdc,
   xorg + ppointlinkFirst->ppoint->m_x,
   yorg + ppointlinkFirst->ppoint->m_y);

SelectObject(hdc, hpenOld);
DeleteObject(hpen);

ReleaseDC(g_hwndClient, hdc);
}
```

Creating Properties

A property represents an attribute of an object. Each property has a pair of accessor functions—a function to get the property value and a function to set the property. Properties may receive arguments, though this is less common than with methods.

The CCalc object exposes the Accum property. This property is implemented by the following member functions (CPOLY.CPP):

```
void _export PASCAL CCalc::CArith::PutAccum(long 1)
{
    m_accum = 1;
}


long _export PASCAL CCalc::CArith::GetAccum()
{
    return m_accum;
}
```

The accessor functions for a single property have the same dispatch ID (DISPID). The purpose of each function is indicated by attributes set for the function. These attributes can be set in the METHODDATA structure or in the ODL description of the function as shown in the following table:

Purpose of function	METHODDATA flag (*wFlags*)	ODL attribute
Return a value	DISPATCH_PROPERTYGET	**propget**
Set a value	DISPATCH_PROPERTYPUT	**propput**
Set a reference	DISPATCH_PROPERTYPUTREF	**propputref**

For example, the following two descriptions are equivalent:

```
// Using METHODDATA -- resides in a file compiled with C compiler
static METHODDATA rgmdataCalc[]
{
    {"Accum", &pdataACCUM, DISPID_VALUE, IMETH_ACCUM, CC_PASCAL, 1, DISPATCH_PROPERTYPUT,
VT_EMPTY},
    {"Accum", 0, DISPID_VALUE, IMETH_ACCUM + 1, CC_PASCAL, 0, DISPATCH_PROPERTYGET, VT_I4}
};

// Using ODL -- resides in .ODL file compiled with MkTypLib.
[id(0), propput]
void Accum([in] long l);
[id(0), propget]
long Accum();
```

Passing Formatted Data

There are many situations where an application may wish to accept some type of formatted data as an argument to a method or property. Examples include a bitmap, formatted text, or a spreadsheet range. To do this, applications should pass an object which implements the OLE **IDataObject** interface.

Using this interface, applications can retrieve data of any Clipboard format from the **IDataObject** object. Since an **IDataObject** can provide data of more than one format, a caller can provide data of several formats, and have the called object choose which format is most appropriate (like the Clipboard).

If the object passed implements **IDispatch**, it should be passed using the VT_DISPATCH flag. If the data object does not support **IDispatch**, it should be passed with the VT_UNKNOWN flag.

The Application Object

Document-based, user-interactive applications that provide OLE Automation objects should expose an Application object.

As previously discussed, the Application object identifies the application and provides a way for OLE Automation controllers to bind to and navigate an application's exposed objects. The Application object is identified by the [appobject] attribute in the object description language (ODL) script.

In addition, the Application object is initialized as the active object when the application starts. See "Initializing the Active Object" earlier in this chapter for details.

See Chapter 4, "Standards and Guidelines," for more on recommended objects, properties, and methods.

The Value Property

The Value property defines the default behavior of an object if no property or method is specified. For example, the following DispTest code returns the default property of the CCalc object. In the case of CCalc, this is the number displayed on the calculator.

```
Dim Calc As Object
Set Calc = CreateObject("DispCalc.CCalc")
Print Calc
```

The Value property is identified by the dispatch ID DISPID_VALUE. In an ODL file, the Value property has the attribute **id**(0).

See Chapter 4, "Standards and Guidelines," for more on recommended objects, properties, and methods.

Returning Objects

To return an object from a property or method, return a pointer to the object's implementation of the **IDispatch** interface. The data type of the return value should be VT_DISPATCH.

Restricting Access

You can restrict access to properties and methods by not providing documentation for the property or method. Furthermore, you can prevent the item from appearing in type library browsers by specifying the **restricted** attribute in ODL or by specifying the flag FUNCFLAG_FRESTRICTED in the FUNCDESC structure for the method or property.

Restricted properties and methods can be invoked by OLE Automation controllers, but are not visible to the end user who may be using languages such as Visual Basic. To restrict access even further, require a password argument for a method that returns an object. The returned object can provide methods and properties to perform actions that should not be available to all customers.

For example:

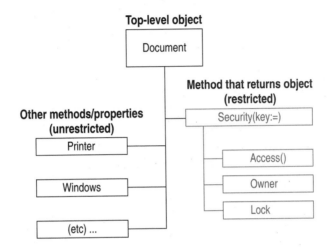

The preceding figure shows the Security method, which returns an object with the method Access and the properties Owner and Lock. Security, Access, Owner, and Lock all have the **restricted** attribute. In addition, the Security method requires an argument, *key*, to gain access to subordinate methods and properties.

Creating Collection Objects

The defining characteristic of a collection object is the ability to iterate over the items it contains. OLE Automation defines the **IEnumVARIANT** interface to provide a standard way for OLE Automation controllers to iterate over collections. In addition, a collection object must expose a _NewEnum method to let OLE Automation controllers know that the object supports iteration.

Implementing IEnumVARIANT

The **IEnumVARIANT** interface provides a way to iterate through the objects contained by a collection object. Collection objects must include this interface in addition to the **IUnknown** and **IDispatch** interfaces discussed in previous sections. Collection objects do not need an **IClassFactory** implementation, since they are built from elements that have their own class factories.

The **IEnumVARIANT** interface defines these member functions:

- **Next**—retrieves one or more elements in a collection, starting with the current element.
- **Skip**—skips over one or more elements in a collection.
- **Reset**—resets the current element to the first element in the collection.
- **Clone**—copies the current state of the enumeration so you can return to the current element after using **Skip** or **Reset**.

In the SPoly2 example, CEnumPoint is the iteration interface for CPoint objects. CEnumPoint implements the following member functions in addition to the member functions inherited from **IUnknown** and **IDispatch** (CENUMPT.CPP):

```
STDMETHODIMP CEnumPoint::Next(
    ULONG celt,
    VARIANT FAR rgvar[],
    ULONG FAR* pceltFetched)
{
    UINT i;
    LONG ix;
    HRESULT hresult;

    for(i = 0; i < celt; ++i)
      VariantInit(&rgvar[i]);

    for(i = 0; i < celt; ++i){
      if(m_iCurrent == m_celts){
        hresult = ReportResult(0, S_FALSE, 0, 0);
      goto LDone;
        }

      ix = m_iCurrent++;
      hresult = SafeArrayGetElement(m_psa, &ix, &rgvar[i]);
      if(FAILED(hresult))
      goto LError0;
      }

    hresult = NOERROR;

LDone:;
```

```
        *pceltFetched = i;

        return hresult;

LError0:;

        for(i = 0; i < celt; ++i)
          VariantClear(&rgvar[i]);

        return hresult;
}


STDMETHODIMP CEnumPoint::Skip(ULONG celt)
{
        m_iCurrent += celt;

        if(m_iCurrent > m_celts)
         m_iCurrent = m_celts;

        return (m_iCurrent == m_celts)
          ? ReportResult(0, S_FALSE, 0, 0) : NOERROR;
}


STDMETHODIMP CEnumPoint::Reset()
{
        m_iCurrent = 0;

        return NOERROR;
}


STDMETHODIMP CEnumPoint::Clone(IEnumVARIANT FAR* FAR* ppenum)
{
        HRESULT hresult;
        SAFEARRAY FAR* psa;
        CEnumPoint FAR* penum;

        hresult = SafeArrayCopy(m_psa, &psa);
        if(FAILED(hresult))
          return hresult;

        hresult = CEnumPoint::Create(psa, &penum);
        if(FAILED(hresult))
          goto LError0;

        // Assert(penum->m_celts == m_celts);
        penum->m_iCurrent = m_iCurrent;

        return NOERROR;
```

```
LError0:
    SafeArrayDestroy(psa);

    return hresult;
}
```

See Chapter 4, "Standards and Guidelines," for more information about collection objects.

Implementing the _NewEnum Method

The _NewEnum method identifies an object as supporting iteration through the **IEnumVARIANT** interface. The _NewEnum method has the following requirements:

- Must be named "_NewEnum" and not be localized.
- Return a pointer to the collection object's IUnknown interface (VT_UNKNOWN)

See Chapter 4, "Standards and Guidelines," for more information about collection objects.

Creating Type Information

Type information is the OLE Automation standard for describing exposed objects, properties, and methods to an application or programming tool that accesses an exposed object. You provide type information as a type library written in Microsoft Object Description Language (ODL) and compiled by MkTypLib or as a data structure exported at run time.

OLE Automation also supports the creation of alternative tools that compile and access type information. See Chapter 9, "Type Building Interfaces," for more information on creating such tools.

The following figure illustrates the differences between exporting type information and creating a type library.

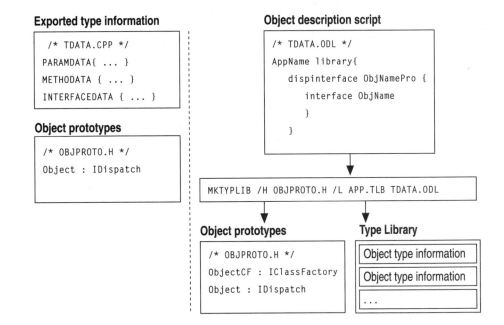

Exported type information

```
/* TDATA.CPP */
PARAMDATA{ ... }
METHODATA { ... }
INTERFACEDATA { ... }
```

Object prototypes

```
/* OBJPROTO.H */
Object : IDispatch
```

Object description script

```
/* TDATA.ODL */
AppName library{
    dispinterface ObjNamePro {
        interface ObjName
        }
    }
```

```
MKTYPLIB /H OBJPROTO.H /L APP.TLB TDATA.ODL
```

Object prototypes

```
/* OBJPROTO.H */
ObjectCF : IClassFactory
Object : IDispatch
```

Type Library

| Object type information |
| Object type information |
| ... |

Type libraries provide more features than type information exported from the application itself. Using type libraries is the standard way to describe a programmable interface. The following table compares the relative advantages of type libraries and exported type information.

Type library	Exported type information
Provides compile-time and run-time access to information.	Provides run-time access only.
Supports browsing and provides Help information on objects, properties, and methods.	Can't be browsed and does not provide Help.
Type information is stored in a file that is separate from the .EXE file. However, the type library may be bound with a DLL using the resource compiler.	Type information is part of the .EXE file or the DLL.

Creating a Type Library

A type library stores complete type information for all of an application's exposed objects. It may be included as a resource in a DLL or remain as a stand-alone file (.TLB).

▶ **To create a type library**

1. Write an object description script for the objects you expose.

2. Build the type library (.TLB) and class description header file (.H) from the script using MkTypLib.

Writing an Object Description Script

An object description script is essentially an annotated header file.

```
[helpfile("SPOLY.HLP"), helpstring("Help for SPOLY objects."),
helpcontext(2475)]

library SPoly {
    [ uuid (906B0CE0-C70B-1067-B317-00DD010662DA),
    version(1.0),helpstring("Help for the object CPoly"),
    helpcontext(2480)]
    dispinterface CPoly {
        properties:
            [id(1)] int xOrigin;          // X, Y Origin properties
            [id(2)] int yOrigin;
            [id(3)] long RGB;             // RGB color value of polygon
            [id(4)] int Width;            // Width polygonmethod
            [id(5)] void Draw(void);      // Draw method
            [id(6)] void Reset(void);
            [id(7)] HRESULT AddPoint([in] short x, [in] short y);
            [id(8)] void Dump(void);      // Debug method
    };
    .
    .                                     // Other objects omitted.
    .

}
```

Note that the AddPoint method has arguments with the [in] attribute. These arguments supply a value and are read-only. If an argument returns a value, it has the [out] attribute. If it supplies and returns a value, specify both attributes.

For more information on the Microsoft Object Description Language, see Chapter 7, "Object Description Language."

Building the Type Library

The MkTypLib tool builds type libraries. Information on this tool's options is available in Chapter 7, "Object Description Language."

▶ **To create a type library from an object description script**

1. From Windows, run the MKTYPLIB tool on the script. For example:

```
MKTYPLIB /TLB output.tlb /H output.h inscript.odl
```

Note that MkTypLib requires Windows. If you run it from NMAKE, you must use the WX server support provided with OLE. For example, start WXSRVR in Windows and use the following command line in your NMAKE script:

```
WX MKTYPLIB /o odlscrip.err /TLB output.tlb /h output.h inscript.odl
```

Alternately, you can add the MkTypLib tool to the Tools menu in the Microsoft C programming environment. If you do this, be sure to check the Arguments check box, so the programming environment will prompt you for the options and input file before running the tool.

After creating the type library (.TLB), you can include it in the resource step of building your application or leave it as a stand-alone file. In either case, the resulting file name must be included in the registration file. See the section "Creating a Registration File" later in this chapter for information on registering the type library.

▶ **To build an application using a type library**

1. Include the header file output by MKTYPLIB in your project.

2. Compile the project.

3. Optionally, bind the type library with your compiled project using the Resource Compiler. You can bind the type library with DLLs, but not with .EXE files.

The following figure shows an example of this process.

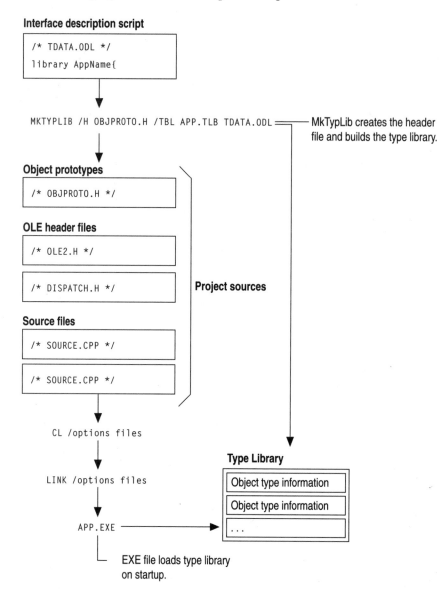

Interface description script

```
/* TDATA.ODL */
library AppName{
```

`MKTYPLIB /H OBJPROTO.H /TBL APP.TLB TDATA.ODL` — MkTypLib creates the header file and builds the type library.

Object prototypes

```
/* OBJPROTO.H */
```

OLE header files

```
/* OLE2.H */
```

```
/* DISPATCH.H */
```

Project sources

Source files

```
/* SOURCE.CPP */
```

```
/* SOURCE.CPP */
```

`CL /options files`

`LINK /options files`

`APP.EXE`

Type Library

| Object type information |
| Object type information |
| ... |

EXE file loads type library on startup.

Exporting Type Information from Your Application

You export type information by creating C data definitions, and by compiling and linking those definitions with your application. Type information exported from an application is a subset of the information available in a type library.

The data structures you must create are:

- INTERFACEDATA—information about the interface (in this case, the class CPoly).
- METHODDATA—each element contains information about a method or property in an interface.
- PARAMDATA—each element contains information about one argument for a method or property.

The following examples are shown in reverse order from the way they must appear in source code. It is easier to discuss them in this order.

```
INTERFACEDATA g_idataCPoly =
{
    rgmdataCPoly, DIM(rgmdataCPoly)
};
```

The METHODDATA structure for the Draw method is included in the rgmdataCPoly[] array. This array contains all of the methods for the CPoly object.

```
static METHODDATA rgmdataCPoly[] =
{
    // void CPoly::Draw(void)
    {
    "Draw",                 // Name.
    NULL,                   // Pointer to array of parameters.
    IDMEMBER_CPOLY_DRAW, // Member ID.
    IMETH_CPOLY_DRAW,       // Method index.
    CC_PASCAL,              // Calling convention.
    0,                      // Number of arguments.
    DISPATCH_METHOD,        // Property/method flag.
    VT_EMPTY                // Return type.
    },
    .
    .          // Structures for other members omitted.
    .
};
```

If the Draw method took an argument, its type information would also include a PARAMDATA structure, as shown for the X and Y properties in the next example.

To expose a property, you define the same structures as for a method. Each accessor function has a flag set in the METHODDATA structure to identify whether it gets or sets the property. For example:

```
static PARAMDATA rgpdataCPointSetX[] =
{
    { "X",  IDPARAM_CPOINT_SETX_X,  VT_I2 }
};

static PARAMDATA rgpdataCPointSetY[] =
{
    { "Y",  IDPARAM_CPOINT_SETY_Y,  VT_I2 }
};

static METHODDATA rgmdataCPoint[] =
{
    // CPoint::GetX()
    {
    "X",
    NULL,
    IDMEMBER_CPOINT_GETX,
    IMETH_CPOINT_GETX,
    CC_PASCAL,
    0,
    DISPATCH_PROPERTYGET,        // Flag -- get property.
    VT_I2
    },

    // CPoint::SetX()
    {
    "X",
    rgpdataCPointSetX,
    IDMEMBER_CPOINT_SETX,
    IMETH_CPOINT_SETX,
    CC_PASCAL,
    DIM(rgpdataCPointSetX),
    DISPATCH_PROPERTYPUT,        // Flag -- set property.
    VT_EMPTY
    },
    .
    .              // Other properties omitted.
    .
};

INTERFACEDATA g_idataCPoint =
{
    rgmdataCPoint, DIM(rgmdataCPoint)
};
```

In order to translate these data definitions into type information, you must call **CreateDispTypeInfo** when you create the first instance of an object. For example:

```
CPoly FAR* CPoly::Create()
{
    HRESULT hresult;
    CPoly FAR* ppoly;
    ITypeInfo FAR* ptinfo;
    POLYLINK FAR* ppolylink;
    extern INTERFACEDATA g_idataCPoly;

    if((ppolylink = new FAR POLYLINK) == (POLYLINK FAR*)NULL)
      return (CPoly FAR*)NULL;
    if((ppoly = new FAR CPoly()) == (CPoly FAR*)NULL)
      return (CPoly FAR*)NULL;

    ppoly->AddRef();

    // create and attach its TypeInfo
    hresult = CreateDispTypeInfo(&g_idataCPoly, LOCALE_SYSTEM_DEFAULT,
        &ptinfo);
    if(hresult != NOERROR)
      goto LError0;

    ppoly->m_ptinfo = ptinfo;
    ppoly->m_lcid = LOCALE_SYSTEM_DEFAULT;

    // Push the new polygon onto the front of the polygon list.
    ++g_cPoly;
    ppolylink->ppoly = ppoly;
    ppolylink->next = g_ppolylink;
    g_ppolylink = ppolylink;
    SBprintf(g_psb, "#poly = %d", g_cPoly);
    return ppoly;
LError0:;
    ppoly->Release();
    return NULL;
}
```

Creating a Registration File

In order to use OLE and OLE Automation, the OLE tools must be registered with the user's system. OLE provides sample registration files to perform this task for OLE tool and the sample applications.

▶ **To create a registration file for your application**

1. Copy DISPCALC.REG.

2. Rename and edit the file: add entries for your application's type information.

The following sections describe the syntax used for registering OLE Automation applications.

Registering Classes (Objects)

The registration file uses this syntax for each class of each object your application

libname.typename = {*UUID*}
\CLSID
    \{*UUID*}=*long_typename*
    \{*UUID*}**LocalServer** =*appname* [/**Automation**]
\{*UUID*}**ProgID** =*libname.typename*

libname
    The name of the type library, as used in the library statement within the application's object description script. For applications that export type information, this is the application's base file name.

typename
    The name of the class as entered in the type library. For applications that export type information, this is the class name used in the application. The programmatic ID *libname.typename* is used by programmer's to access the object identified by this registration database entry.

UUID
    The universally unique ID for the class (CLSID). To generate a universally unique ID for your class, run the utility UUIDGEN.EXE provided in the OLE2 \TOOLS directory.

long_typename
    The spelled-out version of the object's class, as you want it to appear to users in dialogs such as the Insert Object dialog included by many applications.

appname
> The full file name of the application that contains the object. The optional /Automation switch tells the application it was launched for automation purposes. For more information on /Automation, see the section "Initializing the Active Object" earlier in this chapter.

Naming Programmatic IDs

The programmatic ID (ProgID) you create in the system registry should follow consistent naming guidelines across all of your applications.

Version Independent

AppName.ObjectName

For example: Word.Document, Excel.Sheet.

Version Dependent

AppName.ObjectName.vnumber

For example: Word.Basic.v6

Registering Type Library Information

In addition to entering a programmability name for each class, applications that support programmability need to register their type libraries. All type library information is registered under the top level key **\TypeLibs**. The information registered for a type library is as follows:

\TypeLib   ·
> \{*libUUID*}=
>> **\DIR**=*typelib_path*
>> *major.minor*=*localized_typelib_filename*
>> **\HELPDIR**=*helpfile_path*
>> *LCID*=*localized_typelib_filename*

libUUID
> The universally unique ID of the type library.

major.minor
> This is a two-part version number of the type library. If only the minor version number increases, all the features of the previous type library are supported in a compatible way. If the major version number changes, code that compiled against the type library must be recompiled. This version number is probably different from the version number of the application since the application will make every attempt to stay compatible and not have to change the major version number.

localized_typelib_filename
> The full name of the localized type library.

helpfile_path
> The directory where the Help file(s) for the types in the type library can be found. Note that if type libraries for multiple languages are shipped, they may refer to different file names in this directory.

LCID
> This is a hexadecimal string representation of the locale ID (LCID). It is 4 hexadecimal digits with no 0x prefix. The application can explicitly register the file names of type libraries for different languages. This allows a client to find the language they want without having to open all type libraries with a given name. The LCID may have a neutral sublanguage. A client who wants to find the type library for Australian English (0x0309) would first look for 0x0309 and, if that fails, see if there is an entry for Standard English (0x0009). If there is no entry for Standard English, the client looks for the LANG_SYSTEM_DEFAULT (0x0000). For more information on LCIDs and locale support, see Chapter 10, "National Language Support Functions."

Note You can generate the correct registration entries for a type library by calling the **LoadTypeLib** function on the type library. You can then use REGEDIT to write the registration entries to a text file from your system registration database.

Registration File Example

DSPCALC2 uses the following entries to register it's Application object (CCalc) and it's type library (DSPCALC.TLB) with the system (DSPCALC2.REG):

```
REGEDIT

; registration info DspCalc2.Application (defaults to DspCalc2.Application.1
HKEY_CLASSES_ROOT\Dspcalc2.Application = OLE Automation Dspcalc2 Application
HKEY_CLASSES_ROOT\Dspcalc2.Application\Clsid = {00020469-0000-0000-C000-000000000046}

; registration info DspCalc2.Application.1
HKEY_CLASSES_ROOT\Dspcalc2.Application.1 = OLE Automation Dspcalc2 1.0 Application
HKEY_CLASSES_ROOT\Dspcalc2.Application.1\Clsid = {00020469-0000-0000-C000-000000000046}

; registration info DspCalc2 1.0
HKEY_CLASSES_ROOT\CLSID\{00020469-0000-0000-C000-000000000046} = OLE Automation Dspcalc2
1.0 Application
HKEY_CLASSES_ROOT\CLSID\{00020469-0000-0000-C000-000000000046}\ProgID =
Dspcalc2.Application.1
```

```
HKEY_CLASSES_ROOT\CLSID\{00020469-0000-0000-C000-000000000046}\VersionIndependentProgID =
Dspcalc2.Application
HKEY_CLASSES_ROOT\CLSID\{00020469-0000-0000-C000-000000000046}\LocalServer = dspcalc2.exe
/Automation

; registration info DspCalc2 TypeLib
HKEY_CLASSES_ROOT\TypeLib\{00020470-0000-0000-C000-000000000046}
HKEY_CLASSES_ROOT\TypeLib\{00020470-0000-0000-C000-000000000046}\1.0 = OLE Automation
DspCalc2 1.0 Type Library
HKEY_CLASSES_ROOT\TypeLib\{00020470-0000-0000-C000-000000000046}\1.0\HELPDIR =
;Localized language is US english
HKEY_CLASSES_ROOT\TypeLib\{00020470-0000-0000-C000-000000000046}\1.0\409\win16 =
DSPCALC2.TLB
HKEY_CLASSES_ROOT\TypeLib\{00020470-0000-0000-C000-000000000046}\1.0\409\win32 =
DSPCALC2.TLB

HKEY_CLASSES_ROOT\Interface\{00020442-0000-0000-C000-000000000046} = _DCalculator
HKEY_CLASSES_ROOT\Interface\{00020442-0000-0000-C000-000000000046}\ProxyStubClsid =
{00020420-0000-0000-C000-000000000046}
HKEY_CLASSES_ROOT\Interface\{00020442-0000-0000-C000-000000000046}\NumMethod = 7
HKEY_CLASSES_ROOT\Interface\{00020442-0000-0000-C000-000000000046}\BaseInterface =
{00020400-0000-0000-C000-000000000046}
```

Releasing OLE

▶ **To release OLE on exit**

1. Release active object by calling **RevokeActiveObject**.

2. Release the classes of your exposed objects by calling **CoRevokeClassObject**.

3. Reset OLE by calling **OleUninitialize**.

The following code releases CPoint and CPoly classes, then unloads OLE:

```
void UninitOle()
{
    RevokeActiveObject(g_dwRegister, NULL);

    // Tell OLE to release our class factory.
    if(g_dwPolyCF != 0L)
      CoRevokeClassObject(g_dwPolyCF);

    OleUninitialize();
}
```

Supporting Multiple National Languages

It is likely that an application will expose a set of objects whose members have names that differ across localized versions of the product. This poses a problem for programming languages that want to access such objects because it means that late binding will be sensitive to the locale of the application. The **IDispatch** interface has been designed to allow the class implementor a range of solutions which vary in cost of implementation and quality of natural language support. All methods of the **IDispatch** interface that are potentially sensitive to language are passed a locale ID (LCID). See Chapter 10, "National Language Support Functions" for more information on LCIDs.

These are some of the possible approaches a class implementation may take:

- Accept any LCID, and use the same member names in all locales. This is acceptable if the interface being accessed will typically be accessed only by very advanced users. For example, the member names for OLE 2 interfaces will never be localized.

- Accept all LCIDs supported by all versions of the product. This means that the implementation of **GetIDsOfNames** would need to interpret the passed array of names based on the given LCID. This is by far the strongest solution, and means that a user would be able to write code in their natural language and run the code on any localized version of the application.

At the very least, the application must check the LCID before interpreting member names. Also note that **Invoke** is also passed an LCID to enable methods that take parameters whose meaning is dependent on locale the ability to interpret them properly in the caller's national language. For example, a spreadsheet application might interpret the arguments to a SetFormula method differently depending on the LCID.

If you receive an LCID your application does not recognize, your application should use LANG_SYSTEM_DEFAULT (0x0000).

CHAPTER 3

Accessing OLE Automation Objects

Applications that access OLE Automation objects are called *OLE Automation controllers*. OLE Automation controllers can create OLE Automation objects that reside in another application, and they can manipulate those objects using the properties and methods that the OLE Automation object supports.

You can create OLE Automation controllers using DispTest, Microsoft Visual Basic, Microsoft Visual C++, and other programming languages that are compatible with the OLE 2 DLLs.

Note DISPTEST.EXE is a subset of Microsoft Visual Basic, version 3.0. Visual Basic provides a more complete programming environment for creating Windows applications. DispTest is provided for testing OLE Automation objects.

You use the **IDispatch** interface to bind to exposed objects at run time. You use the **ITypeComp** interface to bind to exposed objects when compiling an application.

▶ **Using IDispatch to access exposed objects for OLE Automation involves the following steps:**

1. Initialize OLE.

2. Instantiate the object you wish to access. If the object's application is not yet running, OLE starts it and initializes the object.

3. Obtain a reference to the object's **IDispatch** interface (if it has implemented one).

4. Manipulate the object through the methods and properties exposed in its **IDispatch** interface.

5. Terminate the object by invoking the appropriate method in its **IDispatch** interface.

6. Uninitialize OLE.

This chapter illustrates various ways of accessing OLE objects with the sample application DispCalc. In the next few sections, accessing DispCalc with DispTest is contrasted to accessing it using the OLE interfaces directly.

Manipulating Remote Objects with DispTest

DispTest is a tool, similar to Visual Basic,™ whose programming language manipulates the exposed OLE objects of other applications. Internally, DispTest accomplishes this by using the OLE Automation **IDispatch** interface. Thus it is a good example of the type of programming approach appropriate for end users who are familiar with high-level programming languages, or who use macro languages to automate applications. With DispTest, implementing and initializing the remote object is very straightforward, requiring only the declaration of an object variable and assigning the return of a **CreateObject** or **GetObject** function call to the variable. The syntax for the two appropriate DispTest statements is as follows:

Dim *ObjectVar* **As Object**
Set *ObjectVar* = **CreateObject**(*"ProgID.Objectname"*)
Set *ObjectVar* = **GetObject**(*"Filename"* , *"ProgID.Objectname"*)

Use **Dim** to declare a single variable, or **ReDim** to declare an array of object variables. **GetObject** can be used to reestablish the reference to the most recently used object corresponding to the *Filename* and *Programname.Objectname* specification. For example, if **CreateObject** is used to get a reference to assign a reference to an object in a local variable, **GetObject** could be used to obtain a reference to that object after the original variable has gone out of scope.

The DispCalc sample application included in the OLE 2 SDK accepts only mouse input; it has no keyboard interface. The figure below shows a simple DispTest application called CalcKey that adds a keyboard interface to DispCalc. The form appears as a title bar with a system box. (The form also includes an invisible command button that has no function except to make sure that, when a user presses the Enter key, the message is passed to the CalcKey form.) CalcKey illustrates creation and manipulation of DispCalc from within DispTest.

DispCalc Keypad Enabled

The following CalcKey code manipulates DispCalc at its highest level, through its Button and Quit methods. In Form_Load, CalcRef.accum is set to 0 to illustrate setting a property in the remote object:

```
' Module-level declaration.
Dim CalcRef As Object

Sub Form_Load ()
  Set CalcRef = CreateObject("DISPCALC.ccalc")
    ' Enable form-level key trapping
```

```
      Form.Keypreview = True
        ' Make sure Enter is trapped by making command button the Default
      Command1.Default = True
        ' Clear DispCalc's accumulator by setting the accum property to 0
      CalcRef.accum = 0
End Sub

Sub Form_KeyDown (Keycode As Integer, Shift As Integer)

    If Shift = 1 And Keycode = 187 Then Keycode = 107      ' "+" sign


    ' Figure out which key was pressed and send to DispCalc
    If 12 <= Keycode And Keycode <= 46 Then               ' NumLock not on
        Call ConvertForNumPad(Keycode)                    ' so map keys
    End If
    Select Case Keycode
      Case 96 To 105             ' Keypad w/ Numlock on
        ' Calculate character constant Dispcalc expects
        AsciiChar = Keycode - 48
        'End If
      Case 48 To 57     ' Keyboard number row
        AsciiChar = Keycode
      Case Is = 42, 106
      ' DispCalc"*"
        AsciiChar = 42
      Case Is = 43, 107
      ' DispCalc "+"
        AsciiChar = 43
      Case Is = 45, 109, 189
      ' DispCalc "-"
        AsciiChar = 45
      Case Is = 47, 111, 191, 220
      ' DispCalc "/"
        AsciiChar = 47
      Case Is = 187, 13
      ' DispCalc "="
        AsciiChar = 61
      Case Asc("c"), Asc("C")
        AsciiChar = Asc("c")
      Case Else
        Beep
    End Select
    ' Send the key on to DispCalc
    CalcRef.Button AsciiChar
End Sub

Sub Form_Unload (Cancel As Integer)
      ' If user chooses Close from CalcKey's system box, quits DispCalc.
      CalcRef.Quit
End Sub
```

The preceding code waits for a user to press a key. If Keycode represents a key on the keypad, for example, an equal sign (=), the letter "c" (to clear the calculator), or Enter, the Keycode is converted to an argument appropriate to DispCalc's Button method. (Button looks like a method within the language, but it is defined within the code of the remote object.) The Basic programmer writing this code would need to know the program name and class name of the object, and have documentation of the object's Button and Quit methods in order to call them appropriately. For example, the documentation would need to specify the precise name of the Button and Quit method and the type of any arguments expected. If the object being accessed provides a type library, you could also obtain information needed to access the object by viewing the type library with an object browser similar to the browser TIBROWSE or OLE2VIEW provided as a sample in the OLE 2 SDK.

The following sections show C++ code that uses the same type of access method as the preceding code, but without benefit of DispTest's powerful **CreateObject** and **GetObject** statements.

Accessing Remote Objects Using OLE Interfaces

This section discusses using OLE interfaces to directly access a remote object like DispCalc. Although more complicated than the preceding DispTest code, the approach is similar. Note, however, that this section shows the minimum code necessary to access and manipulate a remote object. A more object-oriented approach is shown in the sample application DispDemo, in which a class mirrors the remote object.

From a C/C++ program, the **CoCreateInstance**, **IUnknown::QueryInterface**, and **IDispatch::GetIDsOfNames** functions shown in the following table can be used to specify, initialize, and prepare to manipulate a remote object. **OleInitialize** and **OleUninitialize** are necessary to start and release OLE.

Function	Purpose	Interface
OleInitialize	Initializes OLE.	OLE API function.
CoCreateInstance	Creates an instance of the class represented by the specified class ID (CLSID_CCalc in the code below). Also places a pointer to the **IUnknown** interface in a caller-allocated variable (punk in code below) to use in a **QueryInterface** call.	Component object API function.

Function	Purpose	Interface
QueryInterface	Call **QueryInterface** on the interface pointed to by the punk obtained from **CoCreateInstance**. When you specify IID_IDispatch, **QueryInterface** checks that **IDispatch** has been implemented for the object, and if so, places a pointer in a caller-allocated variable (pdisp in code below) to the **IDispatch** implementation for the remote object.	**IUnknown.**
GetIDsOfNames	Uses the **IDispatch** pointer from **QueryInterface** to give access to the dispids for names of exposed properties, methods, and their parameters.	**IDispatch.**
Invoke	Executes the method, or sets or gets the property in or from the remote object.	**IDispatch.**
Release	Decrements the reference count for an **IUnknown** or **IDispatch** object.	**IUnknown.**
OleUninitialize	Releases the OLE connection.	OLE API function.

The following fragments could appear in a windows or QuickWin type program, but the function must be preceded by the #include directives shown. Error checking is omitted to save space, but would normally be used where an HRESULT is returned. The macro DEFINE_GUID places a universally unique ID in the CLSID type variable CLSID_CCalc which is passed to **CoCreateInstance**.

```
#include <windows.h>

#include <ole2.h>
#include <compobj.h>
DEFINE_GUID(CLSID_CCalc, 0x00020467, 0x84A9, 0x1068, ,0xF1, 0x00, 0xDD,
0x01, 0x0E, 0xDF, 0x05)
#include <dispatch.h>
#include <olenls.h>

#include "calc.h"

void sendnumbers(void)
{
    int count, buttoncode ;
    HRESULT hresult;
    IUnknown FAR* punk;
    IDispatch FAR* pdisp = (IDispatch FAR*)NULL;
    char FAR* pbpushName = "Button";            // Button method name
    char FAR* pquitName = "Quit";               // Quit method name
```

```
char FAR* paccumName = "Accum";                    // Accum property name
char FAR* pdisplayName = "Display";                // Display method name
DISPID dispidBUTTON;               //Dispatch ID for Button method
DISPID dispidQUIT;                 //Dispatch ID for Quit method
DISPID dispidACCUM;                //Dispatch ID for Accum property
DISPID dispidDISPLAY;              //Dispatch ID for Display method
 // Use this for methods that expect no arguments
DISPPARAMS dispparamsNoArgs = {NULL, NULL, 0, 0};
DISPPARAMS dispparams;
VARIANTARG varg[1] ; // Single element array to hold variant arg

// Initialize OLE
hresult = OleInitialize(NULL);
if (hresult != NOERROR)
  goto EndAll;

// Pass in the DispCalc class ID & retrieve pointer to IUnknown
hresult = CoCreateInstance(CLSID_CCALC, NULL,
        CLSCTX_LOCAL_SERVER, IID_IUnknown, (void FAR* FAR*)&punk);

// Use the punk to find out if IDispatch is implemented for DispCalc
hresult = punk->QueryInterface(IID_IDispatch,
                                (void FAR* FAR*)&pdisp);

// Release the pointer to IUnknown
punk->Release();

// Retrieve a dispatch ID for the Button method
  hresult = pdisp->GetIDsOfNames(
    IID_NULL,
    &pbpushName,
    1, LOCALE_SYSTEM_DEFAULT,
    &dispidBUTTON) ;
```

.
.
.

After **GetIDsOfNames** supplies the appropriate dispatch ID, you can operate DispCalc by calling its Button method with **Invoke**. However, since Button takes an argument you need to fill a DISPPARAMS structure to pass as the last argument to invoke. DISPPARAMS structures have the following form:

```
typedef struct tagDISPPARAMS DISPPARAMS;
struct tagPARAMS{
    VARIANTARG * rgvarg;        // Array of arguments
    DISPID * rgdispidNamedArgs; // dispids of named arguments
    UINT cArgs;                 // Number of arguments
    UINT cNamedArgs;            // Number of named arguments
};
```

The named arguments fields are discussed elsewhere, and do not apply to DispCalc. The cArgs field specifies the count of positional arguments; the rgvarg field is a pointer to an array of VARIANTARG structures. Each element of the array specifies one of the arguments whose position in the array corresponds to its position in the parameter list of the method definition. Although VARIANTARG has five fields, only the first and fifth are used. The first specifies the argument's type, and the fifth specifies its actual value.

```
typedef struct tagVARIANTARG  {
    VARTYPE vt;
    WORD wReserved1;
    WORD wReserved2;
    WORD wReserved3;
    union {
        short iVal;                // VT_I2
  .
  .    // The rest of this union specifies numerous other types
  .

    };
} VARIANTARG;
```

To call DispCalc's Button method, the vt and iVal fields of the VARIANTARG rgvarg structure are filled with VT_I2 (short integer) and the actual value of the argument (initialized below to 0). NULL and 0 are assigned to the named argument fields, and 1 is assigned to cArgs, the field representing the count of positional arguments. Continuing with the sendnumber function shown above, significant DISPPARAMS fields are filled; then **Invoke** is called:

.
.
.

```
VariantInit(&varg); // Initialize variant.
// First put together the initial DISPPARAMS type parameter list
dispparams.rgvarg = &varg;              // Put address in VARIANTARG
dispparams.rgvarg[0].vt = VT_I2;        // Put type in VARIANTARG
dispparams.rgvarg[0].iVal = 0;          // Put value in VARIANTARG
dispparams.rgdispidNamedArgs = NULL;    // Don't use named args
dispparams.cArgs = 1;                   // Only one positional arg
dispparams.cNamedArgs = 0;              // No named args

// Codes for number buttons = ASCII char codes for numbers 1-9
buttoncode = 48;                        // ACCII code for zero

// Call invoke with a different ASCII char code each iteration
for (count = 1; count < 9; count++){          // Start for loop
    // Put a new value into the argument
    dispparams.rgvarg[0].iVal = buttoncode + count;

// Call Invoke on DispCalc's IDispatch implementation --- Each call
// puts another number into the DispCalc's display: 123456789
    hresult = pdisp->Invoke(
    dispidBUTTON,
    IID_NULL,
    LOCALE_SYSTEM_DEFAULT,
    DISPATCH_METHOD,
    &dispparams, NULL, NULL, NULL);
}                                            // End of for loop
```

.
.
.

You can also access DispCalc's properties and other exposed methods, for example, the Accum property (the calculator's accumulator) and the Display method (which displays the accumulator). Setting or retrieving a property is similar to invoking a method, except that the fourth argument to **Invoke** has to specify one of the following: DISPATCH_PROPERTYPUT, DISPATCH_PROPERTYGET, or DISPATCH_PROPERTYPUTREF. Note that the same DISPPARAMS structure can be used since the type of the argument is the same; a new value is simply assigned to the rgvarg[0].ival member. The next fragment continues the sendnumber function, but places a value in the accumulator, then displays it:

```
// First retrieve a dispatch ID for the Accum property:
  hresult = pdisp->GetIDsOfNames(
    IID_NULL,
    &paccumName,
    1, LOCALE_SYSTEM_DEFAULT,
    &dispidACCUM) ;

    // Now Use invoke to put a new value in the accum property.
    // First put new value into the dispparam's argument value field
    dispparams.rgvarg[0].iVal = 3;

    // Now call Invoke with DISPATCH_PROPERTYPUT as arg #4
     hresult = pdisp->Invoke(
    dispidACCUM,
    IID_NULL,
    LOCALE_SYSTEM_DEFAULT,
    DISPATCH_PROPERTYPUT,                        // IMPORTANT!
    &dispparams, NULL, NULL, NULL);

// You have to use the Display method to show value in accumulator
// First, retrieve a dispatch ID for the Display method
  hresult = pdisp->GetIDsOfNames(
    IID_NULL,
    &pdisplayName,
    1, LOCALE_SYSTEM_DEFAULT,
    &dispidDISPLAY) ;

// Use invoke to show the new value by calling the Display method
     hresult = pdisp->Invoke(
    dispidDISPLAY,
    IID_NULL,
    LOCALE_SYSTEM_DEFAULT,
    DISPATCH_METHOD,
    &dispparamsNoArgs, NULL, NULL, NULL);
```

```
// Close DispCalc by invoking its Quit method;
//  First retrieve a dispatch ID for the Quit method
  hresult = pdisp->GetIDsOfNames(
    IID_NULL,
    &pquitName,
    1, LOCALE_SYSTEM_DEFAULT,
    &dispidQUIT) ;

     hresult = pdisp->Invoke(
    dispidQUIT,
    IID_NULL,
    LOCALE_SYSTEM_DEFAULT,
    DISPATCH_METHOD,
    &dispparamsNoArgs, NULL, NULL, NULL);

  // Release the calculator; then release OLE
EndAll::;
    pdisp->Release();  // Decrement refcount for the object

    OleUninitialize();
}
```

The preceding code initializes OLE, creates a DispCalc instance, and retrieves a pointer to **IUnknown**. It calls **QueryInterface** on the **IUnknown** pointer (punk) to determine whether **IDispatch** has been implemented for DispCalc. If it has, a pointer to DispCalc's **IDispatch** interface is placed in pdisp. The pdisp pointer is then used to get the dispatch IDs for some DispCalc methods and a property. **Invoke** is called on pdisp to display numbers on DispCalc and terminate DispCalc. To write this code, you need access to several pieces of DispCalc documentation:

- Class ID for DispCalc. Stored in the external variable CLSID_CCalc, this ID is generated with the DEFINE_GUID macro.

- Name of the Button method and whether it expects an integer representing a character constant.

- Name of the Accum property and whether it can be both set and retrieved.

- Name of the Display and Quit methods and whether they expect arguments.

Note Filling in the DISPPARAMS structure can be simplified by using the **DispBuildParams** and **DispFreeParams** functions that appear in the sample application DispDemo. They are declared and defined in the files disphelp.cpp and disphelp.h. Defining dispparamsnoargs simplifies using **Invoke** for a method that has no arguments.

Other OLE Features of DispTest

As shown at the beginning of this chapter, the OLE Automation features of DispTest let you do much more than share data. From within DispTest, you can easily access and manipulate objects that are exposed by other applications. You can use DispTest to orchestrate custom solutions that utilize data and features from applications that support OLE Automation.

Similarly, the OLE toolkit contains an OLE custom control (MSOLE2.VBX) that can be incorporated into DispTest applications to permit using embedded and linked OLE objects in DispTest applications.

Creating an Invisible Object

At the beginning of the chapter, DispTest was used to access and program a keyboard interface for DispCalc to make it easier to use. Some applications may provide objects that are never displayed to the user. For example, a word processing application may expose its spelling checker engine as an object. This object supports a method called **CheckWord** that takes a string as an argument. If the string is spelled correctly, **True** is returned; otherwise, the method returns **False**. If the string is spelled incorrectly, then you could pass it to another (hypothetical) method called **SuggestWord** that takes a misspelled word as an argument and returns a suggestion for its correct spelling. The code might look something like this:

```
Sub CheckSpelling ()
    Dim ObjVar As Object
    Dim MyWord, Result

    MyWord = "potatoe"

    ' Create the object.
    Set ObjVar = CreateObject("WordProc.SpellCheck")

    ' Check the spelling.
    Result = ObjVar.CheckWord MyWord

    ' If False, get suggestion.
    If Not Result Then
        MyWord = ObjVar.SuggestWord MyWord
    End If
End Sub
```

In the above example, the spelling checker is never displayed to the user. Its functionality is exposed through the properties and methods of the spelling checker object.

As shown in the example, you create and reference invisible objects the same way as any other type of object. Use the **CreateObject** function to create the object and then reference the object using an object variable.

Using Existing Objects

Objects can exist on your system in several ways. Applications that create OLE Automation objects can save objects in files on disk. This section shows you how to access objects that already exist on your system.

Accessing Linked and Embedded Objects

You use the OLE control to create and display linked and embedded objects in a DispTest application. Some applications that supply objects support both linking and embedding and OLE Automation. If you use the OLE control to create a linked or embedded object and that object supports OLE Automation, you can access that object's properties and methods in DispTest using the Object property. The Object property returns the object in the OLE control. This property refers to an OLE object in the same way an object variable created using the **CreateObject** or **GetObject** functions refers to the object variable.

For example, an OLE control named Ole1 contains an object that supports OLE Automation. This object has an **Insert** method, a **Select** method, and a Bold property. In this case, you could write the following code to manipulate the OLE control's object:

```
' Insert text in the object.
Ole1.Object.Insert "Hello, world."
' Select the text.
Ole1.Object.Select
' Format the text as bold.
Ole1.Object.Bold = True
```

Activating an Object from a File

In the beginning of this chapter, **GetObject** was used to retrieve a reference to an object that had previously been instantiated with **CreateObject**. Many OLE Automation applications allow the user to save objects in files. For example, a spreadsheet application that supports worksheet objects allows the user to save the worksheet in a file. The same application may support a chart object that the user can also save in a file. You use the **GetObject** function to activate an object that has been saved to a file.

To activate an object from a file, first declare an object variable. You then call the **GetObject** function using the following syntax:

GetObject (*filename*[, *class*])

The *filename* argument is a string containing the full path and name of the file you want to activate. For example, an application named SPDSHEET.EXE creates an object that was saved in a file called REVENUE.SPD. The following code invokes SPDSHEET.EXE, loads the file REVENUE.SPD, and assigns REVENUE.SPD to an object variable:

```
Dim Spreadsheet As Object
Set Spreadsheet = GetObject("C:\ACCOUNTS\REVENUE.SPD")
```

As shown earlier, if the *filename* argument is set to an empty string (""), the **GetObject** function returns the currently active object of the specified *class*. If there is no object of that type active, an error occurs.

The preceding fragment shows how to activate an entire file. However, some applications let you activate part of an object. To specify that you want to activate part of a file, add an exclamation point (!) or a backslash (\) to the end of the file name followed by a string that identifies the part of the file you want to activate. See the object's application documentation for information on how to create this string.

For example, SPDSHEET.EXE is a spreadsheet application that uses R1C1 syntax. The following code could be used to activate a range of cells within REVENUE.SPD:

```
Set Spreadsheet = GetObject("C:\ACCOUNTS\REVENUE.SPD!R1C1:R10C20")
```

In previous examples, an application is invoked and an object is activated. Notice that in these examples the application name (SPDSHEET.EXE) is never specified. When you use **GetObject** to activate an object, the registry files determine the application to invoke and the object to activate based on the file name you provide. Some files, however, may support more than one class of object. Suppose the spreadsheet file, REVENUE.SPD, supports three different classes of objects: an Application object, a worksheet object, and a toolbar object, all of which are part of the same file. To specify which object in a file you want to activate, you supply an argument for the optional *Class* parameter. Here's an example of activating the toolbar object in the file REVENUE.SPD:

```
Set Spreadsheet = GetObject("C:\REVENUE.SPD", "SPDSHEET.TOOLBAR")
```

Note When you use the **GetObject** function and do not include the *Class* of the object to be activated, then the default object of the specified file is activated.

Manipulating Objects

Once you have created a variable that references an OLE object, the object can be manipulated in DispTest the same way as any DispTest object (such as a control). You use the *object.property* syntax to get and set the object's properties or to perform methods on the object.

Accessing an Object's Properties

To assign a value to a property of an object, put the object variable and property name on the left side of an assignment and the desired property setting on the right side. For example:

```
Dim ObjVar as Object
Dim RowPos, ColPos
Set ObjVar = CreateObject("MyApplication.MyObjectType")

ObjVar.Text = "Hello, world"
ObjVar.Cell(RowPos, ColPos) = "This property accepts two arguments."
```

You can also retrieve property values from an object:

```
Dim X

X = ObjVar.Text
X = ObjVar.Range(12, 32)

' Sets the font for ObjVar.Selection.
ObjVar.Selection.Font = 12
```

Note All arguments to OLE Automation objects use the **Variant** data type. When retrieving a value from a property or method, OLE Automation objects always return values with the **Variant** data type.

If you assign a variable with a data type other than **Variant** when setting a property value or performing a method, the variable is coerced to the **Variant** data type when the property is set or the method is performed.

Invoking Methods

As illustrated earlier, in addition to getting and setting properties, you can manipulate an object using the methods it supports. Some methods may return a value, as in the following example:

```
' IsBold method returns True or False.
X = ObjVar.Text.IsBold
If X Then
    ObjVar.Text = "The text is bold."
```

```
Else
    ObjVar.Text = "The text is not bold."
End If

' This method requires two arguments.
ObjVar.Move XPos, YPos
```

Methods that do not return a value behave like a subroutine. If you assign such a method to a variable, an error occurs.

Some objects contain subobjects. For example, a cell could be considered a subobject of a spreadsheet object. You can include multiple objects, properties, and methods on the same line of code using the dot syntax, just as you would with a DispTest object (for example, Form.Control.Property). For example:

```
ObjVar.Cell(1,1).FontBold = True
```

Limitations in DispTest

Some OLE objects support features that can't be accessed using DispTest. This section discusses those features.

Arrays and Arrays of User-defined Types

Some objects have properties and methods that either return an array of data or an array of user-defined type, or take an array or array of user-defined type as an argument. The following is a list of DispTest's limitations when using arrays or user-defined types with OLE objects. You can't:

- Use an array or a user-defined type as an argument to a method.
- Set a property using an array or a user-defined type.
- Assign an array variable or a variable of a user-defined type to the return value of a property or method.

When a property or method returns an array, you can use the **LBound** and **UBound** functions to determine the size of an array. You can then access the individual elements of the array. For example:

```
Dim I, Value

For I = LBound(ObjVar.Selection) To UBound(ObjVar.Selection)
    Value = ObjVar.Selection(I)
Next
```

Named Arguments

You can't use named arguments when calling an object's methods in DispTest.
Some objects have methods that require many arguments, some of which are
optional. These methods are typically used to display one of the application's
dialogs. The arguments for the method correspond to selections in the dialog.
Such methods often allow you to set any desired arguments using predefined
names. When calling a method using named arguments, the order in which the
arguments appear does not matter. In DispTest, however, you can't use named
arguments. When calling a method that supports named arguments, you must
specify each argument in the correct order. If you want to omit an optional
argument, leave it blank.

For example, an object supports a method called **FileOpen** that is used to display
the object's File Open dialog. The following code shows how the method is called
using named arguments and how to call the method from within DispTest:

Not Valid in DispTest

```
' When using named arguments, the order does not matter.
FileOpen Name = "MYDOC.DOC", ReadOnly = 0, Password = "Mahler"
FileOpen ReadOnly = 0, Name = "MYDOC.DOC", Password = "Mahler"
```

Valid in DispTest

```
' Each argument must be specified in the correct order.
ObjVar.FileOpen "MYDOC.DOC", 0, "Mahler"
' To omit the second argument, insert a comma in its place.
ObjVar.FileOpen "MYDOC.DOC", , "Mahler"
```

Collection Objects

A collection object contains zero or more items. For example, a Menu object may
have a Menus object that is a collection of all the menus in the object's
application. Collection objects are usually specified using the plural form of an
object. For example, the collection object for Row objects would be called Rows.

All collection objects support a property called Count. This property returns the
number of elements in the collection. For example, in the code
`x = ObjVar.Rows.Count`, x equals the number of rows in the object referenced
by the object variable `ObjVar`.

You specify an individual element of a collection object using an index. For
example, in a 1-based collection object, Rows(1) specifies the first row in an
object and Rows(Rows.Count) specifies the last row.

Iterating Through Collection Objects

You should be aware of several factors when iterating through a collection of an OLE object:

- There is no guarantee the iterator of a collection object is numeric.

- If a collection object does provide a numeric iterator, there is no guarantee that the numbers are contiguous.

- If a change is made to an element of a collection object, the positions of the elements may change. This differentiates collection objects from arrays, in which the positions of the elements are guaranteed to be the same unless explicitly changed.

DispTest and Visual Basic, version 3.0, do not provide a mechanism to reliably iterate over objects contained by a collection object. In order to iterate over a collection using these tools, the collection object must provide a contiguous numeric Index method or some other mechanism to iterate over the object in the collection.

For example:

```
For i = 1 to Windows.Count
    Window(i).Minimize   ' Index returns a contained object
Next i
```

In the preceding example, Index accepts the numbers 1 to Windows.Count. Other collection objects may or may not support this method. Consult the application's object documentation to see if a particular collection object supports this method.

Some collection objects do not use numeric iterators. For example, an object has a collection of styles. Instead of using numeric iterator, the Styles collection might use string subscripts. In code, the collection might look like this:

```
ObjVar.Styles("Normal")
ObjVar.Styles("Ex")
ObjVar.Styles("Heading")
```

Visual Basic, Applications edition (shipped in Microsoft Excel and other applications), provides a **For Each** language construct to reliably iterate over the elements in all types of collections. For example:

```
For Each x In Windows
    x.Minimize
Next x
```

Using Visual Basic for Scripting Your Application

Visual Basic, version 3.0, is an OLE Automation controller. It lets you create stand-alone .EXE files that you can distribute to your customers. This makes it easy to customize your applications for specific client needs. In fact, completely new applications can be easily assembled from OLE Automation objects using Visual Basic.

Visual Basic includes database access, performance enhancements, additional documentation, and many other advantages over DispTest.

Creating Type Information Browsers

Although you can use the type description interfaces directly to expose objects in your applications, an easier way to do this is to write an Object Description Language (.ODL) source file, then process that file with MkTypLib to produce a type library (see Chapter 7, "Object Description Language," for more information on MkTypLib and .ODL source files). Typically, the type description interfaces are used by type browsers, compilers, and interpreters to read type libraries created with MkTypLib. The following code illustrates the way a browser might access a type library, in the course of displaying type information to a user. This function is culled from the sample application OLE2BROWSE sample application included with the OLE 2 SDK.

```
// TOFILE.CPP
    .
 .   // Portions omitted for brevity.
    .
BOOL TypeInfoToFile( HFILE  hfile, LPTYPEINFO lpTypeInfo )
{
    char szBuf[512] ;

    Assert( hfile != HFILE_ERROR ) ;
    Assert( lpTypeInfo ) ;

    #define MAX_NAMES    128

    HRESULT         hr ;
    BSTR            bstrName, bstrDoc, bstrHelp ;
    DWORD           dwHelpID ;
    BSTR            rgbstrNames[MAX_NAMES] ;
    int             cNames ;
    WORD            cFuncs, cVars ;
    LPFUNCDESC      pFuncDesc ;
    WORD            iIndex ;
```

```
    hr = lpTypeInfo->GetDocumentation( MEMBERID_NIL, &bstrName,
&bstrDoc, &dwHelpID, &bstrHelp ) ;
  if (SUCCEEDED(hr))
  {
      wsprintf( szBuf,    "' ----------------------------------------
----------------------\r\n"\
                          "' %s\r\n"\
                          "'    %s\r\n\r\n",
                 (LPSTR)(bstrName ? bstrName : ""),
                 (LPSTR)(bstrDoc ? bstrDoc : "") ) ;

      _lwrite( hfile, szBuf, lstrlen( szBuf ) ) ;

      SysFreeString( bstrName ) ;
      SysFreeString( bstrDoc ) ;
      SysFreeString( bstrHelp ) ;
  }
  else
  {
      wsprintf( szBuf, "GetDocumenation for TypeInfo FAILED: %s",
(LPSTR)HRtoString( hr ) ) ;
      _lwrite( hfile, szBuf, lstrlen( szBuf ) ) ;
      return FALSE ;
  }

  LPTYPEATTR  pTA = NULL ;
  hr = lpTypeInfo->GetTypeAttr( &pTA ) ;
  if (FAILED( hr ))
  {
      wsprintf( szBuf, "GetTypeAttr FAILED: %s", (LPSTR)HRtoString( hr
) ) ;
      _lwrite( hfile, szBuf, lstrlen( szBuf ) ) ;
      return FALSE ;
  }

  cVars = pTA->cVars ;
  cFuncs = pTA->cFuncs ;
  lpTypeInfo->ReleaseTypeAttr( pTA ) ;

  short    cParams ;
  short    cParamsOpt ;
  char     szFunc[128] ;   // Function/Sub name
  LPSTR    szParams ;
  LPSTR    lpsz ;

  //
  // Enumerate through all FUNCDESCS
  for ( iIndex = 0 ; iIndex < cFuncs ; iIndex++)
  {
      hr = lpTypeInfo->GetFuncDesc( iIndex, &pFuncDesc ) ;
```

```
      if (FAILED(hr))
      {
            wsprintf( szBuf, "GetFuncDesc FAILED for function #%u
(%s)\r\n", iIndex, (LPSTR)HRtoString( hr ) ) ;
            _lwrite( hfile, szBuf, lstrlen( szBuf ) ) ;
            continue ;
      }

      hr = lpTypeInfo->GetDocumentation( pFuncDesc->memid, &bstrName,
&bstrDoc, &dwHelpID, &bstrHelp ) ;
      if (SUCCEEDED(hr))
      {
          if (bstrDoc)
              wsprintf( szBuf, "' %s\r\n"\
                              "'    %s\r\n",
                (LPSTR)(bstrName ? bstrName : ""),
                (LPSTR)(bstrName ? bstrDoc : "") ) ;
          else
              wsprintf( szBuf, "' %s\r\n",
                (LPSTR)(bstrName ? bstrName : "") ) ;

          _lwrite( hfile, szBuf, lstrlen( szBuf ) ) ;
          SysFreeString( bstrName ) ;
          SysFreeString( bstrDoc ) ;
          SysFreeString( bstrHelp ) ;
      }

      cParams = pFuncDesc->cParams ;
      cParamsOpt = abs(pFuncDesc->cParamsOpt) ;

      // Get the names of the function and it's parameters into
rgbstrNames.
      // cNames gets the number of parameters + 1.
      //
      hr = lpTypeInfo->GetNames( pFuncDesc->memid, rgbstrNames,
MAX_NAMES, (UINT FAR*)&cNames );
      if (SUCCEEDED( hr ))
      {
          // rgbstrNames[0] is the name of the function
          if (cNames > 0)
          {
              lstrcpy( szFunc, (LPSTR)rgbstrNames[0] ) ;
              SysFreeString( rgbstrNames[0] ) ;
          }

          // Allocate a string buffer that should be able to hold
          // all of our parameter types and names.
          //
          if (NULL == (szParams = GlobalAllocPtr( GPTR,
max(cNames,cParams) * (64) )))
```

```
                    {
                        MessageBox( NULL, "GlobalAlloc Failed!", "Yikes!", MB_OK
) ;

                        wsprintf( szBuf, "GlobalAlloc failed!\r\n" ) ;
                        _lwrite( hfile, szBuf, lstrlen( szBuf ) ) ;
                        return FALSE ;
                    }

                    // For each parameter get the type and name.
                    // The "max(cNames-1,cParams)" should handle the case
                    // where a function has optional parameters (i.e. cParamsOpt
is
                    // non-zero).
                    //
                    lstrcpy( szParams, "(" ) ;

                    // For each required parameter
                    //
                    for ( int n = 0 ; n < cParams - cParamsOpt ; n++ )
                    {
                        if (n+1 < cNames)
                            lpsz = rgbstrNames[n+1] ;
                        else
                            lpsz = NULL ;
                        BuildParam( szParams+lstrlen(szParams),
                                    &pFuncDesc->lprgelemdescParam[n], lpsz ,
FALSE ) ;

                        if (n+1 < cNames)
                            SysFreeString( rgbstrNames[n+1] ) ;

                        // If it's the last one then no comma
                        if (n + 1 != max(cNames-1,cParams))
                            lstrcat( szParams, ", " ) ;
                    }

                    // For each optional parameter
                    //
                    for (n = cParams - cParamsOpt ; n < cParams ; n++)
                    {
                        if (n+1 < cNames)
                            lpsz = rgbstrNames[n+1] ;
                        else
                            lpsz = NULL ;
                        BuildParam( szParams+lstrlen(szParams),
                                    &pFuncDesc->lprgelemdescParam[n], lpsz ,
TRUE ) ;

                        if (n+1 < cNames)
                            SysFreeString( rgbstrNames[n+1] ) ;
```

```
                          // If it's the last one then no comma
                          if (n + 1 != max(cNames-1,cParams))
                              lstrcat( szParams,  ", " ) ;
                      }

                  lstrcat( szParams , ")" ) ;

                  // Is it a function or sub?
                  //
                  if (pFuncDesc->elemdescFunc.tdesc.vt == VT_EMPTY ||
                      pFuncDesc->elemdescFunc.tdesc.vt == VT_NULL ||
                      pFuncDesc->elemdescFunc.tdesc.vt == VT_VOID)
                  {
                      // Declare Sub <subname>(<arglist>)
                      wsprintf( szBuf, "Declare Sub %s ", (LPSTR)szFunc ) ;
                      _lwrite( hfile, szBuf, lstrlen(szBuf) ) ;
                      _lwrite( hfile, szParams, lstrlen(szParams) ) ;
                      _lwrite( hfile, "\r\n\r\n", 4 ) ;
                  }
                  else
                  {
                      // Declare Function <funcname>(<arglist>) As
<returntype>
                      wsprintf( szBuf, "Declare Function %s ", (LPSTR)szFunc )
;
                      _lwrite( hfile, szBuf, lstrlen(szBuf) ) ;
                      _lwrite( hfile, szParams, lstrlen(szParams) ) ;
                      wsprintf( szBuf, " As %s\r\n\r\n", (LPSTR)VTtoString2(
pFuncDesc->elemdescFunc.tdesc.vt ) ) ;
                      _lwrite( hfile, szBuf, lstrlen(szBuf) ) ;
                  }

                  GlobalFreePtr( szParams ) ;
              }
              else
              {
                  wsprintf( szBuf, "GetNames (%lu) FAILED: %s", pFuncDesc-
>memid, (LPSTR)HRtoString( hr ) ) ;
                  _lwrite( hfile, szBuf, lstrlen( szBuf ) ) ;
              }
              lpTypeInfo->ReleaseFuncDesc( pFuncDesc ) ;
          }

      // '
      // ' <varname>
      // ' Documentation: <docstring>
      // ' Help for this property can be found in <helpfile>
      // ' The help ID for this property is <helpid>
      // Dim <varname> As <vartype>
```

```
    // '
    // ' <varname>
    // ' Documentation: <docstring>
    // ' Help for this property can be found in <helpfile>
    // ' The help ID for this property is <helpid>
    // Const <varname> As <vartype> = <value>
    LPVARDESC pVarDesc ;
    for (iIndex = 0 ; iIndex < cVars ; iIndex++)
    {
        hr = lpTypeInfo->GetVarDesc( iIndex, &pVarDesc ) ;
        if (FAILED(hr))
        {
            wsprintf( szBuf, "GetVarDesc FAILED for variable #%u
(%s)\r\n", iIndex, (LPSTR)HRtoString( hr ) ) ;
            _lwrite( hfile, szBuf, lstrlen( szBuf ) ) ;
            continue ;
        }
        else
        {
            hr = lpTypeInfo->GetDocumentation( pVarDesc->memid,
&bstrName, &bstrDoc, &dwHelpID, &bstrHelp ) ;
            if (SUCCEEDED(hr))
            {
                if (bstrDoc)
                    wsprintf( szBuf, "' %s\r\n"\
                                     "'   %s\r\n",
                        (LPSTR)(bstrName ? bstrName : ""),
                        (LPSTR)(bstrName ? bstrDoc : "") ) ;
                else
                    wsprintf( szBuf, "' %s\r\n",
                        (LPSTR)(bstrName ? bstrName : "") ) ;

                _lwrite( hfile, szBuf, lstrlen( szBuf ) ) ;
                SysFreeString( bstrName ) ;
                SysFreeString( bstrDoc ) ;
                SysFreeString( bstrHelp ) ;
            }
            hr = lpTypeInfo->GetNames( pVarDesc->memid, rgbstrNames, 1,
(UINT FAR*)&cNames ) ;
            if (SUCCEEDED( hr ))
            {

                if (pVarDesc->varkind == VAR_CONST)
                {
                    // Const constname [As type] = expression
                    wsprintf( szBuf, "Const %s As %s = ",
                                (LPSTR)rgbstrNames[0],
                                (LPSTR)TYPEDESCtoString( &pVarDesc-
>elemdescVar.tdesc )
                                        ) ;
```

```
                            VARIANT varValue ;
                            VariantInit( &varValue ) ;
                            hr = VariantChangeType( &varValue, pVarDesc-
>lpvarValue, 0, VT_BSTR ) ;
                            if (FAILED(hr))
                                lstrcat( szBuf, (LPSTR)HRtoString( hr ) ) ;
                            else
                            {
                                lstrcat( szBuf, varValue.bstrVal ) ;
                                SysFreeString( varValue.bstrVal ) ;
                            }
                        }
                        else
                        {
                            // Dim varname[([subscripts])][As type]
                            wsprintf( szBuf, "Dim %s ", (LPSTR)rgbstrNames[0] )
;
                            if ((pVarDesc->elemdescVar.tdesc.vt & 0x0FFF) ==
VT_PTR &&
                                (pVarDesc->elemdescVar.tdesc.lptdesc->vt &
0x0FFF) == VT_SAFEARRAY)
                            {
                                lstrcat( szBuf, "() As " ) ;
                                lstrcat( szBuf, VTtoString2( pVarDesc-
>elemdescVar.tdesc.vt ) ) ;
                            }
                            else
                            {
                                lstrcat( szBuf, "As " ) ;
                                lstrcat( szBuf, TYPEDESCtoString( &pVarDesc-
>elemdescVar.tdesc ) ) ;
                            }
                        }
                        SysFreeString( rgbstrNames[0] ) ;
                        lstrcat( szBuf, "\r\n\r\n" ) ;
                        _lwrite( hfile, szBuf, lstrlen( szBuf ) ) ;
                    }
                    else
                    {
                        wsprintf( szBuf, "GetNames (%lu) FAILED: %s\r\n",
pVarDesc->memid, (LPSTR)HRtoString( hr ) ) ;
                        _lwrite( hfile, szBuf, lstrlen( szBuf ) ) ;
                    }

                    lpTypeInfo->ReleaseVarDesc( pVarDesc ) ;
            }
        }


    return TRUE ;
}
```

CHAPTER 4

Standards and Guidelines

This chapter describes the standard OLE Automation objects and describes naming guidelines for creating objects that are unique to applications, especially user-interactive applications that support a multiple-document interface. However, if your OLE Automation object is not user-interactive or supports only a single document interface, you should adapt the standards and guidelines as appropriate.

- *Standard objects* comprise a standard set of objects defined by OLE and should be used as appropriate to your application. The objects described in this chapter are oriented toward document-based, user-interactive applications. Other applications (such as non-interactive database servers) may have requirements different from those described here.

- *Naming guidelines* are recommendations meant to improve consistency across applications.

This chapter discusses each of these points in turn. Examples are shown in a hypothetical syntax derived from DispTest and Visual Basic.

Note Additions to these standards and guidelines are likely.

Standard Objects

The following table lists the OLE Automation standard objects and their methods and properties. Although none of these objects is absolutely required, user-interactive applications with subordinate objects should include an Application object.

Object name	Description
Application	Top-level object that provides a standard way for OLE Automation controllers to retrieve and navigate an application's subordinate objects.

Object name	Description
Document	Provides a way to open, print, change, and save an application document.
Documents	For multiple document interface (MDI) applications, this collection provides a way to iterate over and select open documents.
Font	Describes fonts that are used to display or print text.

The following figure shows how the standard objects fit into the organization of the objects an application provides.

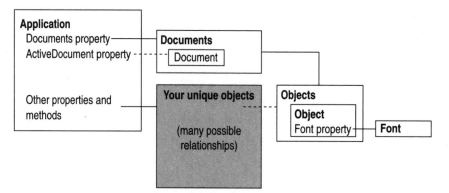

The following sections describe the standard properties and methods for all objects, all collection objects, and each of the standard objects. These sections list only standard methods and properties for each object, as well as the standard arguments for those properties and methods.

Note You may define additional application-specific properties and methods for each object. You may also provide additional optional arguments for any of the listed properties or methods; however, such optional arguments should follow the standard arguments in a positional argument list.

All Objects

All objects, including the Application object and collection objects, must provide the following properties:

Property name	Description
Application	Returns the Application object. VT_DISPATCH; read only.
Parent	Returns the creator of the object. VT_DISPATCH; read only.

Note The Application and Parent properties of the Application object return the Application object.

All Collection Objects

A collection provides a set of objects over which iteration can be performed. All collection objects must provide the following properties:

Property name	Return type	Description
Count	VT_I4	Returns the number of items in a collection; read only.

Collection Methods

Methods for collections are described in the following table. Methods shown in **bold** are required; other methods are optional.

Method name	Return type	Description
Add	VT_DISPATCH or VT_EMPTY	Adds an item to a collection. Returns VT_DISPATCH if object is created (object cannot exist outside the collection) or VT_EMPTY if no object is created (object can exist outside the collection).
Item	Varies with type of collection	Returns the indicated item in the collection. Item may take one or more arguments to indicate the element within the collection to return. Item is the default member (DISPID_VALUE) for the collection object.
_NewEnum	VT_DISPATCH	A special method that returns an object that implements **IEnumVARIANT**.
Remove	VT_EMPTY	Removes an item from a collection. Uses indexing arguments in the same way as the Item method.

All collection objects must provide at least one form of indexing through the Item method. The dispatch ID of the Item method is DISPID_VALUE. Since it is the default member, it can be used in the following convenient form:

```
ThirdDef = MyWords(3).Definition     ' Equivalent to
                                     ' MyWords.Item(3).Definition
```

The Item method takes one or more arguments to indicate the index. Indexes may be numbers, strings, or other types. For example:

```
DogDef = MyWords("dog").Definition
```

Important Within the application's type library, the _NewEnum method has a special dispatch ID: DISPID_NEWENUM. The name "_NewEnum" should not be localized.

The Add method may take one or more arguments. For example, if `MyWord` is an object with the properties `Letters` and `Definition`:

```
Dim MyWord As New Word
Dim MyDictionary as Words
MyWord = "dog"
MyWord.Letters = "Dog"
MyWord.Definition = "My best friend."
MyDictionary.Add MyWord
MyDictionary.Remove("Dog")
```

For more information on creating collection objects, see Chapter 2, "Exposing OLE Automation Objects."

Kinds of Collections

The standard for collections is flexible enough to describe two kinds of collections, depending on whether or not it is logical for the collected object to exist outside the collection.

If the Object Can't Exist Outside the Collection

It may not be logical for a collected object to exist independently of its collection. For example, if the Documents collection contains all currently open Document objects, it is not logical for any of the Document objects to exist independently of the collection. The close relationship between the collection and the collected objects can be shown in the following ways:

- Documents.Add creates an object and adds it to the collection. Since an object is created, a reference to it is returned:

  ```
  Set MyDoc = Documents.Add
  ```

- Document.Close removes an item from the collection:

  ```
  Set SomeDoc = Documents(3)
  SomeDoc.Close
  ```

If the Object Can Exist Outside the Collection

For other collections, it is logical for the collected objects to exist outside the collection. For example, a Mail application might have Name objects, and many collections of these Name objects. The Name object would have the user's email name, the user's full name, and possibly other information. The Name object could have the following string-type properties:

- EmailName
- FullName

The application might have the following collections of Name objects:

- A collection for the "to" list on each piece of mail
- A collection of the names of all of the people to whom a user has sent mail

The collections of Name objects could be indexed by using either the EmailName or the FullName.

For such a collection, it is not logical for Add to create an object because the object already exists. Thus, the Add method should take an object as an argument and should not return a value. Assuming the existence of two collections (AddressBook and ToList), a user might execute the following line of code to add a Name object to the ToList collection:

```
Dim Message as Object
Dim AddressBook as Object
Dim NameRef as Object
...
Set NameRef = AddressBook.Names("Fred Funk")
Message.ToList.Add    NameRef
```

The name object already exists and is contained in the AddressBook collection. The first line of code gets a reference to the Name object for "Fred Funk" and makes NameRef point to it. The second line of code adds a reference to the object to the ToList collection. No new object is created, so no reference is returned from the Add method. Unlike the relationship between Documents and Document, there is no way for the collected object (the Name) to know how to remove itself from the collections in which it is contained. Thus, to remove an item from a collection, the Remove method is used:

```
Message.ToList.Remove("Fred Funk")
```

This line of code removes the Name object having the FullName "Fred Funk". The "Fred Funk" object may exist in other collections. These other collections will be unaffected.

Application Object

The Application object should have the following properties. Properties shown in **bold** are required; other properties are optional.

Property name	Return type	Description
ActiveDocument	VT_DISPATCH, VT_EMPTY	Returns the active document object or VT_EMPTY if none; read only.
Application	VT_DISPATCH	Returns the Application object; read only.
Caption	VT_BSTR	Sets or returns the title of the application window. Setting the Caption to VT_EMPTY returns control to the application; read/write.
DefaultFilePath	VT_BSTR	Sets or returns the default path specification used by the application for opening files; read/write.
Documents	VT_DISPATCH	Returns a collection object for the open documents; read only.
FullName	VT_BSTR	Returns the file specification for the application, including path. For example, `C:\DRAWDIR\SCRIBBLE.EXE`; read only.
Height	VT_R4	Sets or returns the distance between the top and bottom edge of the main application window; read/write.
Interactive	VT_BOOL	Sets or returns whether or not the application accepts actions from the user; read/write.
Left	VT_R4	Sets or returns the distance between the left edge of the physical screen and the main application window; read/write.
Name	VT_BSTR	Returns the name of the application, such as "Microsoft Excel." The Name property is the default member (DISPID_VALUE) for the Application object; read only.
Parent	VT_DISPATCH	Returns the Application object; read only.
Path	VT_BSTR	Returns the path specification for the application's executable file. For example, `C:\DRAWDIR` if the executable is `C:\DRAWDIR\SCRIBBLE.EXE`; read only.
StatusBar	VT_BSTR	Sets or returns the text displayed in the status bar; read/write.
Top	VT_R4	Sets or returns the distance between the top edge of the physical screen and main application window; read/write.

Property name	Return type	Description
Visible	VT_BOOL	Sets or returns whether the application is visible to the user. The default is False when application is started with /Automation command-line switch; read/write.
Width	VT_R4	Sets or returns the distance between the left and right edges of the main application window; read/write.

If a type library is used, the Application object should be the object that has the [appobj] attribute specified. Some OLE Automation controllers will use this information to allow unqualified access to the Application object's members. For this reason, it is important to avoid overloading the Application object with too many members.

The Application object should provide the following methods. Methods shown in **bold** are required; other methods are optional.

Method name	Return type	Description
Help	VT_EMPTY	Displays online Help. May take three optional arguments: *helpfile* (VT_BSTR), *helpcontextID* (VT_I4), and *helpstring* (VT_BSTR). The *helpfile* argument specifies the Help file to display; if omitted the main Help file for the application is displayed. The *helpcontextID* and *helpstring* arguments specify a help context to display, and only one of them may be supplied; if both are omitted, the default Help topic is displayed.
Quit	VT_EMPTY	Exits the application and closes all open documents.
Repeat	VT_EMPTY	Repeats the previous action in the user interface.
Undo	VT_EMPTY	Reverses the previous action in the user interface.

Document Object

If your application is document-based, you should provide a Document object. You should use the name "Document" for this object unless that name is inappropriate for your application. This name may be inappropriate if your application uses highly technical or otherwise specialized terminology within its user interface.

The Document object should have the following properties. Properties shown in **bold** are required; other properties are optional.

Property name	Return type	Description
Application	VT_DISPATCH	Returns the Application object; read only.
Author	VT_BSTR	Sets or returns the summary information about the document's author; read/write.
Comments	VT_BSTR	Sets or returns summary information comments for the document; read/write.
FullName	VT_BSTR	Returns the file specification of the document, including path; read only.
Keywords	VT_BSTR	Sets or returns summary information keywords associated with the document; read/write.
Name	VT_BSTR	Returns the file name of the document, not including the file's path specification; read only.
Parent	VT_DISPATCH	Returns the parent of the Document object; read only.
Path	VT_BSTR	Returns the path specification for the document, not including the file name or file name extension; read only.
ReadOnly	VT_BOOL	Returns True if the file is read only and False if otherwise; read only.
Saved	VT_BOOL	Returns True if the document has never been saved, but has not changed since it was created. Returns True if it has been saved and has not changed since last save. Returns False if it has never been saved and has changed since it was created; or if it was saved, but has changed since last save; read only.
Subject	VT_BSTR	Sets or returns the summary information about the subject of the document; read/write.
Title	VT_BSTR	Sets or returns the summary information about the title of the document; read/write.

The Document object should have the following methods. Methods shown in **bold** are required, other methods are optional.

Method name	Return type	Description
Activate	VT_EMPTY	Activates the first window associated with a given document.
Close	VT_EMPTY	Closes all windows associated with a given document and removes the document from the Documents collection. Takes two optional arguments, *saveChanges* (VT_BOOL) and *fileName* (VT_BSTR). The *fileName* argument specifies the name of the file in which to save the document.
NewWindow	VT_EMPTY	Creates a new window for the given document.
Print	VT_EMPTY	Prints the document. Takes three optional arguments: *from* (VT_I2), *to* (VT_I2), and *copies* (VT_I2). The *from* and *to* arguments specify the page range to print.
PrintOut	VT_EMPTY	Same as Print method, but provides an easier way to use the method in Visual Basic, version 3.0, since **Print** is a Visual Basic 3.0 keyword.
PrintPreview	VT_EMPTY	Previews the pages and page breaks of the document. Equivalent to choosing Print Preview from the File menu.
RevertToSaved	VT_EMPTY	Reverts to the last saved copy of the document, discarding any changes.
Save	VT_EMPTY	Saves changes to the file specified in the document's FullName property.
SaveAs	VT_EMPTY	Saves changes to a file. Takes one optional argument, *filename* (VT_BSTR). The *filename* argument may or may not include a path specification.

Documents Collection Object

If your application is document-based, you should provide a Documents collection object. You should use the name "Documents" for this collection unless that name is inappropriate for your application.

The Documents collection object should have the following properties. Names shown in **bold** are required; other properties are optional.

Property name	Return type	Description
Application	VT_DISPATCH	Returns the Application object; read only.
Count	VT_I4	Returns the number of items in the collection; read only.
Parent	VT_DISPATCH	Returns the parent of the Documents collection object; read only.

The Documents collection object should have the following methods. Names shown in **bold** are required, other methods are optional.

Method name	Return type	Description
Add	VT_DISPATCH	Creates a new document and adds it to the collection. Returns the document that was created.
Close	VT_EMPTY	Closes all documents in the collection.
Item	VT_DISPATCH or VT_EMPTY	Returns a Document object from the collection or VT_EMPTY if the document does not exist. Takes an optional argument, *index*. The *index* argument may take a string (VT_BSTR) indicating the document name, a number (VT_I4) indicating the ordered position within the collection, or either (VT_VARIANT). If *index* is omitted, returns the Document collection. Item is the default member (DISPID_VALUE).
Open	VT_DISPATCH or VT_EMPTY	Opens an existing document and adds it to the collection. Returns the document that was opened or VT_EMPTY if the object could not be opened. Takes one required argument, *filename*, and one optional argument, *password*. Both arguments have type VT_BSTR.
_NewEnum	VT_DISPATCH	A special method that returns an object that implements **IEnumVARIANT**.

Font Object

The Font object should have the following properties. Properties shown in **bold** are required, other properties are optional.

Property name	Return type	Description
Application	VT_DISPATCH	Returns the Application object; read only.
Bold	VT_BOOL	Sets or returns whether or not the font is boldface; read/write.
Color	VT_I4	Sets or returns the RGB color of the font; read/write.
Italic	VT_BOOL	Sets or returns whether the font is italic; read/write.
Name	VT_BSTR	Returns the name of the font; read only.
OutlineFont	VT_BOOL	Sets or returns whether the font is scaleable. For example, bitmapped fonts are not scaleable, whereas TrueType fonts are scaleable; read/write.
Parent	VT_DISPATCH	Returns the parent of the Font object; read only.
Shadow	VT_BOOL	Sets or returns whether the font appears with a shadow; read/write.
Size	VT_R4	Sets or returns the size of the font in points; read/write.
Strikethrough	VT_BOOL	Sets or returns whether the font appears with a line running through it; read/write.
Subscript	VT_BOOL	Sets or returns whether the font is subscripted; read/write.
Superscript	VT_BOOL	Sets or returns whether the font is superscripted; read/write.

Naming Conventions

Choose names for your exposed objects, properties, and methods that can be easily understood by the users of your application. The guidelines in this section apply to all the items you expose:

- Objects (implemented as classes in your application)
- Properties and methods (implemented as members of a class)
- Named arguments (implemented as named parameters in a member function)
- Constants and enumerations (implemented as settings for properties and methods)

Use entire words or syllables whenever possible

Use	Don't use
Application	App
Window	Wnd

It is easier for users to remember complete words than to remember whether you abbreviated Window as Wind, Wn, or Wnd.

When you need to abbreviate because an identifier would be much too long, try to use complete initial syllables. For example, use AltExpEval instead of AlternateExpressionEvaluation.

Use mixed case

All identifiers should use mixed case, rather than underscores, to separate the words in the identifier.

Use	Don't use
ShortcutMenus	Shortcut_Menus, Shortcutmenus, SHORTCUTMENUS, SHORTCUT_MENUS
BasedOn	basedOn

Use the same word you use in the interface

Use	Don't use
Name	Lbl

Use consistent terminology; don't use names like HWND that are based on Hungarian notation. Try to use the same word your users would use to describe a concept.

Collection classes should use the correct plural for class name, when appropriate

Use	Don't use
Axes	Axiss
SeriesCollection	CollectionSeries
Windows	ColWindow

For example, if you have a class named Axis, a collection of Axis objects is stored in a Axes class. Similarly, a collection of Vertex objects is stored in a Vertices class. In rare cases where English uses the same word for the plural, append the word "Collection."

Using plurals rather than inventing new names for collections reduces the number of items a user must remember. It also simplifies the selection of names for collections.

Note, however, that for some collections this may not be appropriate, especially where a set of objects exists independently of the collection. For example, a Mail program might have a Name object that exists in multiple collections: ToList, CCList, and so forth. In this case, you might specify the individual name collections as ToNames and CCNames.

CHAPTER 5

Dispatch Interfaces

The dispatch interfaces provide a way to expose and access objects within an application. The dispatch interfaces include:

- **IDispatch** interface—Exposes objects, methods, and properties to OLE Automation programming tools and other applications.
- Dispatch functions—Simplify the implementation of an **IDispatch** interface. You can use these functions to automatically generate an **IDispatch** interface.
- **IEnumVARIANT** interface—Provides a way for OLE Automation controllers to iterate over collection objects.

Overview of Interfaces

The following table describes the member functions of each of the dispatch interfaces.

Interface	Member name	Purpose
IDispatch	**Invoke**	Provides access to properties and methods exposed by the object.
	GetIDsOfNames	Maps a single member name and an optional set of argument names to a corresponding set of integer DISPIDs which may then be used on subsequent calls to **Invoke**.
	GetTypeInfo	Retrieves the type information for an object.
	GetTypeInfoCount	Retrieves the number of type information interfaces that an object provides (either 0 or 1).

Interface	Member name	Purpose
IEnumVARIANT	**Clone**	Creates a copy of the current enumeration state.
	Next	Gets the next item(s) in the enumeration sequence, and returns them through the array.
	Reset	Resets the enumeration sequence back to the beginning.
	Skip	Skips over the next item(s) in the enumeration sequence.

Overview of Functions

The dispatch functions are summarized in the following table. All of these functions are provided in OLE2DISP.DLL. The header file is DISPATCH.H and the import library is OLE2DISP.LIB.

Category	Function name	Purpose
Dispatch interface creation	**CreateDispTypeInfo**	Creates simplified type information for an object.
	CreateStdDispatch	Creates a standard **IDispatch** implementation for an object.
	DispGetIDsOfNames	Converts a set of names to DISPIDs.
	DispGetParam	Retrieves and coerces elements from a DISPPARAM structure.
	DispInvoke	Calls a member function of an **IDispatch** interface.
Active object initialization	**GetActiveObject**	Retrieves an instance of an object that is initialized with OLE.
	RegisterActiveObject	Initializes a running object with OLE. (Use when application starts.)
	RevokeActiveObject	Revokes a running application's initialization with OLE. (Use when application ends.)

IDispatch Interface

Implemented by	Used by	Header file name	Import library name
Applications that expose programmable objects.	Applications that access programmable objects	DISPATCH.H	None

The **IDispatch** interface is implemented by OLE Automation objects to expose them for access by OLE Automation controllers, such as Microsoft Visual Basic. The object's properties and methods can be accessed using **IDispatch::GetIDsOfNames** and **IDispatch::Invoke**.

The following paragraphs show how to access an OLE Automation object through the **IDispatch** interface; these examples are abbreviated and omit error handling.

```
// Declarations of variables used.
DEFINE_GUID(CLSID_Hello,
HRESULT hresult;
IUnknown * punk;
IDispatch * pdisp;
char FAR* szMember = "SayHello";
DISPID dispid;
DISPPARAMS dispparamsNoArgs = {NULL, NULL, 0, 0}
```

In the following lines, **OleInitialize** loads the OLE DLLs and **CoCreateInstance** initializes the OLE Automation object's class factory. For more information on these two functions, see the *OLE 2 Programmer's Reference, Volume 1*.

```
// Initialize OLE DLLs.
hresult = OleInitialize(NULL);

// OLE function CoCreateInstance starts application using GUID.
hresult = CoCreateInstance(CLSID_Hello, &punk);
```

QueryInterface checks if the object supports **IDispatch**. (As with any call to **QueryInterface**, the returned pointer must be released when it is no longer needed.)

```
// QueryInterface to see if it supports IDispatch.
hresult = punk->QueryInteface(IID_IDispatch, &pdisp);
```

GetIDsOfNames retrieves the dispatch identifier for the indicated method or property (*szMember*).

```
// Retrieve the dispatch identifier for the SayHello method.
// Use defaults where possible.
hresult = pdisp->GetIDsOfNames(
                IID_NULL,
                &szMember,
```

```
                1,
                LOCALE_SYSTEM_DEFAULT,
                &dispid);
```

In the following call to **Invoke**, the dispatch identifier (*dispid*) indicates the property or method to invoke. If the property or method takes parameters, they would be provided in the fifth argument as a DISPPARAMS structure.

```
// Invoke the method. Use defaults where possible.
hresult = pdisp->Invoke(
                dispid,
                IID_NULL,
                LOCALE_SYSTEM_DEFAULT,
                DISPATCH_METHOD,
                &dispparamsNoArgs,
                NULL,
                NULL,
                NULL);
```

Data Types, Structures, and Enumerations

The **IDispatch** interface uses these data types and structures:

Name	Purpose
BSTR	A length-prefixed string.
CALLCONV	Identifies the calling convention used by a member function.
CURRENCY	Provides a precise data type of monetary data.
DISPID	Identifies a method or property to **Invoke**.
DISPPARAMS	Contains arguments passed to a method or property.
EXCEPINFO	Describes an error that occurred during **Invoke**.
INTERFACEDATA	Describes the members of an interface.
LCID	Provides locale information for international string comparisons and localized member names.
METHODDATA	Describes a method or property.
PARAMDATA	Describes a parameter to a method.
VARIANT	Describes a VARIANTARG that can't have the VT_BYREF bit set. Since VT_BYREF is not set, data of type VARIANT can't be passed within DISPPARAMS.
VARIANTARG	Describes arguments that may be passed within DISPPARAMS.
VARTYPE	Identifies the available variant types.

BSTR

A length-prefixed string used by OLE Automation data manipulation functions.

```
typedef char * BSTR;
```

For details on this data type, see Chapter 6, "Data Manipulation Functions."

CALLCONV

Identifies the calling convention used by a member function described in METHODDATA.

```
typedef enum tagCALLCONV {
    CC_CDECL = 1,
    CC_MSCPASCAL,
    CC_PASCAL = CC_MSCPASCAL,
    CC_MACPASCAL,
    CC_STDCALL,
    CC_RESERVED,
    CC_SYSCALL,
    CC_MAX              // End of enumeration marker
} CALLCONV;
```

For the Windows 16-bit operating system, functions implemented with the CC_CDECL calling convention can't have return type float or double. This includes functions returning DATE, which is a floating-point type.

CURRENCY

A currency number is stored as an 8-byte, two's complement integer, scaled by 10,000 to give a fixed-point number with 15 digits to the left of the decimal point and 4 digits to the right. This representation provides a range of ±922337203685477.5807. The currency data type is extremely useful for calculations involving money, or for any fixed-point calculation where accuracy is particularly important.

```
typedef char CURRENCY[8];
```

A structure is defined for working with currency more conveniently:

```
typedef struct {
    unsigned long Lo;
    long  Hi;
} CY;
```

DISPID

Used by **IDispatch::Invoke** to identify the methods, properties, and arguments.

```
typedef LONG DISPID;
```

The following DISPIDs have special meaning:

DISPID	Description
DISPID_VALUE	The default member for the object. This is the property or method that gets invoked if the object name is used from an OLE Automation controller without specifying a property or method.
DISPID_NEWENUM	The _NewEnum method. This special, restricted method is required for collection objects. It returns the collection object and should have the flag FUNCFLAG_FRESTRICTED.
DISPID_EVALUATE	Implicitly invoke this method when the OLE Automation controller encloses the arguments in square brackets. For example, the following two lines are equivalent:
	`x.[A1:C1].value = 10` `x.Evaluate("A1:C1").value = 10`
	In the preceding example, the Evaluate method has the dispatch ID: DISPID_EVALUATE.
DISPID_PROPERTYPUT	Indicates the parameter that receives the value of an assignment in a property "put."
DISPID_UNKNOWN	Value returned by **IDispatch::GetIDsOfNames** to indicate that a member or parameter name was not found.

DISPPARAMS

Used by **IDispatch::Invoke** to contain the arguments passed to a method or property. For more information, see **IDispatch::Invoke** later in this section.

```
typedef struct tagDISPPARAMS DISPPARAMS;
struct tagPARAMS{
    VARIANTARG FAR* rgvarg;              // Array of arguments
    DISPID FAR* rgdispidNamedArgs;       // Dispatch IDs of named
arguments
    unsigned int cArgs;                  // Number of arguments
    unsigned int cNamedArgs;             // Number of named
arguments
};
```

EXCEPINFO

Describes an exception that occurred during **IDispatch::Invoke**. See the section
"**IDispatch::Invoke**" for more information on exceptions.

```
typedef struct tagEXCEPINFO {
    unsigned short wCode;          // Error code
    unsigned short wReserved;
    BSTR bstrSource;               // Source of error (usually application
name)
    BSTR bstrDescription;          // Description of error
    BSTR bstrHelpFile;             // Help file name
    unsigned long dwHelpContext;   // Help context ID
    void * pvReserved;
    // Pointer to function that fills in Help and description info
    HRESULT (*pfnDeferredFillIn)(EXCEPINFO * pexcepinfo);
    SCODE scode;
} EXCEPINFO;
```

Name	Type	Description
wCode	**unsigned short**	An error code identifying the error. Error codes should be greater than 1000.
wReserved	**unsigned short**	Reserved value. This value should be set to 0.
bstrSource	BSTR	A textual, human-readable name of the source of the exception. Typically this will be an application name.
bstrDescription	BSTR	A textual, human-readable description of the error intended for the customer. If no description is available, NULL should be used.
bstrHelpFile	BSTR	The fully qualified drive, path, and file name of a Help file with more information about the error. If no Help is available, NULL should be used.
dwHelpContext	**unsigned long**	The Help context of the topic within the Help file. This field should be filled in if and only if the *bstrHelpFile* field is not NULL.
pvReserved	**void FAR***	Must be set to NULL.
pfnDeferredFillIn		Use of this field allows an application to defer filling in the *bstrDescription*, *bstrHelpFile*, and *dwHelpContext* fields until they are needed. This field might be used, for example, if loading the string for the error is a time-consuming operation. To use deferred fill-in, the application should put a function pointer in this slot and not fill any of the other fields except *wCode* (which is required in any case). When and if the caller wants the additional information, it passes the EXCEPINFO structure back to the *pexcepInfo* callback function, which fills in the additional information. If deferred fill-in is not desired, this field should be set to NULL. When the OLE Automation object and the OLE Automation controller are in different processes, the OLE Automation object will call *pfnDeferredFillIn* before returning to the controller.
scode	SCODE	An SCODE describing the error.

INTERFACEDATA

Describes the OLE Automation object's properties and methods.

```
struct tagINTERFACEDATA {
    METHODDATA FAR* pmethdata;    // Pointer to an array of METHODDATAs
    unsigned int cMembers;        // Count of members
} INTERFACEDATA;
```

LCID

Identifies a locale for national language support. Locale information is used for international string comparisons and localized member names. For information on LCID, see Chapter 10, "National Language Support Functions."

```
typedef unsigned long LCID;
```

METHODDATA

Used to describe a method or property.

```
typedef struct tagMETHODDATA {
    TCHAR FAR* szName;          // Member name
    PARAMDATA FAR* ppdata;      // Pointer to array of PARAMDATAs
    DISPID dispid;              // Member ID
    unsigned int iMeth;         // Method index
    CALLCONV cc;                // Calling convention
    unsigned int cArgs;         // Count of arguments
    unsigned short wFlags;      // Whether this is a method or
                                // a property get, put, or putref
    VARTYPE vtReturn;           // Return type
} METHODDATA;
```

Name	Type	Description
szName	TCHAR FAR*	The method name.
ppdata	PARAMDATA FAR*	The parameters for the method. *ppdata*[0] is the first parameter and so on.
dispid	DISPID	The ID of the method as used in **IDispatch**.
iMeth	unsigned int	The index of the method in the interface's vtable. The indexes start with 0.
cc	unsigned int	The calling convention. Cdecl and Pascal calling conventions are supported by the dispatch interface creation functions, such as **CreateStdDispatch**.
cArgs	unsigned int	The number of arguments for the method.

Name	Type	Description
wFlags	unsigned short	These flags indicate whether the method is used for getting or setting a property. The flags are the same as in **IDispatch::Invoke**. DISPATCH_METHOD indicates this is not used for a property, DISPATCH_PROPERTYGET indicates the member function should be used for retrieving a property value. DISPATCH_PROPERTYPUT indicates the method is used to set the value of a property. DISPATCH_PROPERTYPUTREF indicates the method is used to make the property refer to a passed-in object.
vtReturn	VARTYPE	Return type for the method.

PARAMDATA

Used to describe a parameter accepted by a method or property.

```
typedef struct tagPARAMDATA {
    char FAR* szName;    // Parameter name
    VARTYPE vt;          // Parameter type
} PARAMDATA;
```

Name	Type	Description
szName	char *	The parameter name. It is recommended that this should follow reasonable standard conventions for programming language access; that is, no spaces or control characters in the name, 32 characters or fewer. This is a localized name, because each type description describes names for a particular locale.
vt	VARTYPE	The VARTYPE that will be used by the receiver. If more than one parameter type is accepted, VT_VARIANT should be specified.

VARIANT and VARIANTARG

Use VARIANTARG to describe arguments passed within DISPPARAM. Use VARIANT to specify variant data that can't be by reference; the VARIANT type may not have the VT_BYREF bit set.

```
typedef struct FARSTRUCT tagVARIANT VARIANT;
typedef struct FARSTRUCT tagVARIANT VARIANTARG;

typedef struct tagVARIANT  {
    VARTYPE vt;
    unsigned short wReserved1;
    unsigned short wReserved2;
```

```
        unsigned short wReserved3;
        union {
            short        iVal;              /* VT_I2                    */
            long         lVal;              /* VT_I4                    */
            float        fltVal;            /* VT_R4                    */
            double       dblVal;            /* VT_R8                    */
            VARIANT_BOOL bool;              /* VT_BOOL                  */
            SCODE        scode;             /* VT_ERROR                 */
            CY           cyVal;             /* VT_CY                    */
            DATE         date;              /* VT_DATE                  */
            BSTR         bstrVal;           /* VT_BSTR                  */
            IUnknown     FAR* punkVal;      /* VT_UNKNOWN               */
            IDispatch    FAR* pdispVal;     /* VT_DISPATCH              */

            short        FAR* piVal;        /* VT_BYREF|VT_I2           */
            long         FAR* plVal;        /* VT_BYREF|VT_I4           */
            float        FAR* pfltVal;      /* VT_BYREF|VT_R4           */
            double       FAR* pdblVal;      /* VT_BYREF|VT_R8           */
            VARIANT_BOOL FAR* pbool;        /* VT_BYREF|VT_BOOL         */
            SCODE        FAR* pscode;       /* VT_BYREF|VT_ERROR        */
            CY           FAR* pcyVal;       /* VT_BYREF|VT_CY           */
            DATE         FAR* pdate;        /* VT_BYREF|VT_DATE         */
            BSTR         FAR* pbstrVal;     /* VT_BYREF|VT_BSTR         */
            IUnknown FAR* FAR* ppunkVal;    /* VT_BYREF|VT_UNKNOWN      */
            IDispatch FAR* FAR* ppdispVal;  /* VT_BYREF|VT_DISPATCH     */

            SAFEARRAY    FAR* parray;       /* VT_ARRAY|*               */
            VARIANT      FAR* pvarVal;      /* VT_BYREF|VT_VARIANT      */

            void         FAR* byref;        /* Generic ByRef            */
        };
} ;
```

In order to simplify extracting values from VARIANTARGs , a set of functions for manipulating VARIANTARGs is provided. Use of these functions is highly recommended, in order that applications use consistent coercion rules. These functions are described in Chapter 6, "Data Manipulation Functions."

The *vt* value governs the interpretation of the union as follows:

Value	Description
VT_EMPTY	No value was specified.
	If an argument is left blank, you should **not** return VT_EMPTY for the argument. Rather, you should return the VT_ERROR: DISP_E_MEMBERNOTFOUND.
VT_EMPTY | VT_BYREF	Illegal.
VT_I2	A 2-byte integer was specified; its value is in iVal.
VT_I2 | VT_BYREF	A reference to a 2-byte integer was passed; a pointer to the value is in piVal.

Value	Description
VT_I4	A 4-byte integer was specified; its value is in lVal.
VT_I4	VT_BYREF	A reference to a 4-byte integer was passed; a pointer to the value is in plVal.
VT_R4	An IEEE 4-byte real is stored in fltVal.
VT_R4	VT_BYREF	A reference to an IEEE 4-byte real was passed; a pointer to the value is in pfltVal.
VT_R8	An 8-byte IEEE real was specified; its value is in dblVal.
VT_R8	VT_BYREF	A reference to an 8-byte IEEE real was passed; a pointer to its value is in pdblVal.
VT_CY	A currency value was specified. A currency number is stored as an 8-byte, two's complement integer, scaled by 10,000 to give a fixed-point number with 15 digits to the left of the decimal point and 4 digits to the right. The value is in cyVal.
VT_CY	VT_BYREF	A reference to a currency value was passed; a pointer to the value is in pcyVal.
VT_BSTR	A string was passed. The string is stored in bstrVal. This pointer must be obtained and freed via the BSTR functions. These functions are described in Chapter 6, "Data Manipulation Functions."
VT_BSTR	VT_BYREF	A reference to a string was passed. A BSTR* which points to a BSTR is in pbstrVal. The referenced pointer must be obtained or freed via the BSTR functions.
VT_NULL	A propagating NULL value was specified. This should not be confused with the NULL pointer. The NULL value is used for tri-state logic as with SQL.
VT_NULL	VT_BYREF	Illegal.
VT_ERROR	An SCODE was specified. The type of the error is specified in scode. Generally, operations on error values should raise an exception or propagate the error to the return value, as appropriate.
VT_ERROR	VT_BYREF	A reference to an SCODE was passed. A pointer to the value is in pscode.
VT_BOOL	A Boolean (True/False) value was specified. A value of 0xFFFF (all bits one) indicates True, a value of 0 (all bits zero) indicates False. No other values of bool are legal.
VT_BOOL	VT_BYREF	A reference to a Boolean value. A pointer to the Boolean value is in pbool.

Value	Description
VT_DATE	A value denoting a date and time was specified. Dates are represented as double-precision numbers, where midnight, January 1, 1900 is 2.0, January 2, 1900 is 3.0, and so on. The value is passed in date.

This is the same numbering system used by most spreadsheet programs, although some incorrectly believe that February 29, 1900 existed, and thus set January 1, 1900 to 1.0. The date can be converted to and from an MS-DOS representation using **VariantTimeToDosDateTime** discussed in Chapter 6, "Data Manipulation Functions." |
VT_DATE I VT_BYREF	A reference to a date was passed. A pointer to the value is in pdate.
VT_DISPATCH	A pointer to an object was specified. The pointer is in pdispVal. This object is only known to implement **IDispatch**; the object can be queried as to whether it supports any other desired interface by calling **QueryInterface** on the object. Objects which do not implement **IDispatch** should be passed using VT_UNKNOWN.
VT_DISPATCH I VT_BYREF	A pointer to a pointer to an object was specified. The pointer to the object is stored in the location referred to by ppdispVal.
VT_VARIANT	Illegal. VARIANTARGs must be passed by reference.
VT_VARIANT I VT_BYREF	A pointer to another VARIANTARG is passed in pvarVal. This referenced VARIANTARG will never have the VT_BYREF bit set in the vt, so only one level of indirection can ever be present. This value can be used to support languages which allow variables passed by reference to have their types changed by the called function.
VT_UNKNOWN	A pointer to an object that implements the **IUnknown** interface is passed in punkVal.
VT_UNKNOWN I VT_BYREF	A pointer to a pointer to the **IUnknown** interface is passed in *ppunkVal*. The pointer to the interface is stored in the location referred to by *ppunkVal*.
VT_ARRAY I <anything>	An array of that data type was passed. (VT_EMPTY and VT_NULL are illegal types to combine with VT_ARRAY). The pointer in pByrefVal points to an array descriptor, which describes the dimensionality, size, and in-memory location of the array. The array descriptor is never accessed directly, but instead is read and modified using the functions described in Chapter 6, "Data Manipulation Functions."

VARTYPE

```
enum VARENUM{
    VT_EMPTY,        // Not specified
    VT_NULL,         // Propagating null
    VT_I2,           // Two-byte signed integer
    VT_I4,           // Four-byte signed integer
    VT_R4,           // Real, with four-byte precision
    VT_R8,           // Real
    VT_CY,           // Currency
    VT_DATE,         // Date
    VT_BSTR,      // String
    VT_DISPATCH, // IDispatch *
    VT_ERROR,        // Error
    VT_BOOL,         // Boolean
    VT_VARIANT,      // A VARIANT
    VT_UNKNOWN       // A pointer to the an implementation of IUNKNOWN

    VT_RESERVED = (int) 0x8000

    // By reference: a pointer to the data is passed
    VT_BYREF   = (int) 0x4000
    VT_ARRAY   = (int) 0x2000   // A safe array of the data is passed
};
typedef unsigned short VARTYPE;
```

IDispatch::GetIDsOfNames

HRESULT IDispatch::GetIDsOfNames(*riid, rgszNames, cNames, lcid, rgdispid*)
REFIID *riid*
char FAR* FAR* *rgszNames*
unsigned int *cNames*
LCID *lcid*
DISPID FAR* *rgdispid*

Maps a single member and an optional set of argument names to a corresponding set of integer DISPIDs which may then be used on subsequent calls to **IDispatch::Invoke**. The dispatch function **DispGetIDsOfNames** provides a standard implementation of **GetIDsOfNames**.

Parameter

riid
Reserved for future use. Must be NULL.

rgszNames
Passed in array of names to be mapped.

cNames

Count of the names to be mapped.

lcid

The locale context in which to interpret the given names.

rgdispid

Caller-allocated array each of whose elements contains an ID corresponding to one of the names passed in the *rgszNames* array. The first element represents the member name; the subsequent elements represent each of the member's parameters.

Return Value

The SCODE obtained from the returned HRESULT is one of the following:

SCODE	Meaning
S_OK	Success.
E_OUTOFMEMORY	Out of memory.
DISP_E_UNKNOWNNAME	One or more of the given names were not known. The returned array of DISPIDs will contain DISPID_UNKNOWN for each entry that corresponds to an unknown name.
DISP_E_UNKNOWNLCID	The given LCID was not recognized.

Comments

An **IDispatch** implementation may choose to associate any positive integer ID value with a given name. Zero is reserved for the default, or "value" property, and −1 is reserved to indicate an unknown name. For example, if **GetIDsOfNames** is called and the implementation does not recognize one or more of the given names, it will return DISP_E_UNKNOWNNAME and the *rgdispid* array will contain DISPID_UNKNOWN for the entries which correspond to the unknown names.

The member and parameter DISPIDs must remain constant for the lifetime of the object. This allows a client to discover the DISPIDs once and cache them for later use.

When **GetIDsOfNames** is called with more than one name, the first name (rgszNames[0]) corresponds to the member name and subsequent names correspond to parameter names on that member.

The same name may map to different DISPIDs depending on context. For example, a name may have a DISPID when it is used as a member name with a particular interface, a different DISPID as a member of a different interface, and different mapping for each time it appears as a parameter.

Instead of using **GetIDsOfNames**, an **IDispatch** client can map names to DISPIDs using the type information interfaces described in Chapter 8, "Type Description Interfaces." This allows a client to bind to members at compile time and avoid calling **GetIDsOfNames** at run time.

The implementation of **GetIDsOfNames** must be case insensitive. Clients that want case-sensitive name mapping should use the type information interfaces to map names to DISPIDs, rather than calling **GetIDsOfNames**.

Example

This code from the SPoly2 sample file CPOLY.CPP implements the **GetIDsOfNames** member function for the CPoly class. (OLE Automation object.)

```
STDMETHODIMP
CPoly::GetIDsOfNames(
    REFIID riid,
    char FAR* FAR* rgszNames,
    unsigned int cNames,
    LCID lcid,
    DISPID FAR* rgdispid)
{
    if(riid != IID_NULL)
      return ResultFromScode(DISP_E_UNKNOWNINTERFACE);

    return DispGetIDsOfNames(m_ptinfo, rgszNames, cNames, rgdispid);
}
```

This code calls **GetIDsOfNames** to get the DISPID of the CPoly Draw method. (OLE Automation controller.)

```
HRESULT hresult;
IDispatch FAR* pdisp = (IDispatch FAR*)NULL;
DISPID dispid;
char FAR* szMember = "draw";

hresult = pdisp->GetIDsOfNames(
    IID_NULL,
    &szMember,
    1, LOCALE_SYSTEM_DEFAULT,
    &dispid) ;
```

See Also   **CreateStdDispatch, DispGetIDsOfNames**

IDispatch::GetTypeInfo

HRESULT IDispatch::GetTypeInfo(*itinfo, lcid, pptinfo*)
unsigned int *itinfo*
LCID *lcid*
ITypeInfo FAR* FAR* *pptinfo*

Retrieves type information for an interface.

Parameter

itinfo

Reserved for future use. Always pass 0.

lcid

The locale ID for the type information. An object may be able to return different type information for different languages. This is important for classes that support localized member names. For classes that don't support localized member names, this parameter can be ignored.

pptinfo

Receives a pointer to the type information object requested.

Return Value

The SCODE obtained from the returned HRESULT is one of the following:

SCODE	Meaning
S_OK	Success; the TypeInfo element exists.
TYPE_E_ELEMENTNOTFOUND	Failure; *itypeinfo* argument was not 0.

Example

This code from the SPoly2 sample file CPOLY.CPP creates type information and implements the **GetTypeInfo** member function for the CPoly class. (OLE Automation object.)

```
// These lines from CPoly::Create create pointer to the type
// information returned by GetTypeInfo.
//
    hresult = CreateDispTypeInfo(&g_idataCPoly, LOCALE_SYSTEM_DEFAULT,
                                 &ptinfo);
    ppoly->m_ptinfo = ptinfo;

// Retrieve the type information for this object.
STDMETHODIMP
CPoly::GetTypeInfo(unsigned int itinfo, LCID lcid, ITypeInfo FAR* FAR*
pptinfo)
{
    if(itinfo != 1)                              // Supports one interface.
      return ResultFromScode(DISP_E_BADINDEX);

    m_ptinfo->AddRef();
    *pptinfo = m_ptinfo;

    return NOERROR;
}
```

See Also

CreateStdDispatch

IDispatch::GetTypeInfoCount

HRESULT IDispatch::GetTypeInfoCount(*pctinfo*)
unsigned int FAR* *pctinfo*

Retrieves the number of type information interfaces that an object provides (either 0 or 1).

Parameter

pctinfo
Points to location that receives the number of type information interfaces that the object provides. If the object provides type information, this number is 1; otherwise the number is 0.

Return Value

The SCODE obtained from the returned HRESULT is one of the following:

SCODE	Meaning
S_OK	Success
E_NOTIMPL	Failure

Comments

The function may return zero, which indicates that the object does not provide any type information. In this case, the object may still be programmable through **IDispatch**, but does not provide type information for browsers, compilers, or other programming tools that access type information. This may be useful for hiding an object from browsers or for preventing early binding on an object.

Example

This code from the SPoly2 sample file CPOLY.CPP implements the **GetTypeInfoCount** member function for the CPoly class. (OLE Automation object.)

```
STDMETHODIMP
CPoly::GetTypeInfoCount(unsigned int FAR* pctinfo)
{
    // This object has a single exposed interface
    *pctinfo = 1;

    return NOERROR;
}
```

See Also

CreateStdDispatch

IDispatch::Invoke

HRESULT IDispatch::Invoke(*dispidMember, riid, lcid, wFlags, pdispparams, pvarResult, pexcepinfo, puArgErr*)
LONG *dispidMember*
REFIID *riid*
LCID *lcid*
unsigned short *wFlags*
DISPPARAMS FAR* *pdispparams*
VARIANT FAR* *pvarResult*
EXCEPINFO FAR* *pexcepinfo*
unsigned int FAR* *puArgErr*

Provides access to properties and methods exposed by the object. The dispatch function **DispInvoke** provides a standard implementation of **IDispatch::Invoke**.

Parameter

dispidMember

Identifies the member. Dispatch identifiers may be retrieved using **GetIDsOfNames**.

riid

Reserved for future use. Must be NULL.

lcid

The locale context in which to interpret arguments. This is used by the **GetIDsOfNames** function, and is also passed to **Invoke** to allow the object to interpret its method arguments in a locale-specific way. Applications that don't support multiple national languages can ignore this parameter. See Chapter 10, "National Language Support Functions," for more information on locale IDs.

wFlags

Flags describing the context of the **Invoke** call. See the following table for a complete list of flags.

Value	Description
DISPATCH_METHOD	The member was accessed as a method. If there is a property of the same name, both this and the DISPATCH_PROPERTYGET flag may be set.
DISPATCH_PROPERTYGET	The member is being retrieved as a property or data member.
DISPATCH_PROPERTYPUT	The member is being changed as a property or data member.
DISPATCH_PROPERTYPUTREF	The member is being changed via a reference assignment, rather than a value assignment. This value is only valid when the property accepts a reference to an object.

pdispparams

Pointer to structure containing array of arguments, array of argument dispatch IDs for named arguments, and counts for number of elements in the arrays. See the Comments section for a description of the DISPPARAMS structure.

pvarResult

NULL if caller expects no result. Otherwise, it points to where result is to be stored. This argument is ignored if DISPATCH_PROPERTYPUT or DISPATCH_PROPERTYPUTREF is specified.

pexcepinfo

A pointer to an structure containing exception information. This structure should be filled in if DISP_E_EXCEPTION is returned.

puArgErr

If result is DISP_E_TYPEMISMATCH, this indicates the index within *rgvarg* of the argument with incorrect type. If more than one argument has an error, this should contain the number of the first argument with an error. Arguments are stored in pdispparams->rgvarg in reverse order so the first argument is the one with the highest index in the array. See the Comments section for details.

Return Value

The SCODE obtained from the returned HRESULT is one of the following:

SCODE	Meaning
S_OK	Success.
DISP_E_BADPARAMCOUNT	The number of elements provided in DISPPARAMS is different from the number of arguments accepted by the method or property.
DISP_E_BADVARTYPE	One of the arguments in DISPPARMS is not a valid variant type.
DISP_E_EXCEPTION	The application wishes to raise an exception. In this case the structure passed in pexcepinfo should be filled in.
DISP_E_MEMBERNOTFOUND	The requested member does not exist.
DISP_E_NONAMEDARGS	This implementation of **IDispatch** does not support named arguments.
DISP_E_OVERFLOW	One of the arguments in DISPPARAMS could not be coerced to the specified type.
DISP_E_PARAMNOTFOUND	One of the parameter IDs does not correspond to a parameter on the method. In this case *puArgErr* should be set to the first argument that contains the error.
DISP_E_TYPEMISMATCH	One or more of the arguments could not be coerced. In this case the index within *rgvarg* of the *first* parameter with the incorrect type is returned in the *puArgErr* parameter.

SCODE	Meaning
DISP_E_UNKNOWNINTERFACE	The interface ID passed in *riid* is not NULL.
DISP_E_UNKNOWNLCID	The member being accessed interprets string arguments according to the locale ID (LCID), and the LCID is not recognized. If the LCID is not needed to interpret arguments, this error should not be returned.
DISP_E_PARAMNOTOPTIONAL	A required parameter was omitted.

You can define your own errors using the MAKE_SCODE macro.

Comments

The *dispidMember* argument identifies which member to access. The dispatch IDs identifying members are defined entirely by the implementor of the class, and can be determined using documentation, the **IDispatch::GetIDsOfNames** function, or by using the **ITypeInfo** interface.

Arguments to the method being invoked are passed using the DISPPARAMS structure. It consists of a pointer to an array of arguments represented as variants, dispatch IDs of arguments that were passed as named arguments, and counts for the number of arguments in each array.

```
typedef struct tagDISPPARAMS DISPPARAMS;
struct tagPARAMS{
    VARIANTARG * rgvarg;     // Array of arguments
    DISPID * rgdispidNamedArgs; // Dispatch IDs of named arguments
    unsigned int cArgs;              // Number of arguments
    unsigned int cNamedArgs;         // Number of named arguments
};
```

The arguments to the member are passed in the array *rgvarg[]*, with the number of arguments passed in *cArgs*. Elements within the array *rgvarg* may be changed if they have the ByRef flag set; otherwise they should be considered read only.

The DispDemo sample file DISPHELP.CPP includes the functions **DispBuildParams** and **DispFreeParams** to help create and destroy DISPPARAMS structures used when calling **Invoke**.

The arguments are in the array from last to first, so rgvarg[0] has the last argument, and rgvarg[cArgs −1] has the first argument.

A dispatch invocation can have named arguments as well as positional arguments. If cNamedArgs is 0, all the elements of rgvarg[] represent positional arguments.

Otherwise, there were cNamedArgs named arguments, and each element of rgdispidNamedArgs[] identifies a named argument DISPID whose value is contained in the matching element of rgvarg[]. The named arguments are always contiguous in rgdispidNamedArgs, and their values are in the first *cNamedArgs* elements of *rgvarg*.

The DISPID of an argument is its zero-based position in the argument list. For example, the following method takes three arguments:

```
BOOL _export CDECL
CCredit::CheckCredit(BSTR bstrCustomerID,    // DISPID = 0
                     BSTR bstrLenderID,      // DISPID = 1
                     CURRENCY cLoanAmt)      // DISPID = 2
{
... // Code omitted.
}
```

Named arguments may be passed to **Invoke** in any order, if you include the DISPID with each named argument. For example, if a method is to be invoked with two positional arguments, followed by three named arguments (A, B, and C) using the hypothetical syntax object.method("arg1", "arg2", A := "argA", B := "argB", C: = "argC"), then cArgs would be 5, and *cNamedArgs* would be 3. The first positional argument would be in rgvarg[4]. The second positional argument would be in rgvarg[3]. The ordering of named arguments should be immaterial to the **IDispatch** implementor, but these are also generally passed in reverse order. The argument named A would be in rgvarg[2], with the DISPID corresponding to A in rgdispidNamedArgs[2]. The argument named B would be in rgvarg[1], with the DISPID corresponding to B in rgdispidNamedArgs[1]. The argument named C would be in rgvarg[0], with the DISPID corresponding to C in rgdispidNamedArgs[0]. This is illustrated as follows.

	0	1	2	3	4
rgvarg	"argC"	"argB"	"argA"	"arg2"	"arg1"
rgNamedArgIDs	ID of C	ID of B	ID of A		

In *pvarResult*, the caller passes a pointer to a caller-allocated VARIANTARG where the return value should be placed. If no return value is expected, NULL is passed. The callee fills this value in with the return value. In general, the return value will not have VT_BYREF set. However, implementors may set this bit and return a pointer to the return value, if the lifetime of the return value is the same as that of the object.

Invoke must return DISP_E_MEMBERNOTFOUND if one of the following conditions occur:

- It can't find a member with the specified name *DISPID* and matching *cArgs* and the member is not optional.

- The referenced member is a void function and the caller didn't set *pvarResult* to NULL.

- The referenced member is not a void function and the caller does set *pvarResult* to NULL.

Invoke should return DISP_E_TYPEMISMATCH if it finds a match, but one of the arguments can't be converted to the desired type, setting *puArgErr to the index within rgvarg of the argument with the inappropriate type. For example, if an OLE Automation method expects a reference to a double-precision number as an argument, but receives a reference to an integer, the argument should be coerced. If, however, that method receives a date, **IDispatch::Invoke** should return DISP_E_TYPEMISMATCH.

OLE Automation provides functions to perform standard conversions of VARIANT, and these should be used for consistent operation. Only if these functions fail should DISP_E_TYPEMISMATCH be returned. For more information on performing conversions, see Chapter 6, "Data Manipulation Functions."

Property members are accessed the same way method members are accessed, except that the DISPATCH_PROPERTYGET or DISPATCH_PROPERTYPUT flag is set in wFlags if the use is a property rather than a method access. Note that some languages can't distinguish between retrieving a property and a method call; both the DISPATCH_PROPERTYGET and DISPATCH_METHOD flags will be set in this case. If the caller wants to get the property's current value, DISPATCH_PROPERTYGET is specified, *dispidMember* corresponds to the property's name, cArgs = 0, and *pvarResult* points to the caller-allocated VARIANT which is to receive the property's value. If the caller wants to change the property's value, DISPATCH_PROPERTYPUT is specified, DISPID corresponds to the property's name, *rgvarg*[0] contains the new value, *rgdispidNamedArgs*[0] = DISPID_PROPERTYPUT, *cArgs* = 1, *cNamedArgs* = 1, and *pvarResult* = NULL.

Indexed properties of any dimension are dealt with similarly, by passing additional arguments which are the indexes. In this case, if an element of a indexed property is being changed, the new value of the property is the first element in the rgvarg[] vector. For example, if a put operation on an indexed property is trying to change the value of Prop[1,2] to 3, rgvarg[0] would contain 3, rgvarg[1] would contain 2, and rgvarg[2] would contain 1.

If the setting of a property or data member operation should be a reference assignment rather than the normal value assignment, set the DISPATCH_PROPERTYPUTREF flag.

The caller is responsible for releasing all strings and objects referred to by *rgvarg[]*, or placed in **pvarResult*. As with other BYVAL parameters, if the callee wishes to maintain access to a string after returning, the string should be copied. Also, as usual, if the callee wishes to have access to a passed object pointer after it returns, it must call **AddRef** on that object. A common example is when an object property is changed to refer to a new object, using the DISPATCH_PROPERTYPUTREF flag.

Important   The callee should *not* change values in the passed *rgvarg* array.

Raising Exceptions During Invoke

When an error occurs during the execution of **IDispatch::Invoke**, the implementor can choose to communicate the error either via the normal return value, or by raising an exception. An exception is a special situation that is normally dealt with by jumping to the nearest enclosing exception handler.

If **IDispatch::Invoke** returns DISP_E_EXCEPTION, it is indicating to its caller that an exception has occurred, and that information about the cause of the exception or error has been placed in the structure pointed to by pexcepinfo. This information can then be used by the caller to understand the cause of the exception and deal with it as necessary.

The information placed in the exception information structure includes an error code number which identifies the kind of exception, a string which describes the error in a human-readable way, and a Help file and Help context number which can be passed to WinHelp for more detail about the error. At a minimum, the error code number must be filled in with a valid number.

If you think of **IDispatch** as another way to call C++ style methods in an interface, EXCEPINFO models the throwing of an exception or longjmp() call by such a method.

Example   This code from the SPoly2 sample file CPOLY.CPP implements the **Invoke** member function for the CPoly class. (OLE Automation object.)

```
STDMETHODIMP
CPoly::Invoke(
    DISPID dispidMember,
    REFIID riid,
    LCID lcid,
    unsigned short wFlags,
    DISPPARAMS FAR* pdispparams,
    VARIANT FAR* pvarResult,
    EXCEPINFO FAR* pexcepinfo,
    unsigned int FAR* puArgErr)
{

    if(riid != IID_NULL)
      return ResultFromScode(DISP_E_UNKNOWNINTERFACE);

    return DispInvoke(
      this, m_ptinfo,
      dispidMember, wFlags, pdispparams,
      pvarResult, pexcepinfo, puArgErr);
}
```

This code calls the SPoly2 **Invoke** member function to invoke the Draw method on a CPoly object. (OLE Automation controller.)

```
HRESULT hresult;
IUnknown FAR* punk;
IDispatch FAR* pdisp = (IDispatch FAR*)NULL;
char FAR* szMember = "draw";
DISPID dispid;
DISPPARAMS dispparamsNoArgs = {NULL, NULL, 0, 0};

hresult = CoCreateInstance(CLSID_CPoly2, NULL, CLSCTX_LOCAL_SERVER,
                              IID_Unknown, (void FAR* FAR*)&punk);

hresult = punk->QueryInterface(IID_IDispatch,
                (void FAR* FAR*)&pdisp);

hresult = pdisp->GetIDsOfNames(IID_NULL, &szMember, 1,
                                LOCALE_SYSTEM_DEFAULT, &dispid) ;

hresult = pdisp->Invoke(
dispid,
IID_NULL,
LOCALE_SYSTEM_DEFAULT,
DISPATCH_METHOD,
&dispparamsNoArgs, NULL, NULL, NULL);
```

See Also   **CreateStdDispatch, DispInvoke, DispGetParam**

Dispatch Interface Creation Functions

Implemented by	Used by	Header file name	Import library name
OLE2DISP.DLL	Applications that expose programmable objects	DISPATCH.H	OLE2DISP.LIB

OLE Automation provides these functions to simplify creating OLE Automation objects.

CreateDispTypeInfo

HRESULT CreateDispTypeInfo (*pinterfacedata, lcid, pptinfo*)
INTERFACEDATA *pinterfacedata*
LCID *lcid*
ITypeInfo FAR* FAR* *pptinfo*

Creates simplified type information for use in an implementation of **IDispatch**.

Parameter

pinterfacedata
   The interface description that this type information describes.

lcid
   The locale ID (LCID) for the names used in the type information.

pptinfo
   Output parameter that will contain a pointer to a type information implementation for use in **DispGetIDsOfNames** and **DispInvoke**.

Return Value

The SCODE obtained from the returned HRESULT is one of the following:

SCODE	Meaning
S_OK	The interface is supported.
E_INVALIDARG	Either the interface description or the locale ID is invalid.
E_OUTOFMEMORY	There was insufficient memory to complete the operation.

Comments
Type information may be constructed at run time using **CreateDispTypeInfo** and the INTERFACEDATA defined to describe the object being exposed.

The type information returned by **CreateDispTypeInfo** does not support full functionality of the type information described in Chapter 9, "Type Building Interfaces." The argument *pInterfaceData* is not a complete description of an interface. It does not include Help information, comments, optional parameters, and other type information that is useful in different contexts. The type information returned by this function is primarily designed to automate the implementation of **IDispatch**.

The recommended method for providing type information about an object is to describe the object using the Object Description Language (ODL) and to compile that description into a type library using MkTypLib.

To use type information from a type library, use the **LoadTypeLib** and **GetTypeInfoOfGuid** functions instead of **CreateDispTypeInfo**. For more information on **LoadTypeLib** and **GetTypeInfoOfGuid**, see Chapter 8, "Type Description Interfaces."

Example
This code from the DispCalc sample file DISPCALC.CPP creates type information from INTERFACEDATA defined in IDATA.CPP to expose the CCalc object.

```
CCalc FAR*
CCalc::Create()
{
    HRESULT hresult;
    CCalc FAR* pcalc;
    ITypeInfo FAR* ptinfo;
    IUnknown FAR* punkStdDisp;
    extern INTERFACEDATA g_idataCCalc;   // Defined in IDATA.CPP

    if((pcalc = new FAR CCalc()) == NULL)
      return NULL;

    hresult = CreateDispTypeInfo(
      &g_idataCCalc, LOCALE_SYSTEM_DEFAULT, &ptinfo);
    if(hresult != NOERROR)
      goto LError0;

    hresult = CreateStdDispatch(
      pcalc,                  // Controlling unknown
      &pcalc->m_arith,        // vtable* to dispatch on
      ptinfo,
      &punkStdDisp);

    ptinfo->Release();

    if(hresult != NOERROR)
```

```
        goto LError0;

    pcalc->m_punkStdDisp = punkStdDisp;

    return pcalc;

LError0::;
    pcalc->Release();

    return NULL;
}
```

CreateStdDispatch

HRESULT CreateStdDispatch (*punkOuter, pvThis, ptinfo, ppunkStdDisp*)
IUnknown FAR* *punkOuter*
void FAR* *pvThis*
ITypeInfo FAR* *ptinfo*
IUnknown FAR* FAR* *ppunkStdDisp*

Creates a standard implementation of the **IDispatch** interface through a single function call. This greatly simplifies exposing objects through OLE Automation.

Parameters

punkOuter
Pointer to the object's **IUnknown** implementation.

pvThis
Pointer to the object to expose.

ptinfo
Pointer to the type information that describes the exposed object.

ppunkStdDisp
Pointer to the location where the implementation of the **IDispatch** interface for this object is returned. This pointer is NULL if the function fails.

Return Value

The SCODE obtained from the returned HRESULT is one of the following:

SCODE	Meaning
S_OK	Success.
E_INVALIDARG	One of the first three arguments is invalid.
E_OUTOFMEMORY	There was insufficient memory to complete the operation.

Comments

You can **CreateStdDispatch** when you create an object instead of implementing the **IDispatch** member functions for that object. The implementation that **CreateStdDispatch** creates has these limitations:

- Supports one national language.
- Supports only dispatch-defined exception codes returned from **Invoke**.

CreateDispTypeInfo and **CreateStdDispatch** comprise the minimum set dispatch components you need to call in order to expose an object using type information provided by the INTERFACEDATA structure.

LoadTypeLib, **GetTypeInfoOfGuid**, and **CreateStdDispatch** comprise the minimum set of functions you need to call in order to expose an object using a type library. For more information on **LoadTypeLib** and **GetTypeInfoOfGuid**, see Chapter 8, "Type Description Interfaces."

Example

This code from the DispCalc sample file DISPCALC.CPP implements the IDispatch interface for the CCalc class using **CreateStdDispatch**. (OLE Automation object.)

```
CCalc FAR*
CCalc::Create()
{
    HRESULT hresult;
    CCalc FAR* pcalc;
    ITypeInfo FAR* ptinfo;
    IUnknown FAR* punkStdDisp;
extern INTERFACEDATA g_idataCCalc;        // Defined in IDATA.CPP

    if((pcalc = new FAR CCalc()) == NULL)
      return NULL;

    hresult = CreateDispTypeInfo(
      &g_idataCCalc, LOCALE_SYSTEM_DEFAULT, &ptinfo);
    if(hresult != NOERROR)
      goto LError0;

    hresult = CreateStdDispatch(
      pcalc,                   // Controlling unknown
      &pcalc->m_arith,            // vtable* to dispatch on
      ptinfo,
      &punkStdDisp);

    ptinfo->Release();

    if(hresult != NOERROR)
      goto LError0;

    pcalc->m_punkStdDisp = punkStdDisp;
```

```
        return pcalc;

LError0::;
    pcalc->Release();

    return NULL;
}
```

This code calls the CCalc **IDispatch** member functions implemented by **CreateStdDispatch**. (OLE Automation controller.)

```
long x = 4;
HRESULT hresult;
IUnknown FAR* punk;
IDispatch FAR* pdisp = (IDispatch FAR*)NULL;
char FAR* szMember = "accum";
DISPID dispid;
DISPPARAMS FAR* pdispparams;
DISPPARAMS dispparamsNoArgs = {NULL, NULL, 0, 0};

hresult = CoCreateInstance(CLSID_DispCalc, NULL,
    CLSCTX_LOCAL_SERVER, IID_IUnknown, (void FAR* FAR*)&punk);

hresult = punk->QueryInterface(IID_IDispatch,
    (void FAR* FAR*)&pdisp);

punk->Release();

szMember = "accum";

hresult = pdisp->GetIDsOfNames(
    IID_NULL,
    &szMember,
    1, LOCALE_SYSTEM_DEFAULT,
    &dispid) ;

hresult = DispBuildParams(&pdispparams, 0, NULL, "I", x);

hresult = pdisp->Invoke(
    dispid,
    IID_NULL,
    LOCALE_SYSTEM_DEFAULT,
    DISPATCH_PROPERTYPUT,
    pdispparams, NULL, NULL, NULL);

DispFreeParams(pdispparams);
```

DispGetIDsOfNames

HRESULT **DispGetIDsOfNames** (*ptinfo, rgszNames, cNames, rgdispid*)
ITypeInfo * *ptinfo*
char FAR* FAR* *rgszNames*
unsigned int *cNames*
DISPID FAR* *rgdispid*

Uses type information to convert a set of names to DISPIDs. This is the recommended implementation of **IDispatch::GetIDsOfNames**.

Parameter

ptinfo
Pointer to the type information for an interface. Note that this type information will be specific to one interface and language code, so it is not necessary to pass an IID or LCID to this function.

rgszNames
An array of name strings. This can be the array passed to **IDispatch** in the DISPATCHARGS structure. If *cNames* is greater than one, the first name will be interpreted as a method name and subsequent names will be interpreted as parameters to that method.

cNames
The number of elements in *rgszNames*.

rgdispid
Pointer to an array of DISPIDs that will get filled in by this function. The first id will correspond to the method name; subsequent names will be interpreted as parameters to the method.

Return Value

The SCODE obtained from the returned HRESULT is one of the following:

SCODE	Meaning
S_OK	The interface is supported.
E_INVALIDARG	One of the arguments is invalid.
DISP_E_UNKNOWNNAME	One or more of the given names were not known. The returned array of DISPIDs will contain DISPID_UNKNOWN for each entry that corresponds to an unknown name.
Other returns	Any of the **ITypeInfo::Invoke** errors may also be returned.

Example   This code from the SPoly2 sample file CPOLY.CPP implements the member function **GetIDsOfNames** for the CPoly class using **DispGetIDsOfNames**.

```
STDMETHODIMP
CPoly::GetIDsOfNames(
    REFIID riid,
    char FAR* FAR* rgszNames,
    unsigned int cNames,
    LCID lcid,
    DISPID FAR* rgdispid)
{
    if(riid != IID_NULL)
      return ResultFromScode(DISP_E_UNKNOWNINTERFACE);

    return DispGetIDsOfNames(m_ptinfo, rgszNames, cNames, rgdispid);
}
```

See Also   **CreateStdDispatch, IDispatch::GetIDsOfNames**

DispGetParam

HRESULT DispGetParam(*dispparams, iPosition, vt, pvarResult, puArgErr*)
DISPPARAMS FAR* *dispparams*
unsigned int *iPosition*
VARTYPE *vt*
VARIANT FAR* *pvarResult*
unsigned int FAR* *puArgErr*

Retrieves a parameter from the *dispparams* structure, checking both named parameters and positional parameters, and coerces it to the specified type.

Parameter   *dispparams*
Pointer to the parameters passed to **IDispatch::Invoke**.

iPosition
The position of the parameter in the parameter list. **DispGetParam** starts at the end of the array, so if *iPosition* is 0, the last parameter in the array will be returned.

vt
The type that the argument should be coerced to when it is copied into *pvarResult*.

pvarResult
Pointer to the variant into which to pass the parameter. This must be a valid VARIANT; any existing contents will be released in the standard way. The contents of this VARIANT should be freed with **VariantFree**.

puArgErr

Pointer to the index of the argument that caused a
DISP_E_TYPEMISMATCH error. This pointer should be returned to **Invoke**
to indicate the position of the argument in DISPPARAMS that caused the
error.

Return Value

The SCODE obtained from the HRESULT is one of the following:

SCODE	Meaning
S_OK	Success.
DISP_E_BADVARTYPE	The variant type *vt* is not supported.
DISP_E_OVERFLOW	The retrieved parameter could not be coerced to the specified type.
DISP_E_PARAMNOTFOUND	Could not find the parameter indicated by *iPosition*.
DISP_E_TYPEMISMATCH	Could not coerce argument to specified type.
E_INVALIDARG	One of the arguments was invalid.
E_OUTOFMEMORY	Insufficient memory to complete operation.

Example

This code from the SPoly sample file CPOINT.CPP shows using **DispGetParam**
to set X and Y properties.

```
STDMETHODIMP
CPoint::Invoke(
    DISPID dispidMember,
    REFIID riid,
    LCID lcid,
    unsigned short wFlags,
    DISPPARAMS FAR* pdispparams,
    VARIANT FAR* pvarResult,
    EXCEPINFO FAR* pexcepinfo,
    unsigned int FAR* pwArgErr)
{
    HRESULT hresult;
    VARIANTARG varg0;
    VARIANT varResultDummy;

    VariantInit(&varResultDummy);

    if(riid != IID_NULL)
      return ResultFromScode(DISP_E_UNKNOWNINTERFACE);
```

```
// It simplifies the following code if the caller
// ignores the return value.
if(pvarResult == NULL)
  pvarResult = &varResultDummy;

VariantInit(&varg0);

// Assume the return type is void, unless we find otherwise.
VariantInit(pvarResult);

switch(dispidMember){
case IDMEMBER_CPOINT_GETX:
  V_VT(pvarResult) = VT_I2;
  V_I2(pvarResult) = GetX();
  break;

case IDMEMBER_CPOINT_SETX:
  hresult = DispGetParam(pdispparams, 0, VT_I2, &varg0, pwArgErr);
  if(hresult != NOERROR)
    return hresult;
  SetX(V_I2(&varg0));
  break;

case IDMEMBER_CPOINT_GETY:
  V_VT(pvarResult) = VT_I2;
  V_I2(pvarResult) = GetY();
  break;

case IDMEMBER_CPOINT_SETY:
  hresult = DispGetParam(pdispparams, 0, VT_I2, &varg0, pwArgErr);
  if(hresult != NOERROR)
    return hresult;
  SetY(V_I2(&varg0));
  break;

default:
  return ResultFromScode(DISP_E_MEMBERNOTFOUND);
}
return NOERROR;
}
```

See Also   **CreateStdDispatch, IDispatch::Invoke**

DispInvoke

> **HRESULT DispInvoke(** _this, ptinfo, dispidMember, wFlags, pparams,
> pvarResult, pexcepinfo, puArgErr**)**
> **void FAR*** _this
> **ITypeInfo FAR*** ptinfo
> **LONG** dispidMember
> **unsigned short** wFlags
> **DISPPARAMS FAR*** pparams
> **VARIANT FAR*** pvarResult
> **EXCEPINFO** pexcepinfo
> **unsigned int FAR*** puArgErr

Automatically calls member functions on an interface, given type information. A developer can describe an interface with type information, and implement **IDispatch::Invoke** for that interface using this single call.

Parameter

_this
A pointer to an implementation of the **IDispatch** interface described by ptinfo.

ptinfo
A pointer to the type information describing the interface.

dispidMember
The member to invoke.

wFlags
Flags describing the context of the **Invoke** call. See following table for complete list of flags.

Value	Description
DISPATCH_METHOD	The member was accessed as a method. If there is ambiguity, both this and the DISPATCH_PROPERTYGET flag may be set.
DISPATCH_PROPERTYGET	The member is being retrieved as a property or data member.
DISPATCH_PROPERTYPUT	The member is being changed as a property or data member.
DISPATCH_PROPERTYPUTREF	The member is being changed via a reference assignment, rather than a value assignment.
Other returns	Any of the **ITypeInfo::Invoke** errors may also be returned.

pparams
Pointer to the parameters passed to **IDispatch::Invoke.**

pvarResult
Pointer to the result VARIANT passed to **IDispatch::Invoke.**

pexcepinfo

> Pointer to the EXCEPINFO passed to **IDispatch::Invoke**. This is not currently used by **DispInvoke**.

puArgErr

> If result is DISP_E_TYPEMISMATCH, this indicates the index within *rgvarg* of the argument with incorrect type. If more than one argument has an error, this should contain the number of the first argument with an error. Remember that arguments are placed in *pdispparams->rgvarg* in reverse order, so the first argument is the one with the highest index in the array.

Return Value

The SCODE obtained from the returned HRESULT is one of the following:

SCODE	Meaning
S_OK	Success.
DISP_E_BADPARAMCOUNT	The number of elements provided in DISPPARAMS is different from the number of arguments accepted by the method or property.
DISP_E_BADVARTYPE	One of the arguments in DISPPARMS is not a valid variant type.
DISP_E_EXCEPTION	The application wishes to raise an exception. In this case the structure passed in pexcepinfo should be filled in.
DISP_E_MEMBERNOTFOUND	The requested member does not exist.
DISP_E_NONAMEDARGS	This implementation of **IDispatch** does not support named arguments.
DISP_E_OVERFLOW	One of the arguments in DISPPARAMS could not be coerced to the specified type.
DISP_E_PARAMNOTFOUND	One of the parameter IDs does not correspond to a parameter on the method. In this case *puArgErr* should be set to the first argument that contains the error.
DISP_E_PARAMNOTOPTIONAL	A required parameter was omitted.
DISP_E_TYPEMISMATCH	One or more of the arguments could not be coerced. In this case the index within *rgvarg* of the *first* parameter with the incorrect type is returned in the *puArgErr* parameter.
DISP_E_UNKNOWNINTERFACE	The interface ID passed in *riid* is not NULL.
DISP_E_UNKNOWNLCID	The member being accessed interprets string arguments according to the locale ID (LCID), and the LCID is not recognized. If the LCID is not needed to interpret arguments, this error should not be returned.
E_INVALIDARG	One of the arguments is invalid.

SCODE	Meaning
E_OUTOFMEMORY	Insufficient memory to complete operation.

Comments   The parameter _this is a pointer to an implementation of the interface being deferred to. **DispInvoke** builds a stack frame, coerces parameters using standard coercions, pushes them on the stack, and calls the correct member function in the virtual function table.

Example

```
STDMETHODIMP CCalc::CDisp::Invoke(
    DISPID dispidMember,
    REFIID riid,
    LCID lcid,
    unsigned short wFlags,
    DISPPARAMS FAR* pdispparams,
    VARIANT FAR* pvarResult,
    EXCEPINFO FAR* pexcepinfo,
    unsigned int FAR* puArgErr)
{
    if(riid != IID_NULL)
      return ReportResult(0, DISP_E_UNKNOWNINTERFACE, 0, 0);

    if(lcid != m_pcalc->m_lcid)
      return ReportResult(0, DISP_E_UNKNOWNLCID, 0, 0);

    return DispInvoke(
      &m_pcalc->m_arith,
      m_pcalc->m_ptinfo,
      dispidMember, wFlags, pdispparams,
      pvarResult, pexcepinfo, puArgErr);
}
```

See Also   **CreateStdDispatch, IDispatch::Invoke**

Active Object Registration Functions

Implemented by	Used by	Header file name	Import library name
OLE2DISP.DLL	Applications that expose or access programmable objects	DISPATCH.H	OLE2DISP.LIB

These functions let you identify a running instance of an object. When an application is started with the /Automation switch, it should initialize its Application object as the active object by calling **RegisterActiveObject**.

Applications may also initialize other top-level objects as the active object. For example, an application that exposes a document object may want to let OLE Automation controllers retrieve and modify the currently active document.

For more information on initializing the active object, see Chapter 2, "Exposing OLE Automation Objects."

GetActiveObject

HRESULT GetActiveObject(*rclsid*, *pvreserved*, *ppunk*)
REFCLSID *rclsid*
void FAR* *pvreserved*
IUnknown FAR* FAR* *ppunk*

Retrieves a pointer to a running application initialized with OLE.

Parameters

rclsid
    Pointer to the class ID of the active object from the OLE registration database.

pvreserved
    Must be NULL. Reserved for future use.

ppunk
    Location in which to return a pointer to the requested active object.

Return Value

The SCODE obtained from the returned HRESULT is one of the following:

SCODE	Meaning
S_OK	Success
Other returns	Failure

RegisterActiveObject

HRESULT RegisterActiveObject (*punk*, *rclsid*, *pvreserved*, *pdwRegister*)
IUknown FAR* *punk*
REFCLSID *rclsid*
void FAR* *pvreserved*
unsigned long FAR* *pdwRegister*

Registers the indicated object (*punk*) as the active object for the class indicated by *rclsid*.

Parameters

punk

    Pointer to the **IUnknown** interface of the active object.

rclsid

    Pointer to the class ID of the active object.

pvreserved

    Reserved for future use. Must be NULL.

pdwRegister

    Pointer to a handle used when initializing and revoking an active object. This handle is created by **RegisterActiveObject** and passed to **RevokeActiveObject** when you want to end an object's status as active.

Return Value

The SCODE obtained from the returned HRESULT is one of the following:

SCODE	Meaning
S_OK	Success
Other returns	Failure

RevokeActiveObject

HRESULT RevokeActiveObject (*dwRegister, pvreserved*)
unsigned long *dwRegister*
void FAR* *pvreserved*

Ends an object's status as active.

Parameters

dwRegister

    A handle previously returned by **RegisterActiveObject**.

pvreserved

    Reserved for future use. Must be NULL.

Return Value

The SCODE obtained from the returned HRESULT is one of the following:

SCODE	Meaning
S_OK	Success
Other returns	Failure

IEnumVARIANT Interface

Implemented by	Used by	Header file name	Import library name
Applications that expose collections of objects	Applications that access collections of objects	DISPATCH.H	None

The **IEnumVARIANT** interface provides a method for enumerating a collection of variants. It can be used to enumerate over heterogeneous collections of objects and intrinsic types. Similarly, **IEnumVARIANT** allows enumerating by clients that can't know (or do not wish to know) the specific type, or types, of the elements in the collection.

The following is the definition that results from expanding the parameterized type IEnumVARIANT:

```
interface IEnumVARIANT : IUnknown {
    virtual HRESULT Next(unsigned long celt,
                         VARIANT rgelt[],
                         unsigned long* pceltFetched) = 0;
    virtual HRESULT Skip(unsigned long celt) = 0;
    virtual HRESULT Reset() = 0;
    virtual HRESULT Clone(IEnumVARIANT ** ppenum) = 0;
    };
```

See the sample file CENUMPT.CPP for an example of how to implement a collection of objects using **IEnumVARIANT**.

IEnumVARIANT::Clone

HRESULT IEnumVARIANT::Clone(*ppenum*)
IEnumVARIANT FAR* FAR* *ppenum*

Creates a copy of the current enumeration state.

Parameter

ppenum
Points to the place in which to return the clone enumerator.

Return Value

The SCODE obtained from the returned HRESULT is one of the following:

SCODE	Meaning
S_OK	Success.
E_OUTOFMEMORY	Insufficient memory to complete the operation.

Comments   Using this function, you can record a particular point in the enumeration sequence, then return to it at a later time. Notice that the enumerator returned is of the same actual interface as the one which is being cloned.

There is no guarantee that *exactly* the same set of VARIANTs will be enumerated the second time as was enumerated the first. Although desirable, whether this is the case depends on the collection being enumerated. Some collections (for example, enumerating the files in a directory) will simply find it too expensive to maintain this condition.

Example

```
STDMETHODIMP CEnumPoint::Clone(IEnumVARIANT FAR* FAR* ppenum)
{
    HRESULT hresult;
    SAFEARRAY FAR* psa;
    CEnumPoint FAR* penum;

    hresult = SafeArrayCopy(m_psa, &psa);
    if(FAILED(hresult))
      return hresult;

    hresult = CEnumPoint::Create(psa, &penum);
    if(FAILED(hresult))
      goto LError0;

    // Assert(penum->m_celts == m_celts);
    penum->m_iCurrent = m_iCurrent;
    return NOERROR;

LError0:
    SafeArrayDestroy(psa);
    return hresult;
}
```

IEnumVARIANT::Next

HRESULT IEnumVARIANT::Next(*celt, rgelt, pceltFetched*)
unsigned long *celt*
VARIANT FAR* *rgelt*
unsigned long FAR* *pceltFetched*

Attempts to get the next *celt* items in the enumeration sequence and return them through the array pointed to by *rgelt*.

Parameter	*celt*

Parameter

celt
    The number of elements to be returned.

rgelt
    An array of at least size *celt* in which the next elements are to be returned.

pceltFetched
    If not NULL, *pceltFetched* points to the number of elements actually returned in *rgelt*.

Return Value

The SCODE obtained from the returned HRESULT is one of the following:

SCODE	Meaning
S_OK	The number of elements returned is *celt*.
S_FALSE	The number of elements returned by is less than *celt*.

Comments

If fewer than the requested number of elements remain in the sequence, return only the remaining elements; the actual number of elements returned is passed through *pceltFetched* (unless it is NULL).

Example

```
STDMETHODIMP CEnumPoint::Next(
    unsigned long celt,
    VARIANT FAR rgvar[],
    unsigned long FAR* pceltFetched)
{
    unsigned int i;
    LONG ix;
    HRESULT hresult;

    for(i = 0; i < celt; ++i)
      VariantInit(&rgvar[i]);

    for(i = 0; i < celt; ++i){
      if(m_iCurrent == m_celts){
         hresult = ReportResult(0, S_FALSE, 0, 0);
      goto LDone;
       }

       ix = m_iCurrent++;
       hresult = SafeArrayGetElement(m_psa, &ix, &rgvar[i]);
       if(FAILED(hresult))
      goto LError0;
       }

    hresult = NOERROR;

LDone:;
    *pceltFetched = i;
    return hresult;
```

```
LError0:;

    for(i = 0; i < celt; ++i)
      VariantClear(&rgvar[i]);
    return hresult;
}
```

IEnumVARIANT::Reset

HRESULT IEnumVARIANT::Reset()

Resets the enumeration sequence back to the beginning.

Return Value   The SCODE obtained from the returned HRESULT is one of the following:

SCODE	Meaning
S_OK	Success
S_FALSE	Failure

Comments   There is no guarantee that *exactly* the same set of VARIANTs will be enumerated the second time as was enumerated the first. Although desirable, whether this is the case depends on the collection being enumerated. Some collections (for example, enumerating the files in a directory) will simply find it too expensive to maintain this condition.

Example
```
STDMETHODIMP CEnumPoint::Reset()
{
    m_iCurrent = 0;
    return NOERROR;
}
```

IEnumVARIANT::Skip

HRESULT IEnumVARIANT::Skip(*celt*)
unsigned long   *celt*

Attempts to skip over the next *celt* elements in the enumeration sequence.

Parameter   *celt*
          The number of elements to be skipped.

Return Value

The SCODE obtained from the returned HRESULT is one of the following:

SCODE	Meaning
S_OK	The specified number of elements could be skipped.
S_FALSE	The end of the sequence was reached first.

Example

```
STDMETHODIMP CEnumPoint::Skip(unsigned long celt)
{
    m_iCurrent += celt;

    if(m_iCurrent > m_celts)
     m_iCurrent = m_celts;

    return (m_iCurrent == m_celts)
       ? ReportResult(0, S_FALSE, 0, 0) : NOERROR;
}
```

CHAPTER 6

Data Manipulation Functions

The data manipulation functions access and manipulate the arrays, strings, and variant types of data used by OLE Automation.

Overview of Functions

The data manipulation functions are summarized in the following table. All of these functions are provided in OLE2DISP.DLL. The header file is DISPATCH.H and the import library is OLE2DISP.LIB.

Category	Function name	Purpose
Array manipulation	**SafeArrayAccessData**	Increments the lock count of an array and returns a pointer to array data.
	SafeArrayAllocData	Allocates memory for a safe array based on a descriptor created with **SafeArrayAllocDescriptor**.
	SafeArrayAllocDescriptor	Allocates memory for a safe array descriptor.
	SafeArrayCopy	Copies an existing array.
	SafeArrayCreate	Creates a new array descriptor.
	SafeArrayDestroy	Destroys an array descriptor.
	SafeArrayDestroyData	Frees memory used by the data elements in a safe array.
	SafeArrayDestroyDescriptor	Frees memory used by a safe array descriptor.
	SafeArrayGetDim	Returns the number of dimensions in an array.
	SafeArrayGetElement	Retrieves an element of an array.
	SafeArrayGetElemsize	Returns the size of an element.
	SafeArrayGetLBound	Retrieves the lower bound for a given dimension.

Category	Function name	Purpose
	SafeArrayGetUBound	Retrieves the upper bound for a given dimension.
	SafeArrayLock	Increments the lock count of an array.
	SafeArrayPutElement	Assigns an element into an array.
	SafeArrayRedim	Resizes a safe array.
	SafeArrayUnAccessData	Frees a pointer to array data and decrements the lock count of the array.
	SafeArrayUnlock	Decrements the lock count of an array.
String manipulation	SysAllocString	Creates and initializes a string.
	SysAllocStringLen	Creates a string of a specified length.
	SysFreeString	Frees a previously created string.
	SysReAllocString	Changes the size and value of a string.
	SysReAllocStringLen	Changes the size of an existing string.
	SysStringLen	Returns the length of a string.
Variant manipulation	VariantChangeType	Converts a variant to another type.
	VariantChangeTypeEx	Converts a variant to another type using a locale ID.
	VariantClear	Releases resources and sets a variant to VT_EMPTY.
	VariantCopy	Copies a variant.
	VariantCopyInd	Copies variants that may contain a pointer.
	VariantInit	Initializes a variant.
	Low-level conversion functions	Convert specific types of variants to other variant types. These functions are called by **VariantChangeType** and **VariantChangeTypeEx**.
Time conversion	DosDateTimeToVariantTime	Converts MS-DOS date and time representations to a variant time.
	VariantTimeToDosDateTime	Converts a variant time to MS-DOS date and time representations.

Array Manipulation Functions

Implemented by	Used by	Header file name	Import library name
OLE2DISP.DLL	Applications that expose or access programmable objects	DISPATCH.H	OLE2DISP.LIB

The arrays passed by **IDispatch::Invoke** within VARIANTARGs are called *safe arrays*. Safe arrays contain information about the number of dimensions and bounds within them. When an argument or return value that is an array is provided or returned, the *parray* member of VARIANTARG points to an array descriptor. This array descriptor should not be accessed directly unless you are creating arrays containing elements with nonvariant data types. Functions **SafeArrayAccessData** and **SafeArrayUnaccessData** are provided for accessing the data. The base type of the array is indicated by the VT_ tag or'ed with the VT_ARRAY bit. Following are the definitions of the safe array descriptor, and the functions to use when accessing the data in the descriptor and the array itself.

The data referred to by an array descriptor is stored in column-major order, which is the same ordering scheme used by Visual Basic and FORTRAN, but different from C and Pascal. *Column-major order* means that the leftmost dimension (as specified in a programming language syntax) changes first.

Subscripts for safe arrays are zero-based.

Data Types and Structures

SAFEARRAY

```
typedef struct tagSAFEARRAY {
    USHORT cDims;         // Count of dimensions in this array.
    USHORT fFeatures;     // Flags used by the SafeArray
                          // routines documented below:
    USHORT cbElements;    // The size of an element of the array --
                          // does not include size of pointed-to data.
    USHORT cLocks;        // Number of times the array has been locked
                          // without corresponding unlock.
    HANDLE handle;        // Handle to the data. Format is private.
    void *pvData;         // Pointer to the data. Valid when cLocks > 0.
    SAFEARRAYBOUND rgsabound[]; // One bound for each dimension.

} SAFEARRAY;
```

The array rgsabound is stored with the leftmost dimension in rgsabound[0] and the rightmost dimension in rgsabound[cdims − 1]. If an array were specified in C-like syntax as a[2][5], it would have two elements in the rgsabound vector. Element 0 has an lLbound of 0 and a cElements of 2. Element 1 has an lLbound of 0 and a cElements of 5.

The fFeatures flags describe attributes of an array which may affect how the array is released. This allows freeing the array without referencing its containing variant. The bits are accessed using the following #define statements.

```
#define FADF_VARIANT // An array of VARIANTs.
#define FADF_DISPATCH   // An array of IDispatch*.
#define FADF_UNKNOWN // An array of IUnknown*.
#define FADF_AUTO       // The array is allocated on the stack and need
                        // not be freed.
#define FADF_STATIC     // The array is statically allocated and need
not
                        // be freed.
#define FADF_BSTR       // An array of BSTRs.
```

For more information, see Chapter 3, "Accessing OLE Automation Objects."

SAFEARRAYBOUND

```
typedef struct tagSAFEARRAYBOUND {
    unsigned long cElements;
    long lLbound;
} SAFEARRAYBOUND;
```

This structure represent the bounds of one dimension of the array. lLbound represents the lower bound on this dimension, and cElements is the count of elements for this dimension.

SafeArrayAccessData

HRESULT SafeArrayAccessData(*psa, ppvdata*)
SAFEARRAY FAR* *psa*
void FAR* HUGEP* *ppvdata*

Increments the lock count of an array and retrieves a pointer to the array data.

Parameters   *psa*

Points to an array descriptor created by **SafeArrayCreate**.

ppvdata

On exit, points to the pointer to the array data. Note that arrays may be larger than 64K, so huge pointers must be used on Windows version 3.1 or later.

| **Return Value** | The SCODE obtained from the returned HRESULT is one of the following: |

SCODE	Meaning
S_OK	Success.
E_INVALIDARG	The argument *psa* was not a valid safe array descriptor.
E_UNEXPECTED	The array could not be locked.

SafeArrayAllocData

HRESULT SafeArrayAllocData(*psa*)
SAFEARRAY FAR* *psa*

Allocates memory for a safe array based on a descriptor created with
SafeArrayAllocDescriptor.

Parameters

psa
Points to an array descriptor created by **SafeArrayAllocDescriptor**.

Return Value

The SCODE obtained from the returned HRESULT is one of the following:

SCODE	Meaning
S_OK	Success.
E_INVALIDARG	The argument *psa* was not a valid safe array descriptor.
E_UNEXPECTED	The array could not be locked.

Example

The following example creates a safe array using the **SafeArrayAllocDescriptor**
and **SafeArrayAllocData** functions.

```
SAFEARRAY FAR* FAR*ppsa;
unsigned int ndim = 2;
HRESULT hresult = SafeArrayAllocDescriptor( ndim, ppsa );
if( FAILED( hresult ) )
    return ERR_OutOfMemory;
(*ppsa)->rgsabound[ 0 ].lLbound = 0;
(*ppsa)->rgsabound[ 0 ].cElements = 5;
(*ppsa)->rgsabound[ 1 ].lLbound = 1;
(*ppsa)->rgsabound[ 1 ].cElements = 4;
hresult = SafeArrayAllocData( *ppsa );
if( FAILED( hresult ) ) {
    SafeArrayDestroyDescriptor( *ppsa )
    return ERR_OutOfMemory;
}
```

See Also   SafeArrayAllocData, SafeArrayDestroyData, SafeArrayDestroyDescriptor

SafeArrayAllocDescriptor

HRESULT SafeArrayAllocDescriptor(*cDims, ppsaOut*)
unsigned int *cDims*
SAFEARRAY FAR* FAR* *ppsaOut*

Allocates memory for a safe array descriptor.

Parameters   *cDims*
> The number of dimensions of the array.

ppsaOut
> Points to a location in which to store the created array descriptor.

Return Value   The SCODE obtained from the returned HRESULT is one of the following:

SCODE	Meaning
S_OK	Success.
E_INVALIDARG	The argument *psa* was not a valid safe array descriptor.
E_UNEXPECTED	The array could not be locked.

Comments   This function lets you create safe arrays containing elements with data type other than those provided by **SafeArrayCreate**. After creating an array descriptor using **SafeArrayAllocDescriptor**, set the element size in the array descriptor and call **SafeArrayAllocData** to allocate memory for the array elements.

Example   The following example creates a safe array using the **SafeArrayAllocDescriptor** and **SafeArrayAllocData** functions.

```
SAFEARRAY FAR* FAR*ppsa;
unsigned int ndim = 2;
HRESULT hresult = SafeArrayAllocDescriptor( ndim, ppsa );
if( FAILED( hresult ) )
    return ERR_OutOfMemory;
(*ppsa)->rgsabound[ 0 ].lLbound = 0;
(*ppsa)->rgsabound[ 0 ].cElements = 5;
(*ppsa)->rgsabound[ 1 ].lLbound = 1;
(*ppsa)->rgsabound[ 1 ].cElements = 4;
hresult = SafeArrayAllocData( *ppsa );
if( FAILED( hresult ) ) {
    SafeArrayDestroyDescriptor( *ppsa )
    return ERR_OutOfMemory;
}
```

See Also **SafeArrayAllocData, SafeArrayDestroyData, SafeArrayDestroyDescriptor**

SafeArrayCopy

HRESULT SafeArrayCopy(*psa, ppsaOut*)
SAFEARRAY FAR* *psa*
SAFEARRAY FAR* FAR* *ppsaOut*

Creates a copy of an existing safe array.

Parameters

psa
> Points to an array descriptor created by **SafeArrayCreate**.

ppsaOut
> Points to a location in which to return the new array descriptor.

Return Value

The SCODE obtained from the returned HRESULT is one of the following:

SCODE	Meaning
S_OK	Success.
E_INVALIDARG	The argument *psa* was not a valid safe array descriptor.
E_OUTOFMEMORY	There was insufficient memory to create the copy.

Comments

SafeArrayCopy calls the string or variant manipulation functions if the array to copy contains either of those data types. If the array being copied contains object references, the reference counts for those objects are incremented.

See Also

SysAllocStringLen, VariantCopy, VariantCopyInd

SafeArrayCreate

SAFEARRAY * SafeArrayCreate(*vt, cDims, rgsabounds*)
VARTYPE *vt*
unsigned int *cDims*
SAFEARRRAYBOUND FAR* *rgsabounds*

Creates a new array descriptor, allocates and initializes the data for the array, and returns a pointer to the new array descriptor.

Parameters

vt

The "base" type of the array (the VARTYPE of each element of the array). The VARTYPE is restricted to a subset of the variant types. Neither the VT_ARRAY and VT_BYREF flags can be set. VT_EMPTY and VT_NULL are not valid base types for the array. All other types are legal.

cDims

Number of dimensions in the array. This cannot be changed after the array is created.

rgsabounds

Points to a vector of bounds (one for each dimension) to allocate for the array.

Return Value

Points to the array descriptor, or NULL if the array could not be created.

Example

```
HRESULT PASCAL __export CPoly::EnumPoints(IEnumVARIANT FAR* FAR* ppenum)
{
    unsigned int i;
    HRESULT hresult;
    VARIANT var;
    SAFEARRAY FAR* psa;
    CEnumPoint FAR* penum;
    POINTLINK FAR* ppointlink;
    SAFEARRAYBOUND rgsabound[1];

    rgsabound[0].lLbound = 0;
    rgsabound[0].cElements = m_cPoints;

    psa = SafeArrayCreate(VT_VARIANT, 1, rgsabound);
    if(psa == NULL){
        hresult = ReportResult(0, E_OUTOFMEMORY, 0, 0);
        goto LError0;
    }
    .
    .   // Code omitted here.
    .
LError0:;
    return hresult;
}
```

SafeArrayDestroy

HRESULT SafeArrayDestroy(*psa*)
SAFEARRAY FAR* *psa*

Destroys an existing array descriptor, and all the data in the array. If objects are stored in the array, **Release** is called on each object in the array.

Parameters

psa
> Points to an array descriptor created by **SafeArrayCreate**.

Return Value

The SCODE obtained from the returned HRESULT is one of the following:

SCODE	Meaning
S_OK	Success.
DISP_E_ARRAYISLOCKED	The array is currently locked.
E_INVALIDARG	The item pointed to by *psa* is not a safe array descriptor.

Example

```
STDMETHODIMP_(ULONG) CEnumPoint::Release()
{
    if(--m_refs == 0){
      if(m_psa != NULL)
    SafeArrayDestroy(m_psa);
      delete this;
      return 0;
    }
    return m_refs;
}
```

SafeArrayDestroyData

HRESULT SafeArrayDestroyData(*psa*)
SAFEARRAY FAR* *psa*

Destroys all the data in a safe array. If objects are stored in the array, **Release** is called on each object in the array.

Parameters

psa
> Points to an array descriptor.

Return Value   The SCODE obtained from the returned HRESULT is one of the following:

SCODE	Meaning
S_OK	Success.
DISP_E_ARRAYISLOCKED	The array is currently locked.
E_INVALIDARG	The item pointed to by *psa* is not a safe array descriptor.

Comments   This function is typically used when freeing safe arrays containing elements with data types other than variants.

See Also   **SafeArrayAllocData, SafeArrayAllocDescriptor, SafeArrayDestroyDescriptor**

SafeArrayDestroyDescriptor

HRESULT SafeArrayDestroyDescriptor(*psa*)
SAFEARRAY FAR* *psa*

Destroys a descriptor of a safe array.

Parameters   *psa*
    Points to a safe array descriptor.

Return Value   The SCODE obtained from the returned HRESULT is one of the following:

SCODE	Meaning
S_OK	Success.
DISP_E_ARRAYISLOCKED	The array is currently locked.
E_INVALIDARG	The item pointed to by *psa* is not a safe array descriptor.

Comments   This function is typically used to destroy the descriptor of safe arrays containing elements with data types other than variants. Destroying the array descriptor does not destroy the elements in the array. Call **SafeArrayDestroyData** to free the elements before destroying the array descriptor.

See Also   **SafeArrayAllocData, SafeArrayAllocDescriptor, SafeArrayDestroyData**

SafeArrayGetDim

unsigned int SafeArrayGetDim(*psa*)
SAFEARRAY FAR* *psa*

Returns the number of dimensions in the array.

Parameters

psa
   Points to an array descriptor created by **SafeArrayCreate**.

Return Value   Returns the number of dimensions in the array.

Example

```
HRESULT
CEnumPoint::Create(SAFEARRAY FAR* psa, CEnumPoint FAR* FAR* ppenum)
{
    long lBound;
    HRESULT hresult;
    CEnumPoint FAR* penum;

    // Verify that the SafeArray is the proper shape.
    //
    if(SafeArrayGetDim(psa) != 1)
       return ReportResult(0, E_INVALIDARG, 0, 0);

    // Code omitted here.
.
}
```

SafeArrayGetElement

HRESULT SafeArrayGetElement(*psa, rgIndices, pvData*)
SAFEARRAY FAR* *psa*
long FAR* *rgIndices*
void FAR* *pvData*

Retrieves a single element of the array.

Parameters

psa
   Points to an array descriptor created by **SafeArrayCreate**.

rgIndices
   Points a vector of indexes for each dimension of the array. The rightmost
   (least-significant) dimension is *rgIndices*[0]. The leftmost dimension is stored
   at *rgIndices*[*psa->cDims* – 1]).

pvData
   Points to the location to place the element of the array.

Comments   This function automatically calls **SafeArrayLock** and **SafeArrayUnlock** before and after retrieving the element. The caller must provide a storage area of the correct size for receiving the data. If the data element is a string, object, or variant, a copy of the element is made in the correct way.

Return Value   The SCODE obtained from the returned HRESULT is one of the following:

SCODE	Meaning
S_OK	Success.
DISP_E_BADINDEX	The specified index is invalid.
E_INVALIDARG	One of the arguments is invalid.
E_OUTOFMEMORY	Memory could not be allocated for the element.

Example
```
STDMETHODIMP CEnumPoint::Next(
    ULONG celt,
    VARIANT FAR rgvar[],
    ULONG FAR* pceltFetched)
{
    unsigned int i;
    long ix;
    HRESULT hresult;

    for(i = 0; i < celt; ++i)
      VariantInit(&rgvar[i]);

    for(i = 0; i < celt; ++i){
      if(m_iCurrent == m_celts){
        hresult = ReportResult(0, S_FALSE, 0, 0);
      goto LDone;
        }

      ix = m_iCurrent++;
      hresult = SafeArrayGetElement(m_psa, &ix, &rgvar[i]);
      if(FAILED(hresult))
      goto LError0;
      }
    hresult = NOERROR;

LDone:;
    *pceltFetched = i;
    return hresult;

LError0:;
    for(i = 0; i < celt; ++i)
      VariantClear(&rgvar[i]);
    return hresult;
}
```

SafeArrayGetElemsize

unsigned int SafeArrayGetElemsize(*psa*)
SAFEARRAY FAR* *psa*

Returns the size, in bytes, of the elements of the given array.

Parameters

psa
    Points to an array descriptor created by **SafeArrayCreate**.

SafeArrayGetLBound

HRESULT SafeArrayGetLBound(*psa, nDim, plLbound*)
SAFEARRAY FAR* *psa*
unsigned int *nDim*
long FAR* *plLbound*

Returns the lower bound for the given dimension of the given array.

Parameters

psa
    Points to an array descriptor created by **SafeArrayCreate**.

nDim
    The array dimension for which to get the upper bound.

plLbound
    Pointer to the location to return the lower bound.

Return Value

The SCODE obtained from the returned HRESULT is one of the following:

SCODE	Meaning
S_OK	Success.
DISP_E_BADINDEX	The specified index is out of bounds.
E_INVALIDARG	One of the arguments is invalid.

Example

```
HRESULT
CEnumPoint::Create(SAFEARRAY FAR* psa, CEnumPoint FAR* FAR* ppenum)
{
    long lBound;
    HRESULT hresult;
    CEnumPoint FAR* penum;


    // Verify that the SafeArray is the proper shape.
    //
```

```
              hresult = SafeArrayGetLBound(psa, 1, &lBound);
              if(FAILED(hresult))
                return hresult;
       .
       .      // Code omitted here.
       .

       }
```

SafeArrayGetUBound

HRESULT SafeArrayGetUBound(*psa, nDim, plUbound*)
SAFEARRAY FAR* *psa*
unsigned int *nDim*
long FAR* *plUbound*

Returns the upper bound for the given dimension of the given array.

Parameters   *psa*
              Points to an array descriptor created by **SafeArrayCreate**().

              nDim
              The array dimension for which to get the upper bound.

              plUbound
              Pointer to the location to return the upper bound.

Return Value   The SCODE obtained from the returned HRESULT is one of the following:

SCODE	Meaning
S_OK	Success.
DISP_E_BADINDEX	The specified index is out of bounds.
E_INVALIDARG	One of the arguments is invalid.

Example
```
HRESULT
CEnumPoint::Create(SAFEARRAY FAR* psa, CEnumPoint FAR* FAR* ppenum)
{
    long lBound;
    HRESULT hresult;
    CEnumPoint FAR* penum;

    // Verify that the SafeArray is the proper shape.
    //
    hresult = SafeArrayGetUBound(psa, 1, &lBound);
    if(FAILED(hresult))
      goto LError0;
```

```
      .
      .   // Code omitted
      .
LError0::;
      penum->Release();

      return hresult;
}
```

SafeArrayLock

HRESULT SafeArrayLock(*psa*)
SAFEARRAY FAR* *psa*

Increments the lock count of an array and places a pointer to the array data in *pvData* of the array descriptor.

Parameters

psa
    Points to an array descriptor created by **SafeArrayCreate**.

Comments

The pointer in the array descriptor is valid until a call to **SafeArrayUnlock** is made. Calls to this function can be nested; an equal number of calls to **SafeArrayUnlock** are required.

While an array is locked, the array cannot be deleted.

Return Value

The SCODE obtained from the returned HRESULT is one of the following:

SCODE	Meaning
S_OK	Success.
E_INVALIDARG	The argument *psa* was not a valid safe array descriptor.
E_UNEXPECTED	The array could not be locked.

SafeArrayPutElement

HRESULT SafeArrayPutElement(*psa, rgIndices, pvData*)
SAFEARRAY FAR* *psa*
long FAR* *rgIndices*
void FAR* *pvData*

Assigns a single element into the array.

Parameters

psa

Points to an array descriptor created by **SafeArrayCreate**.

rgIndices

Points a vector of indexes for each dimension of the array. The rightmost (least significant) dimension is *rgIndices*[0]. The leftmost dimension is stored at *rgIndices*[*psa->cDims* – 1]).

pvData

Points to the data to assign into the array. VT_DISPATCH, VT_UNKNOWN, and VT_BSTR variant types are pointers and do not require another level of indirection.

Comments

This function automatically calls **SafeArrayLock** and **SafeArrayUnlock** before and after assigning the element. If the data element is a string, object, or variant, a copy of the element is made correctly. If the existing element is a string, object or variant, it is cleared correctly.

Note that you can have multiple locks on an array, so you can put elements into an array while the array is locked by other operations.

Return Value

The SCODE obtained from the returned HRESULT is one of the following:

SCODE	Meaning
S_OK	Success.
DISP_E_BADINDEX	The specified index was invalid.
E_INVALIDARG	One of the arguments is invalid.
E_OUTOFMEMORY	Memory could not be allocated for the element.

Example

```
HRESULT PASCAL __export CPoly::EnumPoints(IEnumVARIANT FAR* FAR* ppenum)
{
    unsigned int i;
    HRESULT hresult;
    VARIANT var;
    SAFEARRAY FAR* psa;
    CEnumPoint FAR* penum;
    POINTLINK FAR* ppointlink;
    SAFEARRAYBOUND rgsabound[1];
    rgsabound[0].lLbound = 0;
    rgsabound[0].cElements = m_cPoints;

    psa = SafeArrayCreate(VT_VARIANT, 1, rgsabound);

    .
    .    // Code omitted here.
    .
```

```
                    V_VT(&var) = VT_DISPATCH;
                    hresult = ppointlink->ppoint->QueryInterface(
               IID_IDispatch, (void FAR* FAR*)&V_DISPATCH(&var));
                    if(hresult != NOERROR)
                      goto LError1;

                    ix[0] = i;
                    SafeArrayPutElement(psa, ix, &var);

                    ppointlink = ppointlink->next;
                  }

                  hresult = CEnumPoint::Create(psa, &penum);
                  if(hresult != NOERROR)
                    goto LError1;
                  *ppenum = penum;
                  return NOERROR;

               LError1:;
                  SafeArrayDestroy(psa);

               LError0:;
                  return hresult;
               }
```

SafeArrayRedim

HRESULT SafeArrayRedim(*psa, psaboundNew*)
SAFEARRAY FAR* *psa*
SAFEARRAYBOUND FAR* *psaboundNew*

Changes the least significant (rightmost) bound of a safe array.

Parameters   *psa*
         Points to an array descriptor.

psaboundNew
         A pointer to a new safe array bound structure containing the new array bound.
         Only the least significant dimension of an array may be changed.

Return Value   The SCODE obtained from the returned HRESULT is one of the following:

SCODE	Meaning
S_OK	Success.
DISP_E_ARRAYISLOCKED	The array is currently locked.
E_INVALIDARG	The item pointed to by *psa* is not a safe array descriptor.

Comments   If you reduce the bound of an array, **SafeArrayRedim** deallocates the array elements outside the new array boundary. If you increase the bound of an array, **SafeArrayRedim** allocates and initializes the new array elements. The data is preserved for elements that exist in both the old and the new array.

SafeArrayUnaccessData

HRESULT SafeArrayUnaccessData(*psa*)
SAFEARRAY FAR* *psa*

Decrements the lock count of an array and invalidates the pointer retrieved by **SafeArrayAccessData**.

Parameters   *psa*
.Points to an array descriptor created by **SafeArrayCreate**.

Return Value   The SCODE obtained from the returned HRESULT is one of the following:

SCODE	Meaning
S_OK	Success.
E_INVALIDARG	The argument *psa* was not a valid safe array descriptor.
E_UNEXPECTED	The array could not be unlocked.

SafeArrayUnlock

HRESULT SafeArrayUnlock(*psa*)
SAFEARRAY FAR* *psa*

Decrements the lock count of an array so it can be freed or resized.

Parameters	*psa*
	Points to an array descriptor created by **SafeArrayCreate**.
Comments	This function is called after access to the data in an array is finished.
Return Value	The SCODE obtained from the returned HRESULT is one of the following:

SCODE	Meaning
S_OK	Success.
E_INVALIDARG	The argument *psa* was not a valid safe array descriptor.
E_UNEXPECTED	The array could not be unlocked.

String Manipulation Functions

Implemented by	Used by	Header file name	Import library name
OLE2DISP.DLL	Applications that expose or access programmable objects	DISPATCH.H	OLE2DISP.LIB

In order to handle strings which are allocated by one component and freed by another OLE Automation defines a special set of functions for allocating and freeing the strings. These functions use the following data type:

```
typedef char * BSTR;
```

In most cases, these string can be treated just like char *s, in that they are zero terminated. In addition to being zero terminated, a BSTR can be queried for its length without having to scan the string. This allows BSTRs to contain embedded null characters. The length is stored as an integer at the memory location preceding the data in the string. Instead of reading this location directly, those using BSTRs are advised to use supplied functions to access the length of a BSTR. Since BSTR variables may contain multiple null characters, they can be used to pass binary data.

A NULL pointer is a valid value for a BSTR variable; by convention it is always treated the same as a pointer to a BSTR which contains zero characters. Also, by convention, when calling a function which takes a BSTR reference parameter, the pointer whose reference is passed in must be either NULL or point to an allocated BSTR. If the implementation of a function that takes a BSTR reference parameter assigns a new BSTR to the parameter, it must free the previously referenced BSTR.

SysAllocString

BSTR SysAllocString(*sz***)**
char FAR* *sz*

Allocates a new string and copies the passed string into it. Returns NULL if insufficient memory exists or NULL is passed in.

Parameter   *sz*
                       A zero-terminated string to copy.

Return Value   If successful, points to a BSTR containing the string. If insufficient memory exists or *sz* was NULL, returns NULL.

                       Strings created with **SysAllocString** should be freed with **SysFreeString**.

Example
```
inline void CStatBar::SetText(char FAR* sz)
{
    SysFreeString(m_bstrMsg);
    m_bstrMsg = SysAllocString(sz);
}
```

SysAllocStringLen

BSTR SysAllocStringLen(*pch, cch***)**
char FAR* *pch*
unsigned int *cch*

Allocates a new string and copies *cch* characters from the passed string into it, and then appends a null character.

Parameter   *pch*
                       A pointer to *cch* characters to copy, or NULL to keep the string uninitialized.
                       cch
                       Number of characters to copy from *pch**. A null character is placed afterwards, making a total of *cch*+1 bytes allocated.

Return Value   Points to a copy of the string or NULL, if insufficient memory exists.

Comments   If *pch* is NULL, a string of the given length is allocated, but not initialized. The string *pch* can contain embedded null characters, and need not end with a null. The returned string should later be freed with **SysFreeString**.

                       If *pch* points to a buffer with fewer characters than *cch*, **SysAllocString** allocates, but does not initialize, the additional space.

SysFreeString

void SysFreeString(*bstr*)
BSTR *bstr*

Frees a string previously allocated by **SysAllocString**, **SysReAllocString**, **SysAllocStringLen**, or **SysReAllocStringLen**.

Parameter   *bstr*
                      A BSTR allocated earlier or NULL. If NULL, nothing happens.

Return Value None.

Example
```
CStatBar::~CStatBar()
{
    SysFreeString(m_bstrMsg);
}
```

SysReAllocString

BOOL SysReAllocString(*pbstr*, *sz*)
BSTR FAR* *pbstr*
char FAR* *sz*

Allocates a new BSTR and copies the passed string into it, then frees the BSTR currently referenced by *pbstr* and resets *pbstr* to point to the new BSTR. Returns False if insufficient memory exists.

Parameter   *pbstr*
                      Points to a variable containing a BSTR.

                  sz
                      A zero-terminated string to copy.

Return Value Returns False if insufficient memory exists.

SysReAllocStringLen

BOOL SysReAllocStringLen(*pbstr*, *pch*, *cch*)
BSTR FAR* *pbstr*
char FAR* *pch*
unsigned int *cch*

Creates a new BSTR containing a specified number of characters from an old BSTR and frees the old BSTR.

Parameter

pbstr
   Points to a variable containing a BSTR.

pch
   A pointer to *cch* characters to copy, or NULL to keep the string uninitialized.

cch
   Number of character to copy from *pch**. A null character is placed afterwards, making a total of *cch*+1 bytes allocated.

Return Value

Returns True if string is successfully reallocated, False if insufficient memory exists.

Comments

Allocates a new string and copies *cch* characters from the passed string into it and then appends null character. Frees the BSTR currently referenced by *pbstr* and resets *pbstr* to point to the new BSTR. If *pch* is NULL, a string of the given length is allocated, but not initialized.

The string *pch* can contain embedded null characters in it and need not end with a null.

SysStringLen

unsigned int SysStringLen(*bstr*)
BSTR *bstr*

Returns the length of a BSTR previously allocated by**SysAllocString**, **SysReAllocString**, **SysAllocStringLen**, or **SysReAllocStringLen**.

Parameter

bstr
   A BSTR previously allocated. It cannot be NULL.

Return Value

The number of characters in *bstr*, not including a terminating null character.

Comments

The value returned may be different than **_fstrlen**(*bstr*), if the BSTR was allocated with **Sys[Re]AllocStringLen**, and the passed-in characters included a null character in the first *cch* characters. For a BSTR allocated with **Sys[Re]AllocStringLen**, this function always returns the number of characters specified in **cch**.

Example

```
// Draw the status message
//
TextOut(
  hdc,
```

```
rcMsg.left + (m_dxFont / 2),
rcMsg.top + ((rcMsg.bottom - rcMsg.top - m_dyFont) / 2),
m_bstrMsg, SysStringLen(m_bstrMsg));
```

Variant Manipulation Functions

Implemented by	Used by	Header file name	Import library name
OLE2DISP.DLL	Applications that expose or access programmable objects	DISPATCH.H	OLE2DISP.LIB

The following functions are provided to allow applications to manipulate VARIANTARG variables. An implementor of **IDispatch** should test a VARIANTARG for each type of value that the application allows for a given argument, by attempting to coerce the variant to the desired type (using **VariantChangeType** or **VariantChangeTypeEx**). The application should always test for object types before other types, if an object is allowed. If an object type is expected, the application must test (via **IUnknown::QueryInterface**) whether the object is of the type desired.

Although implementors can access and interpret the VARIANTARGs without these functions, using them will ensure that users experience the same conversion and coercion rules for all implementors of **IDispatch**. (For example, these functions automatically coerce numeric arguments to strings and vice versa, when necessary.)

Because variants can contain strings, references to scalars, references to objects and arrays, data ownership rules must be followed. All of the functions described in this section follow the following rules:

1. All VARIANTARGs must be initialized using **VariantInit** before use.

2. For the types VT_I2, VT_I4, VT_R4, VT_R8, VT_BOOL, VT_ERROR, VT_CY, VT_DATE, data is stored within the VARIANT structure. Any pointers to that data will be invalid when the type of the variant is changed.

3. For VT_BYREF | any type, the memory pointed to by the variant is owned and freed by the caller of the function.

4. For VT_BSTR, there is only one owner for the string. All strings in variants must be allocated with the **SysAllocString** function. When releasing or changing the type of a variant with the VT_BSTR type, **SysFreeString** is called on the contained string.

5. For VT_ARRAY | any type, the rule is analogous to the rule for VT_BSTR. All arrays in variants must be allocated with **SafeArrayCreate**. When releasing or changing the type of a variant with the VT_ARRAY flag set, **SafeArrayDestroy** is called.

6. For VT_DISPATCH and VT_UNKNOWN, the pointed-to objects have reference counts which are incremented when they are placed in a variant. When releasing or changing the type of the variant, **Release** is called on the pointed-to object.

VariantChangeType

HRESULT VariantChangeType(*pvargDest, pvargSrc, wFlags, vtNew*)
VARIANTARG FAR* *pvargDest*
VARIANTARG FAR* *pvargSrc*
unsigned short *wFlags*
VARTYPE *vtNew*

This function converts a variant from one type to another.

Parameter

pvargDest
Points to the VARIANTARG to receive the coerced type. This may be the same as *pvargSrc* to convert in place.

pvargSrc
Points to the VARIANTARG to change the type.

wFlags
Flags which control the coercion. The only defined flag is VARIANT_NOVALUEPROP, which prevents the function from attempting to coerce an object to a fundamental type by getting the "value" property. Applications should only set this flag if necessary, since it will make the behavior inconsistent with other applications.

vtNew
The desired type to coerce to. If the return code is S_OK, the *vt* field of the **pvargDest* is guaranteed to be equal to this value.

Return Value

The SCODE obtained from the returned HRESULT is one of the following:

SCODE	Meaning
S_OK	Success.
DISP_E_BADVARTYPE	The variant type *vtNew* is not a valid type of variant.
DISP_E_OVERFLOW	The data pointed to by *pvargSrc* does not fit in the destination type.
DISP_E_TYPEMISMATCH	Could not coerce argument to specified type.
E_INVALIDARG	One of the arguments is invalid.
E_OUTOFMEMORY	Memory could not be allocated for the conversion.

Comments

The **VariantChangeType** function handles coercions between the fundamental types (including numeric-to-string and string-to-numeric coercions). VT_BYREF is coerced to a value by fetching the referenced value. Objects are coerced to values by invoking the object's value property (DISPID_VALUE).

Typically, this function is used by the implementor of **IDispatch::Invoke**, after determining which member is being accessed, to get the value of one or more arguments. For example, if the **IDispatch** call specifies a "SetTitle" member, which takes one string argument, the implementor would call **VariantChangeType** to attempt to coerce the argument to VT_BSTR. If **VariantChangeType** did not return an error, the argument could then be fetched directly from the *bstrVal* field of the VARIANTARG. If **VariantChangeType** did return DISP_E_TYPEMISMATCH, the implementor would set **puArgErr* to 0 (indicating the argument in error) and return DISP_E_TYPEMISMATCH from **IDispatch::Invoke**.

Note that you should not attempt to change the type of a VARIANTARG in the *rgvarg* array in place, since the callee should not change the contents of this array.

Arrays of one type cannot be converted to arrays of another type with this function.

See Also

VariantChangeType

VariantChangeTypeEx

HRESULT **VariantChangeTypeEx**(*pvargDest, pvargSrc, lcid, wFlags, vtNew*)
VARIANTARG FAR* *pvargDest*
VARIANTARG FAR* *pvargSrc*
LCID *lcid*
unsigned short *wFlags*
VARTYPE *vtNew*

This function converts a variant from one type to another using a locale ID.

Parameter

pvargDest
> Points to the VARIANTARG to receive the coerced type. This may be the same as *pvargSrc* to convert in place.

pvargSrc
> Points to the VARIANTARG to change the type of.

lcid
> The locale ID for the variant to coerce. The locale ID is useful when the type of the source or destination VARIANTARG is VT_BSTR, VT_DISPATCH, or VT_DATE.

wFlags

Flags which control the coercion. The only defined flag is VARIANT_NOVALUEPROP, which prevents the function from attempting to coerce an object to a fundamental type by getting the "value" property. Applications should only set this flag if they have a good reason to do so, since it will make the behavior inconsistent with other applications.

vtNew

The desired type to coerce to. If the return code is S_OK, the *vt* field of the **pvargDest* is guaranteed to be equal to this value.

Return Value

The SCODE obtained from the returned HRESULT is one of the following:

SCODE	Meaning
S_OK	Success.
DISP_E_BADVARTYPE	The variant type *vtNew* is not a valid type of variant.
DISP_E_OVERFLOW	The data pointed to by *pvargSrc* does not fit in the destination type.
DISP_E_TYPEMISMATCH	Could not coerce argument to specified type.
E_INVALIDARG	One of the arguments is invalid.
E_OUTOFMEMORY	Memory could not be allocated for the conversion.

Comments

The **VariantChangeTypeEx** function handles coercions between the fundamental types (including numeric to string and string to numeric coercions), changing types with VT_BYREF set to those without VT_BYREF set by fetching the pointed-at values, and coercions from objects to fundamental types by fetching the value of the "value" property.

Typically, this function is used by the implementor of **IDispatch::Invoke**, after determining which member is being accessed, to get the value of one or more arguments. For example, if the **IDispatch** call specifies a "SetTitle" member, which takes one string argument, the implementor would call **VariantChangeTypeEx** to attempt to coerce the argument to VT_BSTR. If **VariantChangeTypeEx** did not return an error, the argument could then be fetched directly from the *bstrVal* field of the VARIANTARG. If **VariantChangeTypeEx** did return DISP_E_TYPEMISMATCH, the implementor would set **puArgErr* to 0 (indicating the argument in error) and return DISP_E_TYPEMISMATCH from **IDispatch::Invoke**.

Note that you should not attempt to change the type of a VARIANTARG in the *rgvarg* array in place, since the callee should not change the contents of this array.

Arrays of one type cannot be converted to arrays of another type with this function.

See Also   **VariantChangeType**

VariantClear

HRESULT VariantClear(*pvarg*)
VARIANTARG FAR* *pvarg*

Clears a variant.

Parameter   *pvarg*
                 Points to the VARIANTARG to clear.

Return Value The SCODE obtained from the returned HRESULT is one of the following:

SCODE	Meaning
S_OK	Success.
DISP_E_ARRAYSLOCKED	The given variant contains an array that is locked.
DISP_E_BADVARTYPE	The variant type *vtNew* is not a valid type of variant.
E_INVALIDARG	One of the arguments is invalid.

Comments   This function clears a VARIANTARG, by setting the *vt* field to VT_EMPTY and
                 the *wReserved* field to 0. The current contents of the VARIANTARG are released
                 first: if the *vt* field is VT_BSTR, the string is freed; if the *vt* field is
                 VT_DISPATCH, the object is released. If the *vt* field has the VT_ARRAY bit set,
                 the array is freed. The function should be used to clear variables of type
                 VARIANTARG (or VARIANT) before the memory containing the
                 VARIANTARG is freed (as when a local goes out of scope).

Example
```
for(i = 0; i < celt; ++i)
    VariantClear(&rgvar[i]);
```

VariantCopy

HRESULT VariantCopy(*pvarDest, pvarSrc*)
VARIANTARG FAR* *pvargDest*
VARIANTARG FAR* *pvargSrc*

Frees the destination VARIANT and makes a copy of the given source
VARIANT.

Parameter   *pvargDest*
                         Points to the VARIANT to receive the copy.

                         pvargSrc
                         Points to the VARIANT to be copied.

Return Value   The SCODE obtained from the returned HRESULT is one of the following:

SCODE	Meaning
S_OK	Success.
DISP_E_ARRAYSLOCKED	The given variant contains an array that is locked.
DISP_E_BADVARTYPE	The source and destination have an invalid variant type (usually uninitialized).
E_OUTOFMEMORY	Memory could not be allocated for the copy.
E_INVALIDARG	The argument *pvargSrc* was VT_BYREF.

Comments   First, any memory owned by *pvargDest* is freed as in **VariantClear** (note that
                         pvargDest must point to a valid initialized variant, and not simply an uninitialized
                         memory location). Then, *pvDest* receives an exact copy of the contents of *pvSrc*.
                         If *pvarSrc* is a VT_BSTR, a copy of the string is made. If *pvSrc* is a VT_BSTR, a
                         copy of the string is created. If *pvSrc* is a VT_DISPATCH or VT_UNKNOWN,
                         an **AddRef** is done on the object and if the VT_ARRAY bit is set, the entire array
                         is copied.

VariantCopyInd

                         HRESULT VariantCopyInd(*pvarDest, pvargSrc*)
                         VARIANT FAR* *pvarDest*
                         VARIANTARG FAR* *pvargSrc*

                         Frees the destination variant and makes a copy of the source VARIANTARG,
                         performing the necessary indirection if the source is specified to be VT_BYREF.

Parameters   *pvDest*
                         Points to the VARIANT to receive the copy.

                         pvargSrc
                         Points to the VARIANTARG to be copied.

Return Value The SCODE obtained from the returned HRESULT is one of the following:

SCODE	Meaning
S_OK	Success.
DISP_E_ARRAYSLOCKED	The given variant contains an array that is locked.
DISP_E_BADVARTYPE	The source and destination have an invalid variant type (usually uninitialized).
E_OUTOFMEMORY	Memory could not be allocated for the copy.
E_INVALIDARG	The argument *pvargSrc* was VT_ARRAY.

Comments This function is useful when you want to make a copy of a variant and guarantee that it is not VT_BYREF, such as when handling arguments within an implementation of **IDispatch::Invoke**.

For example, if the source is a (VT_BYREF | VT_I2), the destination will be a ByVal VT_I2. The same is true for all legal VT_BYREF combinations including VT_VARIANT.

If *pvargSrc* is (VT_BYREF | VT_VARIANT) and the contained variant is also VT_BYREF, the contained variant is also dereferenced.

This function frees any existing contents of *pvarDest*.

VariantInit

void VariantInit(*pvarg*)
VARIANTARG FAR* *pvarg*

Initializes a variant.

Parameter *pvarg*
Points to the VARIANTARG to initialize.

Comments The **VariantInit** function initializes the VARIANTARG by setting the *vt* field to VT_EMPTY and the *wReserved* field to 0. Unlike **VariantClear**, this function does not interpret the current contents of the VARIANTARG. The function should be used to initialize new local variables of type VARIANTARG (or VARIANT).

Example
```
for(i = 0; i < celt; ++i)
VariantInit(&rgvar[i]);
```

Low-Level Variant Conversion Functions

OLE2DISP.DLL provides the following low-level functions for converting variant data types. These functions are used by the higher-level variant manipulation functions, such as **VariantChangeType**, but may be called directly as well.

Convert to type	From type	Function
short	**short**	None
	long	**VarI2FromI4**(*lIn*, *psOut*)
	float	**VarI2FromR4**(*fltIn*, *psOut*)
	double	**VarI2FromR8**(*dblIn*, *psOut*)
	CURRENCY	**VarI2FromCy**(*cyIn*, *psOut*)
	DATE	**VarI2FromDate**(*dateIn*, *psOut*)
	char FAR*	**VarI2FromStr**(*strIn*, *lcid*, *dwFlags*, *psOut*)
	IDispatch FAR*	**VarI2FromDisp**(*pdispIn*, *lcid*, *dwFlags*, *psOut*)
	BOOL	**VarI2FromBool**(*boolIn*, *psOut*)
long	**short**	**VarI4FromI2**(*sIn*, *plOut*)
	long	None
	float	**VarI4FromR4**(*fltIn*, *plOut*)
	double	**VarI4FromR8**(*dblIn*, *plOut*)
	CURRENCY	**VarI4FromCy**(*cyIn*, *plOut*)
	DATE	**VarI4FromDate**(*dateIn*, *plOut*)
	char FAR*	**VarI4FromStr**(*strIn*, *lcid*, *dwFlags*, *plOut*)
	IDispatch FAR*	**VarI4FromDisp**(*pdispIn*, *lcid*, *dwFlags*, *plOut*)
	BOOL	**VarI4FromBool**(*boolIn*, *plOut*)
float	**short**	**VarR4FromI2**(*sIn*, *prOut*)
	long	**VarR4FromI4**(*lIn*, *prOut*)
	float	None
	double	**VarR4FromR8**(*dblIn*, *prOut*)
	CURRENCY	**VarR4FromCy**(*cyIn*, *prOut*)
	DATE	**VarR4FromDate**(*dateIn*, *prOut*)
	char FAR*	**VarR4FromStr**(*strIn*, *lcid*, *dwFlags*, *prOut*)

Convert to type	From type	Function
	IDispatch FAR*	**VarR4FromDisp**(*pdispIn*, *lcid*, *dwFlags*, *prOut*)
	BOOL	**VarR4FromBool**(*boolIn*, *prOut*)
double	**short**	**VarR8FromI2**(*sIn*, *pdblOut*)
	long	**VarR8FromI4**(*lIn*, *pdblOut*)
	float	**VarR8FromR4**(*fltIn*, *pdblOut*)
	double	None
	CURRENCY	**VarR8FromCy**(*cyIn*, *pdblOut*)
	DATE	**VarR8FromDate**(*dateIn*, *pdblOut*)
	char FAR*	**VarR8FromStr**(*strIn*, *lcid*, *dwFlags*, *pdblOut*)
	IDispatch FAR*	**VarR8FromDisp**(*pdispIn*, *lcid*, *dwFlags*, *pdblOut*)
	BOOL	**VarR8FromBool**(*boolIn*, *pdblOut*)
DATE	**short**	**VarDateFromI2**(*sIn*, *pdateOut*)
	long	**VarDateFromI4**(*lIn*, *pdateOut*)
	float	**VarDateFromDate**(*fltIn*, *pdateOut*)
	double	**VarDateFromR8**(*dblIn*, *pdateOut*)
	CURRENCY	**VarDateFromCy**(*cyIn*, *pdateOut*)
	DATE	None
	char FAR*	**VarDateFromStr**(*strIn*, *lcid*, *dwFlags*, *pdateOut*)
	IDispatch FAR*	**VarDateFromDisp**(*pdispIn*, *lcid*, *dwFlags*, *pdateOut*)
	BOOL	**VarDateFromBool**(*boolIn*, *pdateOut*)
CURRENCY	**short**	**VarCyFromI2**(*sIn*, *pcyOut*)
	long	**VarCyFromI4**(*lIn*, *pcyOut*)
	float	**VarCyFromCY**(*fltIn*, *pcyOut*)
	double	**VarCyFromR8**(*dblIn*, *pcyOut*)
	CURRENCY	**VarCyFromCy**(*cyIn*, *pcyOut*)
	DATE	None

Convert to type	From type	Function
	char FAR*	**VarCyFromStr**(*strIn*, *lcid*, *dwFlags*, *pcyOut*)
	IDispatch FAR*	**VarCyFromDisp**(*pdispIn*, *lcid*, *dwFlags*, *pcyOut*)
	BOOL	**VarCyFromBool**(*boolIn*, *pcyOut*)
BSTR	short	**VarBstrFromI2**(*sIn*, *lcid*, *dwFlags*, *pbstrOut*)
	long	**VarBstrFromI4**(*lIn*, *lcid*, *dwFlags*, *pbstrOut*)
	float	**VarBstrFromBstr**(*fltIn*, *lcid*, *dwFlags*, *pbstrOut*)
	double	**VarBstrFromR8**(*dblIn*, *lcid*, *dwFlags*, *pbstrOut*)
	CURRENCY	**VarBstrFromCy**(*cyIn*, *lcid*, *dwFlags*, *pbstrOut*)
	DATE	**VarBstrFromBstr**(*dateIn*, *lcid*, *dwFlags*, *pbstrOut*)
	char FAR*	None
	IDispatch FAR*	**VarBstrFromDisp**(*pdispIn*, *lcid*, *dwFlags*, *pbstrOut*)
	BOOL	**VarBstrFromBool**(*boolIn*, *lcid*, *dwFlags*, *pbstrOut*)
BOOL	short	**VarBoolFromI2**(*sIn*, *pboolOut*)
	long	**VarBoolFromI4**(*lIn*, *pboolOut*)
	float	**VarBoolFromBool**(*fltIn*, *pboolOut*)
	double	**VarBoolFromR8**(*dblIn*, *pboolOut*)
	CURRENCY	**VarBoolFromCy**(*cyIn*, *pboolOut*)
	DATE	**VarBoolFromBool**(*dateIn*, *pboolOut*)
	char FAR*	**VarBoolFromStr**(*strIn*, *lcid*, *dwFlags*, *pboolOut*)
	IDispatch FAR*	**VarBoolFromDisp**(*pdispIn*, *lcid*, *dwFlags*, *pboolOut*)
	BOOL	None

Parameters

sIn, lIn, fltIn, dblIn, cyIn, dateIn, strIn, pdispIn, boolIn
The value to coerce. These parameters have following data types:

Parameter	Data type
sIn	**short**
lIn	**long**
fltIn	**float**
dblIn	**double**
cyIn	CURRENCY
dateIn	DATE
strIn	**char** FAR*
pdispIn	IDispatch FAR*
boolIn	BOOL

lcid
For conversions from string and VT_DISPATCH input, the locale ID to use for the conversion. For a listing of locale IDs, see Chapter 10, "National Language Support Functions."

dwFlags
One or more of the following flags:

Flag	Description
LOCALE_NOUSEROVERRIDE	Use the system default locale settings, rather than custom user locale settings.
VAR_TIMEVALUEONLY	Applies to conversions to or from dates. Omit the date portion of a VT_DATE and return the time only.
VAR_DATEVALUEONLY	Applies to conversions to or from dates. Omit the time portion of a VT_DATE and return the time only.

psOut, plOut, pfltOut, pdblOut, pcyOut, pstrOut, pdispOut, pboolOut
A pointer to the coerced value. These parameters have following data types:

Parameter	Data type
sOut	**short**
lOut	**long**
fltOut	**float**
dblOut	**double**
cyOut	CURRENCY
dateOut	DATE
strOut	**char** FAR*

Parameter	Data type
pdispOut	IDispatch FAR*
boolOut	BOOL

Return Value   The SCODE obtained from the returned HRESULT is one of the following:

SCODE	Meaning
S_OK	Success.
DISP_E_BADVARTYPE	The input parameter is not a valid type of variant.
DISP_E_OVERFLOW	The data pointed to by the output parameter does not fit in the destination type.
DISP_E_TYPEMISMATCH	Argument could not be coerced to specified type.
E_INVALIDARG	One of the arguments is invalid.
E_OUTOFMEMORY	Memory could not be allocated for the conversion.

Time Conversion Functions

OLE2DISP.DLL provides the following functions to convert between dates and times stored in MS-DOS format and the variant representation.

DosDateTimeToVariantTime

int DosDateTimeToVariantTime(*wDOSDate*, *wDOSTime*, *pvtime*)
unsigned short *wDOSDate*
unsigned short *wDOSTime*
double FAR* *pvtime*

Converts the MS-DOS representation of time to the date and time representation stored in variant.

Parameters   *wDOSDate*
    The MS-DOS date to convert.

wDOSTime
    The MS-DOS time to convert.

pvtime
    Pointer to the location to store the converted time.

Return Value   One of the following:

Result	Meaning
True	Success
False	Failure

Comments   MS-DOS records file dates and times as packed 16-bit values. An MS-DOS *date* has the following format:

Bits	Contents
0-4	Day of the month (1-31)
5-8	Month (1 = January, 2 = February, etc.)
9-15	Year offset from 1980 (add 1980 to get actual year)

An MS-DOS time has the following format:

Bits	Contents
0-4	Second divided by 2
5-10	Minute (0-59)
11-15	Hour (0-23 on a 24-hour clock)

VariantTimeToDosDateTime

int VariantTimeToDosDateTime(*pvtime*, *lpwDOSDate*, *lpwDOSTime*)
double *vtime*
unsigned short FAR* *lpwDOSDate*
unsigned short FAR* *lpwDOSTime*

Converts the variant representation of a date and time to MS-DOS date and time values.

Parameters   *vtime*
      The variant time to convert.

lpwDOSDate
      Pointer to location to store the converted MS-DOS date.

lpwDOSTime
      Pointer to location to store the converted MS-DOS time.

C H A P T E R   7

Object Description Language

Type information is described using the Object Description Language (ODL). Scripts written in ODL are compiled to create type libraries. ODL scripts are compiled using the MkTypLib tool, included with the OLE 2 SDK.

This chapter provides a reference to the ODL and the MkTypLib tool.

MkTypLib: Type Library Creation Tool

Vendors of applications can expose OLE Automation objects to permit interoperability with the programs of other vendors. The characteristics of such objects can be made known in several ways:

- They can be published as object and type definitions (for example, as printed documentation).

- They can be coded into a compiled .c or .cpp file and then accessed using **IDispatch** helper functions or implementations of the **ITypeInfo** and **ITypeLib** interfaces.

- They can be placed in a type library created with MkTypLib and then included as a resource in an application's DLL, as a subfile within an OLE compound document file, or as a standalone compound document file.

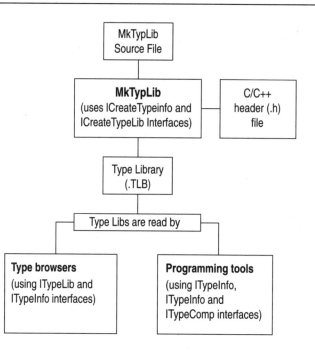

Tools such as object browsers and compilers access type libraries through the **ITypeLib**, **ITypeInfo**, and **ITypeComp** interfaces. Type library generation tools (such as MkTypLib) can be created using the **ICreateTypeLib**, and **ICreateTypeInfo** interfaces.

Creating Type Libraries

MkTypLib accepts a text file as input and produces a type library (a file with a .TLB extension). Type libraries are OLE compound document files containing standard descriptions of data types, modules, and interfaces that can be used to fully expose objects for OLE Automation.

MkTypLib processes the Object Description Language (ODL). In addition to type libraries, MkTypLib can optionally output a C/C++ style header file. See Chapter 2, "Exposing OLE Automation Objects" for more information about header files generated by MkTypLib. MkTypLib uses the **ICreateTypeLib** and **ICreateTypeInfo** interfaces to produce a type library. Type libraries can in turn be accessed by tools such as type browsers and compilers using the **ITypeLib** and **ITypeInfo** interfaces.

Application vendors can ship type libraries in one of the following forms:

- A resource in a DLL. This resource should have the type **typelib**, and the integer ID 1. There can be no more than one resource of this type. Application developers use the resource compiler to combine the TLB file with their own DLL.

- A subfile within a compound document file (sometimes called a "docfile"). The subfile must have the name:

  `"\006typelib"`

  This is a quoted string starting with a control character (ASCII 6) plus the identifier "typelib" (\006 represents 6 within the string, using octal notation).

- A stand-alone compound document file. The file output by MkTypLib (extension .TLB) is a compound document file.

Contents and Structure of a Type Library

The general syntax for a type library is as follows:

[*attributes*] **library** *libraryname* { *librarycontents* };

The *librarycontents* shown in the table below can include data type information such as an alias, enumeration, structure, or union, as well as module, interface, IDispatch interface, and component object class type information that describes an object or objects. Each of these is frequently referred to as a "typeinfo." Type descriptions from other type libraries can be accessed or referenced by specifying the other type libraries with an **importlib** directive for each library.

Enumerations, structures, and unions must be defined with the **typedef** keyword. The *attributes* for a type defined with **typedef** are enclosed in square brackets following the **typedef** keyword. If a simple alias **typedef** has no attributes, it is treated like a #define and the *aliasname* does not appear in the library. Any attribute (use **public** if no others are desired) specified between the **typedef** keyword and the rest of a simple alias definition causes the alias to appear explicitly in the type library. The *attributes* typically include things like a Help string and Help context.

Module, IDispatch interface, interface, and component object class descriptions can include *attributes* by preceding the keyword with the list of attributes in square brackets. Features shown in the table are described in the section "Reference to MkTypLib Statements and Directives," at the end of this chapter.

Category	Library Element	Description
Directive for referencing other type libraries. Must precede all other *librarycontents* entries.	**importlib** (*lib1*)	Specifies an external type library (in this case *lib1*) whose definitions may be referenced in this type library.
Data type declarations used by the objects in this type library. Must appear before any references to the types.	**typedef**[*attributes*]	An alias declared using C syntax. Must have at least one *attribute* to be included in the type library.

Category	Library Element	Description
	typedef [*attributes*] **enum**	An enumeration declared using C **typedef** and **enum** keywords.
	typedef [*attributes*] **struct**	A structure declared using C **typedef** and **enum** keywords.
	typedef [*attributes*] **union**	A union declared using C **typedef** and **union** keywords.
DLL description functions (make querying the DLL possible)	[*attributes*] **module**	Constants and a group of general data functions whose actions are not restricted to any specified class of objects (functions exposed by a DLL and not accessed through Vtable entries).
Interface Descriptions	[*attributes*] **dispinterface**	An **IDispatch** interface describing the methods and properties for an object that can be accessed through **IDispatch::Invoke**.
	[*attributes*] **interface**	Interface describing functions accessed through vtable entries, for example **IUnknown** and **IClassFactory**.
OLE Class Descriptions	[*attributes*] **coclass**	Specifies an implementation of an interface.

Invoking MkTypLib

To start MkTypLib, choose the Run command from the Program Manager or File Manager's File menu, then enter the following command line in the dialog box:

MkTypLib [*options*] *ODLfile*

This form creates a type library file (extension .TLB) based on source text input contained in the file specified by *ODLfile*. It can optionally produce a header file (extension .h) which is a stripped version of the input file suitable for inclusion in C/C++ programs that want to access the types defined in the input file.

The *options* can be a series of - or / prefixed options as follows:

Option	Explanation
/?	Print out command line Help. The *ODLfile* does not need to be specified in this case.
/D *define*[=value]	The *define* is a name to be defined for the C preprocessor. Value is its (optional) value. No space is permitted between the equal sign (=) and the value.
/I *includedir*	*includedir* is the directory where include files are for the C preprocessor.
/tlb *filename*	*filename* is the name of the output TLB file. If not specified, this is the same as the name of the *ODLfile* with the extension .TLB.
/h *filename*	*filename* is the name of a stripped version of the input file. This file can be used as a C/C++ header file. The output is defined in the section .h file output.
/Win16 /Win32 /mac	Specifies type of output type library to produce. Default is /Win16 for the Windows 16-bit version), /Win32 for the Windows NT version, and Mac for the Macintosh version.
/nologo	Disables display of the copyright banner.
/nocpp	If this flag is specified, the C preprocessor is not invoked while MkTypLib is executed.
/cpp_cmd *cpppath*	*cpppath* is the command to run the C preprocessor. Default is to run cl.
/cpp_opt *options*	A set of options to the C preprocessor. Default is **/C /E /D__MKTYPLIB__**.
/o *outputfile*	Redirects output (for example, error messages) to specified *outputfile*.
/w0	Disable warnings.

Error Reporting

MkTypLib offers minimal error reporting. Error messages include accurate line and column number information so that they can be used from within text editors.

MkTypLib Source File Syntax

In general, the description of an alias, enumeration, union, or structure has the following syntax:

typedef [*typeattributes*] *typekind typename* {
   memberdescriptions
};

The description of an interface, IDispatch interface, component object class, or module has this syntax:

[*typeattributes*] *typekind typename* {
   memberdescriptions
};

Note   The square and curly brackets in these descriptions are part of the syntax, not descriptive symbols. The semicolon after the curly brace (}) that terminates the library definition (and all other type definitions) is optional.

The following example illustrates a MkTypLib source file:

```
// Type library specification with preceding attributes in brackets
// Note the library must have a uuid
[uuid(BFB73340-822A-1068-8849-00DD011087E8),
helpfile("MYOBJS.HLP"), helpstring("This is some Help for the library"),
helpcontext(2475)]

library mylibrary {

importlib("STDOLE.TLB");    // Necessary to support IDispatch interfaces
importlib("MYOBLIB.TLB");   // An imported external library

// A typedef used by objects in the library;
    typedef [uuid(BFB73341-822A-1068-8849-00DD011087E8)] DWORD long;

// An enumeration used by objects in the library
    typedef
    [uuid(BFB73342-822A-1068-8849-00DD011087E8), helpstring("Farm
```

```
Animals are friendly"), helpcontext(234)]
    enum {
        [helpstring("Moo")] cows = 1,
        pigs = 2
    } ANIMALS;


// A typedef'd structure used by objects in the library
    typedef
    [uuid(BFB73343-822A-1068-8849-00DD011087E8), helpstring("A task"),
    helpcontext(1019)]
    struct {
        DATE startdate;
        DATE enddate;
        BSTR ownername;
        SAFEARRAY (int) subtasks ;
    } TASKS;


        .
        .
        .

// A description of interface
[odl]
[uuid(BFB73344-822A-1068-8849-00DD011087E8), version(1.0)]
    interface hello {
    void HelloProc([in, string] unsigned char * pszString);
    void Shutdown(void);
    };


// A description of an object, helloPro, exposed for IDispatch
    [ uuid (BFB73345-822A-1068-8849-00DD011087E8),
    version(1.0),helpstring("Hello World Example"),  helpcontext(2480)]
    dispinterface helloPro {
            interface hello;           // hello interface supports
                                       // IDispatch, so declare it here.
                                       // This is shorthand for repeating
                                       // the methods/properties here.

    };
// Description of an implemented OLE style class
    [ uuid(BFB73346-822A-1068-8849-00DD011087E8), version(1.0),
    helpstring("A class"), helpcontext(2481), libglobal]
    coclass myapp {
        interface helloPro;
        dispinterface helloPro;
    };

};
```

The preceding example file creates a library named mylibrary. Help for all of the objects in the library is found in the file MYOBJS.HLP. The overview Help for the library has the context 2475. The file above imports another type library, declares and describes an alias using **typedef** with a uuid attribute, type definitions an enumeration and a structure, and then describes an interface, one object that can be accessed via **IDispatch**, and a component object class. The **IDispatch** object (helloPro) has two properties that are accessed via **IDispatch** using the IDs 1 and 2. It has two methods using the IDs 3 and 11. Many of the descriptions are preceded by typical attributes.

Other Source File Contents

Constants

A constant can be either numeric or a string depending on the attribute.

Numerics

Numeric input is usually an integer (in either decimal or in hex using the standard **0x** format), but may also be a single character constant (\0, for example).

Strings

A string is delimited by double-quotation marks (") and may not span multiple lines. The backslash character (\) acts as an escape character. The backslash character followed by any character (even another backslash) prevents the second character from being interpreted with any special meaning normally associated with it; the backslash is not included in the text.

For example, a double-quotation mark (") may be included in the text without causing it to be interpreted as the closing delimiter by using \". Similarly, \\ can be used to put a backslash into the text. Some examples of valid strings are:

```
"commandName"
"This string contains a \"quote\"."
"Here's a pathname: c:\\bin\\binp"
```

A string can be up to 255 characters long.

Identifiers

Identifiers can be up to 255 characters long. Identifiers must conform to C-style syntax. MkTypLib is case-sensitive, but a generated type library is case-insensitive. Thus, it is possible to define a user-defined type whose name differs from that of a built-in type only by case. However, user-defined type names (and type-member names) that differ only in case refer to the same type or member. Except for property accessor functions, it is illegal for two members of a type to have the same name, regardless of case.

The Globally Unique ID (GUID)

A **uuid** is a globally unique ID (GUID). This number is created by running the command-line program GUIDGEN. GUIDGEN will never produce the same number twice no matter how many times it is run, and how many different machines it runs on. Every entity (such as an interface) that needs to be uniquely identified is identified by a GUID.

Comments

C-style comments are ignored by MkTypLib. This includes comments in block form /*...*/, as well as single-line comments beginning with //. Comments are not preserved in the header file.

Forward Declarations

Forward declarations permit forward references to types and have the following form:

```
typedef struct mydata;
interface aninterface;
dispinterface fordispatch;
```

Intrinsic Types

The following data types are recognized by MkTypLib:

Type	Description
int	A signed integer, whose size is system-dependent.
boolean	A data item that can have the values TRUE or FALSE. The size may be system-dependent.
char	8-bit signed data item.
double	64-bit IEEE floating point number.
float	32-bit IEEE floating point number.
long	32- bit signed integer.
short	16-bit signed integer.
wchar_t	Unicode character accepted only for unicode version of MkTypLib.
LPSTR	A zero-terminated string.
CURRENCY	8-byte fixed-point number.
DATE	64-bit floating point fractional number of days since December 30, 1899.
VARIANT	One of the variant data types as described in Chapter 5, "Dispatch Interfaces."

Type	Description
void	Allowed only as return type for a function or in function parameter list to indicate no arguments.
BSTR	A length-prefixed string, as described in Chapter 5, "Dispatch Interfaces."
HRESULT	Return type used for reporting error information in interfaces, as described in the *OLE 2 Programmer's Reference, Volume 1*.

The keyword **unsigned** may be specified before **int**, **char**, **short**, and **long**.

Array Definitions

MkTypLib accepts both fixed-size (C-style) arrays (*type arrname*[*size*];) and arrays declared as **SAFEARRAY**. The following syntax can be used for a **SAFEARRAY**:

SAFEARRAY (*elementtype*) **arrayname*

A function returning a **SAFEARRAY** has the following syntax:

SAFEARRAY (VARIANT) *myfunction*(*parameterlist*);

String Definitions

Strings can be declared using the **LPSTR** type, which indicates a 0-terminated string, and with the **BSTR** type, which indicates a length-prefixed string (as defined in Chapter 5, "Dispatch Interfaces."

Attribute Descriptions

MkTypLib accepts the following attributes as indicated:

Attribute	Allowed on	Effect	Comments
appobject	coclass	Identifies the Application object.	Attributes that indicate the members of the class may be accessed without qualification when used by programmers accessing this type library.
dllname(*str*)	module		Defines the name of the DLL where the module entry points are.

Attribute	Allowed on	Effect	Comments
entry(*entryid*)	function in a module	The identifier for the entry point in the DLL. If *entryid* is a string, this is a named entry point. If *entryid* is a number, the entry point is defined by an ordinal.	Provides a means of obtaining the address of a function in a module.
helpcontext(*numctxt*)	interface, library, dispinterface, struct, enum, union, module, typedef, method, struct member, enum value, property, coclass, const	Retrieved via the **GetDocumentation** functions in the **ITypeLib** and **ITypeInfo** interfaces.	The *numctxt* is a 32-bit Help context within the Help file.
helpfile(*filenam*)	library	Retrieved via the **GetDocumentation** functions in the **ITypeLib** and **ITypeInfo** interfaces.	All types in a library share the same Help file.
helpstring(*string*)	library, interface, dispinterface, struct, enum, union, module, typedef, method, struct member, enum value, property, coclass, const	Retrieved via the **GetDocumentation** functions in the **ITypeLib** and **ITypeInfo** interfaces.	
id(*num*)	method in dispinterface, property in dispinterface	Identifies the DISPID of the member.	The *num* is a 32-bit integral value.
in	parameter	Parameter receives a value.	If this attribute is listed, parameter is passed in. Parameter may be a pointer (as with char *) but value it refers to is not returned.
lcid(*numid*)	library	Identifies the locale for the library.	The *numid* is a 32-bit locale ID as used in Win32 National Language Support. This is typically entered in hexidecimal.
odl	interface (required)	Identifies an interface as an ODL interface. This attribute must appear on all interfaces.	

Attribute	Allowed on	Effect	Comments
optional	parameter	Parameter may be omitted.	If this attribute is listed, the parameter is optional. Only legal if the parameter is of type VARIANT. All subsequent parameters of the function must be **optional**.
out	parameter	Parameter supplies a value.	If this attribute is listed, parameter is a pointer to memory that will receive a result.
propget	functions; methods in interfaces and dispinterfaces	This attribute causes the INVOKEKIND in the funcdesc to be INVOKE_PROPERTYGET.	If this attribute is listed, the function is a property-accessor function for the property with the same name as the function. At most, one of propget, propput, and propputref can be specified for a function.
propput	functions; methods in interfaces and dispinterfaces	This attribute causes the INVOKEKIND in the funcdesc to be INVOKE_PROPERTYPUT.	If this attribute is listed, the function is a property-setting function for the property with the same name as the function. At most, one of propget, propput and propputref can be specified.
propputref	functions; methods in interfaces and dispinterfaces	This attribute causes the INVOKEKIND in the funcdesc to be INVOKE_PROPERTYPUTREF.	If this attribute is listed, the function is a property-setting function that sets the reference for the property with the name of the function. At most, one of propget, propput and propputref can be specified.
public	aliases declared with **typedef**	If specified , an alias created with **typedef** (and having no other attributes) is included in the type library.	If omitted, an alias created with **typedef** (and having no other attributes) is treated as a **#define**.
readonly		If specified, the variable's VARDESC structure will have its wVarFlags element set with VARFLAG_FREADONLY.	If the flag is set, assignment to the variable should not be allowed.

Attribute	Allowed on	Effect	Comments
restricted	type libraries and members in modules and interfaces	If specified, the FUNCDESC will have its wFuncFlags element set with FUNCFLAG_FRESTRICTED	Indicates the function should not be called from macro languages. Corresponds to FUNCFLAG_FRESTRICTED
string	struct, member, parameter, property		Included only for compatibility with IDL; use **LPSTR** for a zero-terminated string.
uuid(*uuidval*)	library, dispinterface, struct, enum, union, module, typedef, interface, coclass	This value is returned in the TypeAttr structure retrieved via **TypeInfo::GetTypeAttr**	Optional for all but library, coclass, and dispinterface. The *uuidval* is a 16-byte value formatted as hex digits in the following format: 12345678-1234-1234-1234-123456789ABC.
vararg	all functions		If this attribute is listed, last parameter must be a safe array of VARIANT type.
version(*versionval*)	library, struct, module, dispinterface, interface, coclass, enum, union		The argument *versionval* is a real number of the format n.m, where n is a major version number and m is a minor version number.

Note that attribute specifications follow the **typedef** keyword when it is used, but precede the descriptions of other types.

File Names

File names are strings representing either full or partial pathnames. The referenced files are expected to be in directories referenced by the type library registration entries, so partial pathnames are typically used. See Chapter 2, "Exposing OLE Automation Objects" for more information about registration.

Preprocessing

MkTypLib spawns the C preprocessor. The symbol **__MKTYPLIB__** is predefined for the preprocessor.

Reference to MkTypLib Statements and Directives

The coclass Statement

Syntax

[*attributes*]
coclass *classname* {
    [**interface** | **dispinterface**] *interfacename*;
    ...
};

The Microsoft Component Object model defines a class as an implementation that allows QueryInterface between a set of interfaces. The coclass statement describes the GUID and supported interfaces for a component object.

Syntax Elements

attributes

The **uuid** attribute is required on a coclass. This is the same **uuid** that is registered as a CLSID in the system registration database. The **helpstring**, **helpcontext, and appobject** attributes are accepted, but not required, before **coclass** definition. See the section "Attribute Descriptions" for more information on the attributes accepted before a coclass definition. The **appobject** attribute makes the functions and properties of the coclass globally available in the type library.

classname

Name by which the common object is known in the type library.

interfacename

Either an interface declared with the **interface** keyword, or a dispinterface declared with **dispinterface**.

Example

```
[ uuid(BFB73347-822A-1068-8849-00DD011087E8), version(1.0),
helpstring("A class"), helpcontext(2481), appobject]
coclass myapp {
    interface mydocfuncs;
    dispinterface mydocfuncs;
};
```

The dispinterface Statement

Syntax 1

[attributes]
dispinterface *intfname* {
    properties:
        proplist
    methods:
        methlist
};

Syntax 2

[attributes]
dispinterface *intfname* {
    interface *interfacename*
};

Defines a set of properties and methods on which you can call
IDispatch::Invoke. An IDispatch interface (dispinterface) may be defined by
explicitly listing the set of supported methods and properties (Syntax 1) or by
listing a single interface (Syntax 2).

Syntax Elements

attributes
    The **helpstring**, **helpcontext**, **uuid**, and **version** attributes are accepted before
    dispinterface. See the section "Attribute Descriptions" for more information
    on the attributes accepted before a **dispinterface** definition. Attributes
    (including the square brackets) may be omitted. The **uuid** attribute is required.

intfname
    The name by which the **dispinterface** is known in the type library. This name
    must be unique within the type library.

interfacename
    (Syntax 2) The name of the interface to declare as an IDispatch interface.

proplist
    (Syntax 1) An optional list of properties supported by the object, declared in
    the form of variables. This form is shorthand for declaring the property
    functions in the methods list. See the comments section for details.

methlist
    (Syntax 1) A list comprising a function prototype for each method and
    property in the **dispinterface**. Any number of function definitions can appear
    in *methlist*. A function in *methlist* has the following form:

    *[attributes] returntype methname(params)***;**

    The following attributes are accepted on a method in a **dispinterface**:
    helpstring, **helpcontext**, **string** (for compatibility with IDL), and **vararg.** If
    vararg is specified, the last parameter must be a safe array of VARIANT type.

The parameter list is a comma-delimited list, each element of which has the following form:

[*attributes*] *type paramname*

The *type* can be any declared or built-in type, or a pointer to any type. Attributes on parameters are:

in, **out**, **optional**, **string**

If **optional** appears, it must only be specified on the rightmost parameters, and the types of those parameters must be VARIANT.

Comments   Method functions are specified exactly as described in the section "The **module** Statement," except that the **entry** attribute is not allowed. Note that STDOLE.DLL must be imported, since a **dispinterface** inherits from **IDispatch**.

You can declare properties in either the properties or methods lists. Declaring properties in the properties list does not indicate the type of access the property supports (that is, get, put, or putref). Specify the readonly **attribute** for properties that don't support put or putref. If you declare the property functions in the methods list, functions for one property all have the same ID.

Using Syntax 1, the **properties:** and **methods:** tags are required. The **id** attribute is also required on each member. For example:

```
properties:
    [id(0)] int Value;  // Default property.
methods
    [id(1)] void Show();
```

Using Syntax 2, interfaces that support **IDispatch** and that are declared earlier in an ODL file, can be redeclared as **IDispatch** interfaces as follows:

```
dispinterface helloPro {
    interface hello;
};
```

The preceding example declares all of the members of hello and all of the members that hello inherits as supporting **IDispatch**.

Example
```
[ uuid(BFB73347-822A-1068-8849-00DD011087E8), version(1.0),
helpstring("Useful help string."), helpcontext(2480)]
dispinterface MyDispatchObject {
    properties:
        [id(1)] int x; //An integer property named x
        [id(2)] BSTR y; //A string property named y
    methods:
        [id(3)] void show(); //No arguments, no result
        [id(11)] int computeit(int inarg, double *outarg);
};
```

The enum Statement

Syntax

typedef [*attributes*] **enum** [*tag*] {
    enumlist
} *enumname*;

Syntax Elements

attributes
    The **helpstring**, **helpcontext**, and **uuid** attributes are accepted before an
    enum. The **helpstring** and **helpcontext** attributes are accepted on an
    enumeration element. See the section "Attribute Descriptions" for more
    information on the attributes accepted before an enumeration definition.
    Attributes (including the square brackets) may be omitted. If **uuid** is omitted,
    the enumeration is not uniquely specified in the system.

tag
    An optional tag, as with a C **enum**.

enumlist
    List of enumerated elements.

enumname
    Name by which the enumeration is known in the type library.

Comments

The **enum** keyword must be preceded with **typedef**. The enumeration description
must precede other references to the enumeration in the library. If = *value* is not
specified for enumerators, the numbering progresses as with enumerations in C.
The type of the enum elements is **int**, the system default integer. This is
dependent on the target type library specification.

Examples

```
typedef [uuid(DEADF00D-C0DE-B1FF-F001-A100FF001ED), helpstring("Farm
Animals are friendly"), helpcontext(234)]
enum {
    [helpstring("Moo")] cows = 1,
    pigs = 2
} ANIMALS;
```

The importlib Directive

Syntax

importlib(*filename*);

All **importlib** directives must precede the rest of the type descriptions in the
library. The make types are compiled into other type libraries available to the
library in which they appear.

Syntax Elements

filename
    The location of the referenced type library file when MkTypLib is executed.

Comments   The **importlib** directive makes any type defined in the imported library accessible
                      from within the library being compiled. Ambiguity is resolved as follows. The
                      current library is searched for the type. If not found, then the lexically first
                      imported library is used, then the next, and so on. If the developer wants to get to
                      a "shadowed" type name, it is entered as *libname.typename* where *libname* is the
                      library name as it appeared in the **library** statement when that library was
                      compiled.

The interface Statement

Syntax   [*attributes*]
                      interface *interfacename* [*:baseinterface*] {
                         functionlist
                      };

                      An interface is a set of procedure definitions. An interface can inherit from any
                      base interface.

Syntax Elements   *attributes*
                      The **helpstring**, **helpcontext**, **odl**, **uuid**, and **version** attributes are accepted
                      before **interface**. See the section "Attribute Descriptions" for more
                      information on the attributes accepted before an interface definition.

                      The **odl** and **uuid** attributes are required on all interface declarations.

                      interfacename
                      The name by which the interface is known in the type library.

                      baseinterface
                      The name of the interface that is the base class for this interface.

                      functionlist
                      List of function prototypes for each function in the interface. Any number of
                      function definitions can appear in the function list. A function in the function
                      list has the following form:

                      [*attributes*] *returntype* [*calling convention*] *funcname*(*params*);

                      The following attributes are accepted on a function in an interface: **helpstring**,
                      helpcontext, **string**, **propget**, **propput**, **propputref**, **vararg**. If **vararg** is
                      specified, the last parameter must be a safe array of VARIANT type. The
                      optional *calling convention* can be any one of **__pascal/_pascal/pascal** or
                      __cdecl/_cdecl/cdecl, **__stdcall/_stdcall/stdcasll**. In other words, the calling
                      convention specification can include zero, one, or two leading underscores.

The parameter list is a comma separated list of:

[*attributes*] *type paramname*

The *type* can be any previously declared type, built-in type, a pointer to any type, or a pointer to a built-in type. Attributes on parameters are:

in, **out**, **optional**, **string**

If **optional** appears, it must only be specified on the rightmost parameters, and the types of those parameters must be VARIANT.

Comments

Functions in interfaces are exactly as described in the section "The **module** Statement," except that the **entry** attribute is not allowed.

Example

```
[uuid(BFB73347-822A-1068-8849-00DD011087E8), version(1.0)]
interface hello : IUnknown
{
void HelloProc([in, string] unsigned char * pszString);
void Shutdown(void);
};
```

The library Statement

Syntax

[*attributes*] **library** *libname* {
    definitions
};

Describes a type library. This description contains all the other information in a MkTypLib input file.

Syntax Elements

attributes
The **helpstring**, **helpcontext**, and **uuid** attributes are accepted before a **library** statement. See the section "Attribute Descriptions" for more information on the attributes accepted before a library definition. Attributes (including the square brackets) may be omitted. The **uuid** attribute is required.

libname
The name by which the type library is known.

definitions
Descriptions of any imported libraries, data types, modules, interfaces, dispinterfaces, and coclasses relevant to the object being exposed.

Comments

The library statement must precede any other type definitions.

Example

```
[uuid(BFB73349-822A-1068-8849-00DD011087E8), version(1.0)]
[helpfile("MYOBJS.HLP"), helpstring("This is some Help for the
library"), helpcontext(2475)]
library Alibrary {
    [uuid(BFB7334A-822A-1068-8849-00DD011087E8), version(1.0)]
    interface hello
    {
    void HelloProc([in, string] unsigned char * pszString);
    void Shutdown(void);
    };
};
```

The module Statement

Syntax

[*attributes*]
module *modulename* {
    elementlist
};

A module is a set of procedure definitions. Typically it describes a set of DLL entry points.

Syntax Elements

attributes

The **uuid, version, helpstring, helpcontext, and dllname** attributes are accepted before a **module** statement. See the section "Attribute Descriptions" for more information on the attributes accepted before a module definition. Attributes (including the square brackets) may be omitted. If **uuid** is omitted, the module is not uniquely specified in the system.

modulename

The name of the module.

elementlist

List of constant definitions and function prototypes for each function in the DLL. Any number of function definitions can appear in the function list. A function in the function list has the following form:

[*attributes*] *returntype* [*calling convention*] *funcname*(*params*);
[*attributes*] **const** *constname* = *constval*;

Only the **helpstring** and **helpcontext** attributes are accepted for a **const**.

The following attributes are accepted on a function in a module: **helpstring, helpcontext, string, entry** (required when a *dllname* has been specified), **propget, propput, propputref, vararg.** If **vararg** is specified, the last parameter must be a safe array of VARIANT type.

The optional *calling convention* can be one of **__pascal/_pascal/pascal**, **__cdecl/_cdecl/cdecl**, or **__stdcall/_stdcall/stdcall**. The *calling convention* can include zero, one, or two leading underscores.

The parameter list is a comma-delimited list of:

[*attributes*] *type paramname*

The *type* can be any previously declared type or built-in type, or a pointer to any type, or a pointer to a built-in type. Attributes on parameters are:

in, **out**, **optional**

If **optional** appears, it must only be specified on the rightmost parameters, and the types of those parameters must be VARIANT.

Comments
Header file (.h) output for modules is a series of function prototypes. The **module** keyword and surrounding brackets are stripped out of the .h file output, but a comment (// **module** *modulename*) is inserted before the prototypes. The keyword **extern** is inserted before the declarations.

Example
```
[uuid(D00BED00-CEDE-B1FF-F001-A100FF001ED), helpstring("This is not
GDI.EXE"), helpcontext(190), dllname("MATH.DLL")]
module somemodule{
    [helpstring("Color for the frame")] const COLOR_FRAME = 0xH80000006;
    [helpstring("Not a rectangle but a square"), entry(1)] pascal double
square([in] double x);
};
```

The struct Statement

Syntax
typedef [*attributes*]
struct [*tag*] {
   memberlist
} *structname*;

Syntax Elements
attributes
The **helpstring**, **helpcontext**, **uuid,** and **version** attributes are accepted before a **struct** statement. The **helpstring**, **helpcontext**, **string** attributes are accepted on a structure member. See the section "Attribute Descriptions" for more information on the attributes accepted before a structure definition. Attributes (including the square brackets) may be omitted. If **uuid** is omitted, the structure is not uniquely specified in the system.

tag
An optional tag, as with a C **struct**.

memberlist
> List of structure members defined with C syntax.

structname
> Name by which the structure is known in the type library.

Comments   The **struct** keyword must be preceded with **typedef**. The structure description must precede other references to the structure in the library. Members of a **struct** can be of any built-in type, or any type defined lexically as a **typedef** before the **struct**. See the sections "String Definitions" and "Array Definitions" for a description of how strings and arrays can be entered.

Example
```
typedef [uuid(BFB7334B-822A-1068-8849-00DD011087E8), helpstring("A
task"), helpcontext(1019)]
struct {
    DATE startdate;
    DATE enddate;
    BSTR ownername;
    SAFEARRAY (int) subtasks;
    int A_C_array[10];
} TASKS;
```

The typedef Statement

Syntax   **typedef** [*attributes*] *basename aliasname*;

Creates an alias for a type.

Syntax Elements   *attributes*
> Any attribute specifications must follow the **typedef** keyword. If no attributes and no other type (for example **enum**, **struct**, or **union**) are specified, the alias is treated as a **#define** and does not appear in the type library. If no other attribute is desired, **public** can be used to explicitly include the alias in the type library. The **helpstring**, **helpcontext**, **uuid** attributes are accepted before a typedef. See the section "Attribute Descriptions" for more information on the attributes accepted before a typedef definition. Attributes (including the square brackets) may be omitted. If **uuid** is omitted, the typedef is not uniquely specified in the system.

aliasname
> Name by which the type will be known in the type library.

basename
> The type for which the alias is defined.

Comments   The **typedef** keyword must also be used whenever a **struct** or **enum** is defined.

Examples
```
typedef [public]  long DWORD;
```

The preceding example creates a type description for an alias type with the name DWORD.

```
typedef enum {
    cows = 1,
    pigs = 2
} ANIMALS;
```

The second example creates a type description for an enumeration named "animals." The name recorded for the **enum** or **struct** is the typedef name, not the tag for the enumeration. No attributes are required to make sure the alias appears in the type library.

The union Statement

Syntax
typedef [*attributes*] **union** [*tag*] {
    memberlist
} *unionname*;

Syntax Elements   *attributes*
The **helpstring**, **helpcontext**, **uuid,** and **version** attributes are accepted before a **typedef**. The **helpstring**, **helpcontext**, **safe** (on arrays), **string** attributes are accepted on a structure member. See the section "Attribute Descriptions" for more information on the attributes accepted before a union definition. Attributes (including the square brackets) may be omitted. If **uuid** is omitted, the union is not uniquely specified in the system.

tag
An optional tag, as with a C **union.**

memberlist
List of union members defined with C syntax.

unionname
Name by which the union is known in the type library.

Comments   The **union** keyword must be preceded with **typedef**. The union description must precede other references to the structure in the library. Members of a **union** can be of any built-in type, or any type defined lexically as a **typedef** before the **union.** See the sections "String Definitions" and "Array Definitions" for a description of how strings and arrays can be entered.

Example

```
[uuid(BFB7334C-822A-1068-8849-00DD011087E8), helpstring("A task"),
helpcontext(1019)]
typedef union {
    DATE startdate;
    DATE enddate;
    BSTR ownername;
    SAFEARRAY (int) subtasks;
} UNIONSHOP;
```

CHAPTER 8

Type Description Interfaces

The type description interfaces provide a way to read and bind to the descriptions of objects in a type library. The descriptions are used by OLE Automation controllers when they browse, create, and manipulate OLE Automation objects.

The type description interfaces include:

- **ITypeLib**—Used to retrieve information about a type library.
- **ITypeInfo**—Used to read the type information within the type library.
- **ITypeComp**—Used when creating compilers that use type information.

Overview of Interfaces

A type library is a container for type descriptions. **ITypeLib** gives access to information about a type description's containing library. **ITypeInfo** is used to gain access to each type description contained in a type library. The following table describes the member functions of each of the type description interfaces:

Category	Member name	Purpose
ITypeLib	**FindName**	Finds occurrences of a type description in a type library.
	GetDocumentation	Retrieves the library's documentation string, name of the complete Help file path and name, and the context ID for the library Help topic in the Help file.
	GetLibAttr[1]	Retrieves the structure containing the library's attributes.
	GetTypeComp	Retrieves a pointer to the **ITypeComp** for a type library. This enables a client compiler to bind to the library's types, variables, constants and global functions.

Category	Member name	Purpose
	GetTypeInfo	Retrieves the specified type description in the library.
	GetTypeInfoCount	Retrieves the number of type descriptions in the library.
	GetTypeInfoType	Retrieves the type of a type description.
	GetTypeInfoOfGuid	Retrieves the type description corresponding to the specified GUID.
	IsName	Indicates whether a passed-in string contains the name of a type or member described in the library.
	ReleaseTLibAttr	Releases TLIBATTR originally obtained from **ITypeLib::GetLibAttr**.
ITypeInfo	AddressOfMember	Retrieves the addresses of static functions or variables, such as those defined in a DLL.
	CreateInstance	Creates a new instance of a type that describes a component object class (**coclass**).
	GetContainingTypeLib	Retrieves the type library containing a specific type description as well as the index of the type description within the type library.
	GetDllEntry	Retrieves a description or specification of an entry point for a function in a DLL.
	GetDocumentation	Retrieves the documentation string, name of the complete Help file path and name, and the context ID for the Help topic for a specified type description.
	GetFuncDesc[1]	Retrieves the FUNCDESC structure containing information about a specified function.
	GetIDsOfNames	Maps between member names and member IDs and parameter names and parameter IDs.
	GetMops	Retrieves marshaling information.

Category	Member name	Purpose
	GetNames	Retrieves the variable with the specified member ID, or the name of the function and parameter names corresponding to the specified function ID.
	GetRefTypeInfo	If a type description references other type descriptions, this function retrieves the referenced type descriptions.
	GetTypeAttr[1]	Retrieves a TYPEATTR structure containing the attributes of the type description.
	GetTypeComp	Retrieves the ITypeComp interface for the type description, which enables a client compiler to bind to the type description's members.
	GetRefTypeOfImpl-Type	If this type description describes a component object class, this function retrieves the type description of the specified implemented interface types.
	GetVarDesc[1]	Retrieves a VARDESC structure describing the specified variable.
	Invoke	Invokes a method or accesses a property of an object that implements the interface described by the type description.
	ReleaseFuncDesc	Releases a FUNCDESC previously returned by **GetFuncDesc**.
	ReleaseTypeAttr	Releases a TYPEATTR previously returned by **GetTypeAttr**.
	ReleaseVarDesc	Releases a VARDESC previously returned by **GetVarDesc**.
ITypeComp	**Bind**	Maps a name to a member of a type, or binds global variables and functions contained in a type library.
	BindType	Binds to the type descriptions contained within a type library.

Category	Member name	Purpose
Type compilation	**LHashValOfName**	Computes a hash value for a name that can then be passed to: **ITypeComp::Bind** **ITypeComp::BindType** **ITypeComp::IsName**.
	LHashValOfNameSys	Equivalent to **LHashValOfName**.

[1] The caller of a method that returns an object must release the returned object using the object's Release method. The caller of a method that returns a structure must delete the structure by using the Release methods (**ReleaseTLib**, **ReleaseVarDesc**, **ReleaseFuncDesc**, **ReleaseTypeAttr**) provided by the interface that created the structure.

Overview of Functions

TYPELIB.DLL provides functions for loading, registering, and querying type libraries.

Category	Function name	Purpose
Library loading	**LoadTypeLib**	Loads and registers a type library created with MkTypLib.
	LoadRegTypeLib	Uses registry information to load a type library.
Library registration	**RegisterTypeLib**	Adds information about a type library to the system registry.
	QueryPathOfRegTypeLib	Retrieves the pathname of a registered type library.

ITypeLib Interface

Implemented by	Used by	Header file name
TYPELIB.DLL	Tools that need to access the descriptions of objects contained in type libraries	**DISPATCH.H**

Data describing a set of objects is stored in a type library. A type library is typically stored as a resource in a DLL; however, it may also be stored in a compound document file.

A type library contains descriptions of a collection of objects, and is accessed via the **ITypeLib** interface. The descriptions of individual objects are accessed via the **ITypeInfo** interface. The system registry contains a list of all the installed type libraries. Type library organization is illustrated in the following figure:

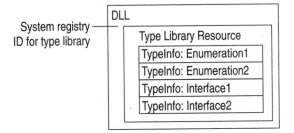

The **ITypeLib** interface provides methods for accessing a library of type descriptions. This interface provides the following:

- Generalized containment support for type information. **ITypeLib** allows iteration over the type descriptions contained in the library.

- Global function and data support. A type library can contain descriptions of a set of modules, each of which is the equivalent of a C/C++ source file that exports data and functions. The type library supports compiling references to this exported data and functions.

- General information, including a user-readable name for the library and Help for the library as a whole.

TLIBATTR Structure

The following structure contains information about a type library. Information from this structure is used to identify the type library and to provide national language support for member names.

```
typedef struct FARSTRUCT tagTLIBATTR {
    GUID guid;                          // Unique ID of the library
    LCID lcid;                          // Language/locale of the library
    SYSKIND syskind;                    // Target hardware platform
    unsigned short wMajorVerNum;        // Major version number
    unsigned short wMinorVerNum;        // Minor version number
    unsigned short wLibFlags;           // Library flags
} TLIBATTR, FAR * LPTLIBATTR;
```

For more information on national language support and LCID, see Chapter 10, "National Language Support Functions."

ITypeLib::FindName

HRESULT ITypeLib::FindName(*szNameBuf, lHashVal, rgptinfo, rgmemid, pcFound*)
LPCSTR *szNameBuf*
unsigned long *lHashVal*
ITypeInfo FAR* FAR* *rgptinfo*
MEMBERID FAR* *rgmemid*
unsigned int FAR*pcFound

Finds occurrences of a type description in a type library. This may be used to quickly verify that a name exists in a type library.

Parameter

rgptinfo

An array of pointers to the type descriptions that contain the name specified in *szNameBuf*. May not be NULL.

rgmemid

An array of the MEMBERIDs of the found items; *rgmemid*[*i*] is the MEMBERID which indexes into the type description specified by *rgptinfo*[*i*]. May not be NULL.

pcFound

On entry, indicates how many instances to look for. For example, you may call with *pcFound* = 1 in order to find the first occurrence. In this case, the search stops when one is found.

On exit, indicates the number of instances that were found. If the in and out values of *pcFound* are identical, there may be more type descriptions that contain the name.

Return Value

The SCODE obtained from the returned HRESULT is one of the following:

SCODE	Meaning
S_OK	Success.
STG_E_INSUFFICIENTMEMORY	Out of memory.
E_OUTOFMEMORY	Out of memory.
E_INVALIDARG	One or more of the arguments is invalid.
TYPE_E_IOERROR	The function could not write to the file.
TYPE_E_INVDATAREAD	The function could not read from the file.
TYPE_E_UNSUPFORMAT	The type library has an old format.
TYPE_E_INVALIDSTATE	The type library could not be opened.
TYPE_E_CANTLOADLIBRARY	The library or DLL could not be loaded.
TYPE_E_ELEMENTNOTFOUND	The element was not found.

Comments   Passing **pcFound* = *n* indicates that there is enough room in the arrays for *n* (*ptinfo*, *memid*) pairs.

ITypeLib::GetDocumentation

HRESULT ITypeLib::GetDocumentation(*index, lpbstrName, lpbstrDocString, lpdwHelpContext, lpbstrHelpFile*)
int *index*
BSTR FAR* *lpbstrName*
BSTR FAR* *lpbstrDocString*
unsigned long FAR* *lpdwHelpContext*
BSTR FAR* *lpbstrHelpFile*

Retrieves the library's documentation string, name of the complete Help file path and name, and the context ID for the library Help topic in the Help file

Parameter   *index*
Index of the type description whose documentation is to be returned; if index is −1, then the documentation for the library itself is returned.

lpbstrName
Returns a BSTR allocated by the caller that contains the name of the specified item. If the caller does not need the item name, then *lpbstrName* can be NULL.

lpbstrDocString
Returns a BSTR allocated by the caller that contains the documentation string for the specified item. If the caller does not need the documentation string, then *lpbstrDocString* can be NULL.

lpdwHelpContext
Returns the Help context ID associated with the specified item. If the caller does not need the Help context ID, then *lpdwHelpContext* can be NULL.

lpbstrHelpFile
Returns a BSTR allocated by the caller that contains the fully qualified name of the Help file. If the caller does not need the Help file name, then *lpbstrHelpFile* can be NULL.

Return Value   The SCODE obtained from the returned HRESULT is one of the following:

SCODE	Meaning
S_OK	Success.
STG_E_INSUFFICIENTMEMORY	Out of memory.
E_INVALIDARG	One or more of the arguments is invalid.

SCODE	Meaning
TYPE_E_IOERROR	The function could not write to the file.
TYPE_E_INVDATAREAD	The function could not read from the file.
TYPE_E_UNSUPFORMAT	The type library has an old format.
TYPE_E_INVALIDSTATE	The type library could not be opened.
TYPE_E_ELEMENTNOTFOUND	The element was not found.

Example

```
for (i = 0; i < utypeinfoCount; i++)
{
    CHECKRESULT(ptlib->GetDocumentation(i, &bstrName, NULL, NULL,
NULL));
    .
    .
    .

    SysFreeString(bstrName);
}
```

ITypeLib::GetLibAttr

HRESULT ITypeLib::GetLibAttr(*lplptlibattr*)
TLIBATTR FAR* FAR* *lplptlibattr*

Retrieves the structure containing the library's attributes.

Parameter

lplptlibattr
   A pointer to a structure containing the library's attributes.

Return Value

The SCODE obtained from the returned HRESULT is one of the following:

SCODE	Meaning
S_OK	Success.
STG_E_INSUFFICIENTMEMORY	Out of memory.
E_OUTOFMEMORY	Out of memory.
E_INVALIDARG	One or more of the arguments is invalid.
TYPE_E_IOERROR	The function could not write to the file.
TYPE_E_INVDATAREAD	The function could not read from the file.
TYPE_E_UNSUPFORMAT	The type library has an old format.
TYPE_E_INVALIDSTATE	The type library could not be opened.

ITypeLib::GetTypeComp

HRESULT ITypeLib::GetTypeComp(*lplptcomp*)
ITypeComp FAR* FAR* *lplptcomp*

Enables a client compiler to bind to the library's types, variables, constants and global functions.

Parameter

lplptcomp
Points to a pointer to the **ITypeComp** instance for this **ITypeLib** that a client compiler can use to bind to types in the **ITypeLib** and to the global functions, variables, and constants defined in the **ITypeLib**.

Return Value

The SCODE obtained from the returned HRESULT is one of the following:

SCODE	Meaning
S_OK	Success.
STG_E_INSUFFICIENTMEMORY	Out of memory.
E_OUTOFMEMORY	Out of memory.
E_INVALIDARG	One or more of the arguments is invalid.
TYPE_E_IOERROR	The function could not write to the file.
TYPE_E_INVDATAREAD	The function could not read from the file.
TYPE_E_UNSUPFORMAT	The type library has an old format.
TYPE_E_INVALIDSTATE	The type library could not be opened.
TYPE_E_WRONGTYPEKIND	Type mismatch.

Comments

The **Bind** function of the returned **TypeComp** binds to global functions, variables, constants, enumerated values, and coclass members. The **Bind** function also binds the names of the TYPEKINDS of TKIND_MODULE, TKIND_ENUM, and TKIND_COCLASS. These names shadow any global names defined within the type information.

ITypeComp::Bind and **ITypeComp::BindType** accept only unqualified names. **ITypeLib::GetTypeComp** returns a pointer to the **ITypeComp** interface which is then used to bind to global elements in the library. The names of some types (TKIND_ENUM, TKIND_MODULE, and TKIND_COCLASS) share the name space with variables, functions, constants, and enumerators. If a member requires qualification to differentiate it from other items in the name space, **GetTypeComp** can be called successively for each qualifier in order to bind to the desired member. This allows programming language compilers to access members of modules, enumerations, and coclasses, even though the member cannot be bound to with a qualified name.

ITypeLib::GetTypeInfo

HRESULT ITypeLib::GetTypeInfo(*index*, *lplpitinfo*)
unsigned int *index*
ITypeInfo FAR* FAR* *lplpitinfo*

Retrieves the specified type description in the library.

Parameters

index
    Index of the **ITypeInfo** to be returned.

lplpitinfo
    If successful, returns a pointer to the **ITypeInfo**.

Return Value

The SCODE obtained from the returned HRESULT is one of the following:

SCODE	Meaning
S_OK	Success.
TYPE_E_ELEMENTNOTFOUND	*Index* is outside the range of 0 to **GetTypeInfoCount**() −1.
STG_E_INSUFFICIENTMEMORY	Out of memory.
E_OUTOFMEMORY	Out of memory.
E_INVALIDARG	One or more of the arguments is invalid.
TYPE_E_IOERROR	The function could not write to the file.
TYPE_E_INVDATAREAD	The function could not read from the file.
TYPE_E_UNSUPFORMAT	The type library has an old format.
TYPE_E_REGISTRYACCESS	There was an error accessing the system registration database.
TYPE_E_INVALIDSTATE	The type library could not be opened.

Example

```
if (dwIndex != LB_ERR)
{
    //Note that the index in the list box is conveniently the same
    //as the one to pass to GetTypeInfo.

    CHECKRESULT(ptlib->GetTypeInfo((unsigned int) dwIndex,
&ptypeinfoCur));
    .
    .
    .
}
```

ITypeLib::GetTypeInfoCount

unsigned int ITypeLib::GetTypeInfoCount( )

Comments   Returns the number of type descriptions in a type library.

ITypeLib::GetTypeInfoType

HRESULT ITypeLib::GetTypeInfoType(*index, ptypekind*)
unsigned int *index*
TYPEKIND FAR* *ptypekind*

Retrieves the type of a type description.

Parameters   *index*
                The index of the type description within the type library.

                ptypekind
                A pointer to the TYPEKIND for the type description.

Return Value   The SCODE obtained from the returned HRESULT is one of the following:

SCODE	Meaning
S_OK	Success.
TYPE_E_ELEMENTNOTFOUND	*Index* is outside the range of 0 to **GetTypeInfoCount**() –1.

ITypeLib::GetTypeInfoOfGuid

ITypeLib::HResult ITypeLib::GetTypeInfoOfGuid(*lpguid, lplpitinfo*)
REFGUID *lpguid*
ITypeInfo FAR* FAR* *lplpitinfo*

Retrieves the type description corresponding to the specified GUID.

Parameters   *lpguid*
                Pointer to the globally unique ID of the type description.

                lplpitinfo
                Pointer to a pointer to the **ITypeInfo**.

Return Value   The SCODE obtained from the returned HRESULT is one of the following:

SCODE	Meaning
S_OK	Success.
TYPE_E_ELEMENTNOTFOUND	No type description was found in the library with the specified *guid*.
STG_E_INSUFFICIENTMEMORY	Out of memory.
E_OUTOFMEMORY	Out of memory.
E_INVALIDARG	One or more of the arguments is invalid.
TYPE_E_IOERROR	The function could not write to the file.
TYPE_E_INVDATAREAD	The function could not read from the file.
TYPE_E_UNSUPFORMAT	The type library has an old format.
TYPE_E_REGISTRYACCESS	There was an error accessing the system registration database.
TYPE_E_INVALIDSTATE	The type library could not be opened.

ITypeLib::IsName

HResult ITypeLib::IsName(*szNameBuf*, *lHashVal*, *lpfName*)
TCHAR FAR* *szNameBuf*
unsigned long *lHashVal*
BOOL *lpfName*

Indicates whether a passed-in string contains the name of a type or member described in the library.

Parameter   *szNameBuf*
   The string to test. If **IsName** is successful, *szNameBuf* is modified to match the case (capitalization) found in the type library.

   lHashVal
   The hash value of *szNameBuf*.

   lpfName
   This argument is set to True if *szNameBuf* is found in the type library.

Return Value   The SCODE obtained from the returned HRESULT is one of the following:

SCODE	Meaning
S_OK	Success.
STG_E_INSUFFICIENTMEMORY	Out of memory.
E_OUTOFMEMORY	Out of memory.
E_INVALIDARG	One or more of the arguments is invalid.

SCODE	Meaning
TYPE_E_IOERROR	The function could not write to the file.
TYPE_E_INVDATAREAD	The function could not read from the file.
TYPE_E_UNSUPFORMAT	The type library has an old format.
TYPE_E_INVALIDSTATE	The type library could not be opened.

Comments   Tests whether a string is the name of a type or member defined in the type library.

ITypeLib::ReleaseTLibAttr

VOID ITypeLib::ReleaseTLibAttr(*lptlibattr*)
TLIBATTR FAR* *lptlibattr*

Releases TLIBATTR originally obtained from **ITypeLib::GetLibAttr**.

Parameter   *lptlibattr*
  Pointer to the TLIBATTR to be freed.

Comments   Releases the specified TLIBATTR. This TLIBATTR was previously obtained with a call to **GetTypeLib::GetLibAttr**.

ITypeInfo Interface

Implemented by	Used by	Header file name
TYPELIB.DLL	Tools that need to access the descriptions of objects contained in type libraries	DISPATCH.H

This section describes **ITypeInfo**, an interface usually used for reading information about objects. For example, an object browser tool could use **ITypeInfo** to extract information about the characteristics and capabilities of objects from type libraries. (An example of typical browser code appears in Chapter 3, "Accessing OLE Automation Objects.")

Type information interfaces are intended to describe the parts of the application that can be called by outside clients, rather than kind of types that might be used internally to build an application.

The **ITypeInfo** interface provides access to the following:

- The set of function descriptions associated with the type; for interfaces, this contains the set of member functions in the interface.

- The set of data member descriptions associated with the type; for structures, this contains the set of fields of the type.

- The general attributes of the type such as whether it describes a structure, an interface, and so forth.

You can use the type description of an **IDispatch** interface to implement the **IDispatch** interface. See the description of **CreateStdDispatch** in Chapter 5, "Dispatch Interfaces," for more information.

An **ITypeInfo** instance provides various information about a type, and is used in different ways. A compiler could use an **ITypeInfo** to compile references to members of the type. A type interface browser could use it to find out information about each member of the type. An **IDispatch** implementor could use it to provide automatic delegation of **IDispatch** calls to an interface.

Type Descriptions

The information associated with an object described by **ITypeInfo** can include a set of functions, a set of data members, and various type attributes. It is essentially the same as the information described by a C++ class declaration. A C++ class declaration can be used to define both interfaces and structures, as well as any combination of functions and data members. In addition to interfaces and structure definitions, the **ITypeInfo** interface is used to describe other types as well, including enumerations and aliases. Since the interface to a C file or library is also just a set of functions and variable declarations, **ITypeInfo** is used to describe these as well.

Type information comprises individual type descriptions. Each type description must have one of the following forms:

Table 8.1   Recognized Type Information

Type description category	ODL keyword	Description
alias	[*attribute*]**typedef**	An alias for another type.
enumeration	**enum**	An enumeration.
structure	**struct**	A structure.
union	**union**	A single data item that can have one of a specified group of types.
module	**module**	Data and functions not accessed through vtable entries.

Table 8.1   Recognized Type Information *(continued)*

Type description category	ODL keyword	Description
IDispatch interface	**dispinterface**	**IDispatch** properties and methods accessed through **IDispatch::Invoke**.
OLE interface	**interface**	OLE member functions accessed through vtable entries.
Component object class	**coclass**	Description of a component object class description. Specifies an implementation of one or more OLE interfaces and one or more **IDispatch** interfaces.

Note that all bit flags that are not specifically used should be set to zero for future compatibility.

Alias

An alias has TypeKind = TKIND_ALIAS. An alias is an empty set of functions, an empty set of data members, and a type description which gives the actual type of the alias.

Enumeration

An enumeration has TypeKind = TKIND_ENUM. An enumeration is an empty set of functions and a set of constant data members.

Structure

A structure description has TypeKind = TKIND_RECORD. A structure is an empty set of functions and a set of per-instance data members.

Union

A union description has TypeKind = TKIND_UNION. A union is an empty set of functions and a set of per-instance data members, each of which has an instance offset of zero.

Module

A module has TypeKind = TKIND_MODULE. A module is a set of static functions and a set of static data members.

OLE-Compatible Interfaces

An interface definition has TypeKind = TKIND_INTERFACE. An interface is a set of pure virtual functions and an empty set of data members. If a type description contains any virtual functions, then the pointer to the virtual function table is the first 4 bytes of the instance.

The type information fully describes the member functions in the vtable, including parameter names and types and function return types. It may inherit from no more than one other interface.

Note that with interfaces and dispinterfaces, all members should have different names, except the accessor functions of properties. For property functions having the same name, the documentation string and Help context should only be set for one of the functions (since they conceptually define the same property).

Dispatch-Only Interfaces

These include objects (TypeKind = TKIND_DISPATCH) that support the **IDispatch** interface with a specification of the dispatch data members (for example, properties) and methods supported through the object's **Invoke** implementation. All members of the dispinterface should have different IDs, except for the accessor functions of properties.

Component Object Class (coclass) Interfaces

These include objects (TypeKind = TKIND_COCLASS) that support a set of implemented interfaces, which can be of either TKIND_INTERFACE or TKIND_DISPATCH.

The **ITypeInfo** interface is used by programming tools and browsers to read the information in type libraries. It can be implemented by applications that wish to expose their objects, but exposing objects through a type library lets OLE Automation controllers browse and retrieve type information without creating an instance of the application. **ITypeInfo** references many structures and enumerations, described in the next several sections.

Structures and Enumerations

Structures and enumerations used by **ITypeInfo** include the following:

ARRAYDESC

A pointer to an ARRAYDESC is contained within the TYPEDESC, which describes a C-style array. The TYPEDESC describes the type of the array's elements and information describing the arrays dimensions. It is defined as follows:

```
typedef struct tagARRAYDESC{
    TYPEDESC tdescElem;          // Element type.
    USHORT cDims;                // Dimension count.
    SAFEARRAYBOUND rgbounds[1];// Variable length array containing one
                                 // element for each dimension.
} ARRAYDESC;
```

ELEMDESC

An ELEMDESC structure includes the type description and process-transfer information for either a variable, a function, or a function parameter. It is defined as follows:

```
typedef struct tagELEMDESC{
TYPEDESC tdesc;      // Type of the element.
IDLDESC idldesc;// Information needed for transferring the
                    // element between processes.
    }  ELEMDESC;
```

FUNCDESC

A FUNCDESC describes a function, and is defined as follows:

```
typedef struct tagFUNCDESC {
MEMBERID memid;          // Function member ID
SCODE FAR* lprgscode;    // Legal SCODES for the function.
ELEMDESC FAR* lprgelemdescParam;  // Array of parameter types
FUNCKIND funckind;       // specifies whether the function is virtual,
                         // static, or dispatch-only.
INVOKEKIND invkind;      // Invocation kind; indicates if this is a
                         // property function and if so what kind.
CALLCONV callconv;       // Specifies the function's calling convention.
short cParams;           // Count of total number of parameters.
short cParamsOpt;        // Count of optional parameters (detailed
                         // description below).
short oVft;              // For FUNC_VIRTUAL, specifies the offset in the
                         // virtual function table.
short cScodes;           // Count of permitted Scodes.
ELEMDESC elemdescFunc;   // Contains the return type of the function.
unsigned short wFuncFlags; // See below for definition of flags.
} FUNCDESC;
```

The field cParams specifies the total number of required and optional parameters.

The *cParamsOpt* field specifies the form of optional parameters accepted by the function, as follows:

- A value of 0 specifies that no optional arguments are supported.

- A value of –1 specifies that the method's last parameter is a pointer to a safe array of variants and that any number of variant arguments greater than *cParams* – 1 must be packaged by the caller into a safe array and passed as the final parameter. This array of optional parameters array must be freed by the caller after control is returned from the call.

- Any other number indicates that the last *n* parameters of the function are variants and need not be specified explicitly by the caller. Those parameters left unspecified should be filled in by the compiler or interpreter as variants of type VT_ERROR with the value DISP_E_PARAMNOTFOUND.

The fields *cScodes* and *lprgscode* store the count and the set of errors that a function can return. If *cScodes* = –1 then the set of errors is unknown. If *cScodes* = –1 or *cScodes* = 0, then *lprgscode* is undefined.

FUNCFLAGS

The FUNCFLAGS enumeration is defined as follows:

```
typedef enum tagFUNCFLAGS {
    FUNCFLAG_FRESTRICTED = 1
} FUNCFLAGS;
```

Set FUNCFLAG_FRESTRICTED flag when the function should not be accessible from macro languages to ensure that crashing is impossible. This flag is intended for system-level functions or functions that you do not want type browsers to display.

FUNCKIND

The FUNCKIND enumeration is defined as follows:

```
typedef enum tagFUNCKIND {
    FUNC_VIRTUAL,
    FUNC_PUREVIRTUAL,
    FUNC_NONVIRTUAL,
    FUNC_STATIC,
    FUNC_DISPATCH,
} FUNCKIND;
```

Value	Description
FUNC_PUREVIRTUAL	The function is accessed via the virtual function table and takes an implicit *this* pointer.
FUNC_VIRTUAL	Same access as PUREVIRTUAL, except the function has an implementation.
FUNC_NONVIRTUAL	The function is accessed by static address and takes an implicit *this* pointer.
FUNC_STATIC	The function is accessed by static address and does not take an implicit *this* pointer.
FUNC_DISPATCH	The function can only be accessed via **IDispatch**.

HREFTYPE

HREFTYPE is a handle that identifies a type description.

```
typedef unsigned long HREFTYPE
```

IDLDESC

An IDLDESC contains information needed for transferring a structure element, parameter, or function return value between processes, and is defined as follows:

```
typedef struct tagIDLDESC{
BSTR            bstrIDLInfo;// Pointer to buffer containing the
                           //additional information.
unsigned short  wIDLFlags;       // in, out, unspecified
} IDLDESC;
```

Note that bstrIDLInfo is reserved for future use and should be set to NULL.

IDLFLAGS

The IDLFLAGS are defined as follows:

```
#define IDLFLAG_NONE 0
#define IDLFLAG_FIN     0x1
#define IDLFLAG_FOUT 0x2
```

Value	Description
IDLFLAG_NONE	Whether the parameter passes or receives information is unspecified. **IDispatch** interfaces can use this flag.
IDLFLAG_FIN	Parameter passes information from the caller to the callee.
IDLFLAG_FOUT	Parameter returns information from the callee to the caller.
IDLFLAGS_FIN I IDLFLAG_FOUT	Parameter passes and returns information.

INVOKEKIND

The INVOKEKIND enumeration is defined as follows:

```
typedef enum tagINVOKEKIND {
    INVOKE_FUNC = DISPATCH_METHOD,
    INVOKE_PROPERTYGET = DISPATCH_PROPERTYGET,
    INVOKE_PROPERTYPUT = DISPATCH_PROPERTYPUT,
    INVOKE_PROPERTYPUTREF = DISPATCH_PROPERTYPUTREF
} INVOKEKIND;
```

Value	Description
INVOKE_FUNC	The member is called using normal function invocation syntax.
INVOKE_PROPERTYGET	The function is invoked via normal property access syntax.

Value	Description
INVOKE_PROPERTYPUT	The function is invoked via property value assignment syntax. Syntactically, a typical programming language might represent changing a property in the same way as assignment; for example: `object.property := value`.
INVOKE_PROPERTYPUTREF	The function is invoked via property reference assignment syntax.

Note that in C, value assignment is written as `*pobj1 = *pobj2`, while reference assignment would be written as `pobj1 = pobj2`. Other languages have other syntactic conventions. A property or data member may support value assignment only, reference assignment only, or both. For a more detailed description of property functions, see Chapter 5, "Dispatch Interfaces." These enumeration constants are the same constants that are passed to **IDispatch::Invoke** to specify the way in which a function is invoked.

MEMBERID

MEMBERID identifies the member in a type description. For **IDispatch** interfaces, this is the same as DISPID.

```
typedef DISPID MEMBERID; // memid
```

TYPEATTR

The TYPEATTR structure contains attributes of an **ITypeInfo**, and is defined as follows:

```
typedef struct FARSTRUCT tagTYPEATTR {
    GUID guid;                 // the GUID of the TypeInfo
    LCID lcid;                 // locale of member names and doc
                               //strings
    unsigned long dwReserved;
    MEMBERID memidConstructor; // ID of constructor, MEMBERID_NIL if
                               //none
    MEMBERID memidDestructor;  // ID of destructor, MEMBERID_NIL if
                               // none
    char FAR* lpstrSchema;     // reserved for future use
    unsigned long cbSizeInstance;// the size of an instance of this type
    TYPEKIND typekind;         // the kind of type this typeinfo
describes
    unsigned short cFuncs;     // number of functions
    unsigned short cVars;      // number of variables / data members
    unsigned short cImplTypes; // number of implemented interfaces
    unsigned short cbSizeVft;  // the size of this types virtual func
                               // table
```

```
    unsigned short cbAlignment;  // the byte-alignment for an instance
                                 // of this type
    unsigned short wTypeFlags;
    unsigned short wMajorVerNum;// major version number
    unsigned short wMinorVerNum;// minor version number
    TYPEDESC tdescAlias;            // if typekind == TKIND_ALIAS this
                                   // specifies the type for which this
                                   // type is an alias
    IDLDESC idldescType;           // IDL attributes of the described type
} TYPEATTR, FAR* LPTYPEATTR;
```

The cbAlignment field indicates how addresses are aligned. A value of 0 indicates alignment on the 64K boundary; 1 indicates no special alignment. For other values, *n* indicates aligned on byte *n*.

TYPEDESC

A TYPEDESC, which describes the type of a variable, the return type of a function, or the type of a function parameter, is defined as follows:

```
typedef struct FARSTRUCT tagTYPEDESC {
    union {
        /* VT_PTR - the pointed-at type */
        struct FARSTRUCT tagTYPEDESC FAR* lptdesc;

        /* VT_CARRAY */
        struct FARSTRUCT tagARRAYDESC FAR* lpadesc;

        /* VT_USERDEFINED - this is used to get a TypeInfo for a user-
        defined type */
        HREFTYPE hreftype;

        }UNION_NAME(u);
        VARTYPE vt;
} TYPEDESC;
```

If the variable is VT_SAFEARRAY or VT_PTR, the union portion of the TYPEDESC contains a pointer to a TYPEDESC that specifies the element type.

TYPEFLAGS

The TYPEFLAGS enumeration is defined as follows:

```
typedef enum tagTYPEFLAGS {
    TYPEFLAG_FAPPOBJECT = 1
    , TYPEFLAG_FCANCREATE = 2
} TYPEFLAGS;
```

TYPEFLAG_FAPPOBJECT may be used on type descriptions with TypeKind = TKIND_COCLASS, and indicates that the type description describes an Application object.

Members of the Application object are globally accessible in that the **Bind** method of the **ITypeComp** instance associated with the library will bind to the members of an Application object just as it does for type descriptions with TypeKind = TKIND_MODULE.

A global variable is implicitly defined by the type description with the same name as the type description with the type described by the type description. This variable is also globally accessible. Specifically, when **Bind** is passed the name of an Application object, a VARDESC is returned describing the implicit variable. The ID of the implicitly created variable is always ID_DEFAULTINST.

When the **CreateInstance** function of an Application object type description is called, it uses **GetActiveObject** to retrieve the Application object. If **GetActiveObject** fails because the application is not running, then **CreateInstance** calls **CoCreateInstance** (which should start the application).

When TYPEFLAG_FCANCREATE is True, **ITypeInfo::CreateInstance** can create an instance of the type. Note that this is currently true only for component object classes for which a GUID has been specified.

TYPEKIND

The TYPEKIND enumeration is defined as follows:

```
typedef enum tagTYPEKIND {
      TKIND_ENUM = 0
    , TKIND_RECORD
    , TKIND_MODULE
    , TKIND_INTERFACE
    , TKIND_DISPATCH
    , TKIND_COCLASS
    , TKIND_ALIAS
    , TKIND_UNION
    , TKIND_MAX          /* end of enum marker */
} TYPEKIND;
```

Value	Description
TKIND_ALIAS	A type that is an alias for another type.
TKIND_COCLASS	A set of implemented component object interfaces.
TKIND_DISPATCH	A set of methods and properties which are accessible via **IDispatch::Invoke**.
TKIND_ENUM	A set of enumerators.
TKIND_INTERFACE	A type that has virtual functions, all of which are pure.
TKIND_MODULE	A module which can only have static functions and data (for instance, a DLL).

Value	Description
TKIND_RECORD	A struct with no methods.
TKIND_UNION	A union, all of whose members have offset zero.

VARDESC

A VARDESC structure describes a variable, constant, or data member, and is defined as follows:

```
typedef struct FARSTRUCT tagVARDESC {
    MEMBERID memid;
    char FAR* lpstrSchema;          /* reserved for future use */
    union {
      /* VAR_PERINSTANCE - the offset of this variable within the
instance */
      unsigned long oInst;

      /* VAR_CONST - the value of the constant */
      VARIANT FAR* lpvarValue;

    }UNION_NAME(u);
    ELEMDESC elemdescVar;
    unsigned short wVarFlags;
    VARKIND varkind;
} VARDESC, FAR* LPVARDESC;
```

VARFLAGS

The VARFLAGS enumeration is defined as follows:

```
typedef enum tagVARFLAGS {
    VARFLAG_FREADONLY   = 1
} VARFLAGS;
```

When VARFLAG_READONLY is set, assignment to the variable should not be allowed.

VARKIND

The VARKIND enumeration is defined as follows:

```
typedef enum tagVARKIND {
    VAR_PERINSTANCE,
    VAR_STATIC,
    VAR_CONST,
    VAR_DISPATCH
} VARKIND;
```

Value	Description
VAR_PERINSTANCE	The variable is a field or member of the type; it exists at a fixed offset within each instance of the type.
VAR_STATIC	There is only one instance of the variable.
VAR_CONST	The VARDESC describes a symbolic constant. There is no memory associated with it.
VAR_DISPATCH	The variable can only be accessed via **IDispatch::Invoke**.

ITypeInfo::AddressOfMember

HRESULT ITypeInfo::AddressOfMember(*memid*, *invkind*, *lplpvoid*)
MEMBERID *memid*
INVOKE_KIND *invkind*
VOID FAR* FAR* *lplpvoid*

Retrieves the addresses of static functions or variables, such as those defined in a DLL.

Parameters

memid
Member ID of the static member whose address is to be retrieved.
Member ID is defined by DISPID.

invkind
Specifies whether the member is a property, and if so, what kind.

lplpvoid
Upon return, points to a pointer to the static member.

Return Value

The SCODE obtained from the returned HRESULT is one of the following:

SCODE	Meaning
S_OK	Success.
STG_E_INSUFFICIENTMEMORY	Out of memory.
E_OUTOFMEMORY	Out of memory.
E_INVALIDARG	One or more of the arguments is invalid.
TYPE_E_IOERROR	The function could not write to the file.
TYPE_E_WRONGTYPEKIND	Type mismatch.
TYPE_E_INVDATAREAD	The function could not read from the file.
TYPE_E_UNSUPFORMAT	The type library has an old format.

SCODE	Meaning
TYPE_E_INVALIDSTATE	The type library could not be opened.
TYPE_E_ELEMENTNOTFOUND	The element was not found.
TYPE_E_DLLFUNCTIONNOTFOUND	The function could not be found in the DLL.
TYPE_E_CANTLOADLIBRARY	The type library or DLL could not be loaded.
STG_E_OLDDLL	The COMPOBJ.DLL is out of date.

Comments   The addresses are valid until the caller releases its reference to the type description. Note that the INVOKE_KIND parameter can be ignored unless the address of a property function is being requested.

ITypeInfo::CreateInstance

HRESULT ITypeInfo::CreateInstance(*punkOuter, riid, ppvObj*)
IUnknown FAR* *punkOuter*
REFIID *riid*
VOID FAR* FAR* *ppvObject*

Creates a new instance of a type that describes a component object class (**coclass**).

Parameters   *punkOuter*
    A pointer to the instance that was created.

riid
    An ID for the interface the caller will use to communicate with the resulting object.

ppvObject
    On return, points to a pointer to an instance of the created object.

Return Value   The SCODE obtained from the returned HRESULT is one of the following:

SCODE	Meaning
S_OK	Success.
STG_E_INSUFFICIENTMEMORY	Out of memory.
E_OUTOFMEMORY	Out of memory.
TYPE_E_WRONGTYPEKIND	Type mismatch.
E_INVALIDARG	One or more of the arguments is invalid.
E_NOINTERFACE	OLE could not find an implementation of one or more required interfaces.
TYPE_E_UNSUPFORMAT	The type library has an old format.

SCODE	Meaning
TYPE_E_INVALIDSTATE	The type library could not be opened.
Other returns	Additional errors may be returned from **GetActiveObject** or **CoCreateInstance**.

Comments

For types that describe a component object class (**coclass**), **CreateInstance** creates a new instance of the class. Normally **CreateInstance** calls **CoCreateInstance** with the type description's GUID. For an Application object, it first calls **GetActiveObject**. If the application is active, **GetActiveObject** returns the active object; otherwise, if **GetActiveObject** fails, **CreateInstance** calls **CoCreateInstance**.

ITypeInfo::GetContainingTypeLib

HRESULT ITypeInfo::GetContainingTypeLib(*lplptlib, lpindex*)
ITypeLib FAR* FAR* *lplptlib*
unsigned int* *lpindex*

Retrieves the containing type library and the index of the type description within that type library.

Parameters

lplptlib
Upon return, points to a pointer to the containing type library.

lpindex
Upon return, points to the index of the type description within the containing type library.

Return Value

The SCODE obtained from the returned HRESULT is one of the following:

SCODE	Meaning
S_OK	Success.
STG_E_INSUFFICIENTMEMORY	Out of memory.
E_OUTOFMEMORY	Out of memory.
E_INVALIDARG	One or more of the arguments is invalid.
E_NOINTERFACE	OLE could not find an implementation of one or more required interfaces.
TYPE_E_IOERROR	The function could not write to the file.
TYPE_E_INVDATAREAD	The function could not read from the file.
TYPE_E_UNSUPFORMAT	The type library has an old format.
TYPE_E_INVALIDSTATE	The type library could not be opened.

ITypeInfo::GetDllEntry

> **HRESULT ITypeInfo::GetDllEntry**(*memid, invkind, lpbstrDllName*,
> *lpbstrName, lpwOrdinal*)
> **MEMBERID** *memid*
> **INVOKEKIND** *invkind*
> **BSTR FAR*** *lpbstrDllName*
> **BSTR FAR*** *lpbstrName*
> **unsigned short FAR*** *lpwOrdinal*

Retrieves a description or specification of an entry point for a function in a DLL.

Parameters

memid
ID of the member function whose DLL entry description is to be returned.

invkind
Specifies kind of member identified by *memid*. This is important for properties, since one *memid* can identify up to three separate functions.

lpbstrDllName
Pointer to a BSTR allocated by the callee. If not NULL, the function sets *lpbstrDllName* to point to the DLL name.

lpbstrName
Pointer to a BSTR allocated by the callee. If not NULL, the function sets *lpbstrName* to point to the name of the entry point; if the entry point is specified by an ordinal, then the passed-in pointer is set to NULL.

lpwOrdinal
If not NULL, and if the function is defined by ordinal, then *lpwOrdinal* is set to point to the ordinal.

Return Value

The SCODE obtained from the returned HRESULT is one of the following:

SCODE	Meaning
S_OK	Success.
STG_E_INSUFFICIENTMEMORY	Out of memory.
E_OUTOFMEMORY	Out of memory.
E_INVALIDARG	One or more of the arguments is invalid.
E_NOINTERFACE	OLE could not find an implementation of one or more required interfaces.
TYPE_E_ELEMENTNOTFOUND	The element was not found.
TYPE_E_IOERROR	The function could not write to the file.
TYPE_E_INVDATAREAD	The function could not read from the file.
TYPE_E_UNSUPFORMAT	The type library has an old format.

SCODE	Meaning
TYPE_E_INVALIDSTATE	The type library could not be opened.
TYPE_E_WRONGTYPEKIND	Type mismatch.

Comments

The caller passes in a MEMID representing the member function whose entry description is desired. If the function has a DLL entry point, the name of the DLL containing the function, and either its name or ordinal identifier are placed in the passed-in pointers allocated by the caller. If there is no DLL entry point for the function, an error is returned.

ITypeInfo::GetDocumentation

HRESULT ITypeInfo::GetDocumentation(*memid, lpbstrName, lpbstrDocString, lpdwHelpContext, lpbstrHelpFile*)
MEMBERID *memid*
BSTR FAR* *lpbstrName*
BSTR FAR* *lpbstrDocString*
unsigned long FAR* *lpdwHelpContext*
BSTR FAR* *lpbstrHelpFile*

Retrieves the documentation string, name of the complete Help file path and name, and the context ID for the Help topic for a specified type description.

Parameters

memid
ID of the member whose documentation is to be returned.

lpbstrName
Pointer to a BSTR allocated by the callee into which the name of the specified item is placed. If the caller does not need the item name, *lpbstrName* can be NULL.

lpbstrDocString
Pointer to a BSTR allocated by the callee into which the documentation string for the specified item is placed. If the caller does not need the documentation string, *lpbstrDocString* can be NULL.

lpdwHelpContext
Pointer to the Help context associated with the specified item. If the caller does not need the Help context, the *lpdwHelpContext* can be NULL.

lpbstrHelpFile
Pointer to a BSTR allocated by the callee into which the fully qualified name of the Help file is placed. If the caller does not need the Help file name, *lpbstrHelpFile* can be NULL.

Return Value

The SCODE obtained from the returned HRESULT is one of the following:

SCODE	Meaning
S_OK	Success.
STG_E_INSUFFICIENTMEMORY	Out of memory.
E_OUTOFMEMORY	Out of memory.
E_INVALIDARG	One or more of the arguments is invalid.
TYPE_E_IOERROR	The function could not write to the file.
TYPE_E_ELEMENTNOTFOUND	The element was not found.
TYPE_E_INVDATAREAD	The function could not read from the file.
TYPE_E_UNSUPFORMAT	The type library has an old format.
TYPE_E_INVALIDSTATE	The type library could not be opened.
TYPE_E_ELEMENTNOTFOUND	The element was not found.

Comments

Provides access to the documentation for the Member specified by the *memid* parameter. If the passed-in *memid* is MEMBERID_NIL, then the documentation for the type description is returned.

Example

```
CHECKRESULT(ptypeinfo->GetDocumentation(idMember, &bstrName, NULL, NULL,
NULL));
```

ITypeInfo::GetFuncDesc

HRESULT ITypeInfo::GetFuncDesc(*index*, *lplpfuncdesc*)
unsigned int *index*
FUNCDESC FAR* FAR* *lplpfuncdesc*

Retrieves the FUNCDESC structure containing information about a specified function.

Parameters

index
    Index of the function whose description is to be returned. The index should be in the range of 0 to 1 less than the number of functions in this type.

lplpfuncdesc
    Upon return, points to a pointer to a FUNCDESC that describes the specified function.

Return Value

The SCODE obtained from the returned HRESULT is one of the following:

SCODE	Meaning
S_OK	Success.
STG_E_INSUFFICIENTMEMORY	Out of memory.
E_OUTOFMEMORY	Out of memory.
E_INVALIDARG	One or more of the arguments is invalid.
TYPE_E_IOERROR	The function could not write to the file.
TYPE_E_INVDATAREAD	The function could not read from the file.
TYPE_E_UNSUPFORMAT	The type library has an old format.
TYPE_E_INVALIDSTATE	The type library could not be opened.

Comments   Provides access to a FUNCDESC which describes the function with the specified index. The number of functions in the type is one of the attributes contained in the TYPEATTR structure.

Example

```
CHECKRESULT(ptypeinfo->GetFuncDesc(i, &pfuncdesc));
idMember = pfuncdesc->elemdescFunc.ID;
CHECKRESULT(ptypeinfo->GetDocumentation(idMember, &bstrName, NULL, NULL,
NULL));
ptypeinfo->ReleaseFuncDesc(pfuncdesc);
pfuncdesc = NULL;
```

ITypeInfo::GetIDsOfNames

HRESULT ITypeInfo::GetIDsOfNames(*rgszNames, cNames, rgmemid*)
char FAR* FAR* *rgszNames*
unsigned int *cNames*
MEMBERID FAR* *rgmemid*

Maps between member names and member IDs, and parameter names and parameter IDs.

Parameters   *rgszNames*
        Passed-in pointer to an array of names to be mapped.

cNames
        Count of the names to be mapped.

rgmemid
        Caller-allocated array in which name mappings are placed.

Return Value   The SCODE obtained from the returned HRESULT is one of the following:

SCODE	Meaning
S_OK	Success.
STG_E_INSUFFICIENTMEMORY	Out of memory.
E_OUTOFMEMORY	Out of memory.
E_INVALIDARG	One or more of the arguments is invalid.
DISP_E_UNKNOWNNAME	One or more of the names could not be found.
DISP_E_UNKNOWNLCID	The LCID could not be found in the OLE DLLs.
TYPE_E_IOERROR	The function could not write to the file.
TYPE_E_INVDATAREAD	The function could not read from the file.
TYPE_E_UNSUPFORMAT	The type library has an old format.
TYPE_E_INVALIDSTATE	The type library could not be opened.
TYPE_E_WRONGTYPEKIND	Type mismatch.

Comments

Maps a member name (*rgszNames*[0]) and parameter names (*rgszNames*[1] ...*rgszNames*[cNames−1]) of the member to the ID of that member (*rgid*[0]), and the IDs of the specified parameters (*rgid*[1] ... *rgid*[*cNames*−1]). Note that the IDs of parameters are 0 for the first parameter in the member function's argument list, 1 for the second, and so on.

If the type description inherits from another type description, **GetIDsOfNames** recurses on the base type description if necessary.

ITypeInfo::GetMops

HRESULT ITypeInfo::GetMops(*memid, lpbstrMops*)
MEMBERID *memid*
BSTR FAR* *lpbstrMops*

Retrieves marshaling information.

Parameters

memid
    Member ID indicating which marshaling information is sought.

lpbstrMops
    Upon return, points to a pointer to the opcode string used in marshaling the fields of the structure described by the referenced type description.

Return Value   The SCODE obtained from the returned HRESULT is one of the following:

SCODE	Meaning
S_OK	Success.
STG_E_INSUFFICIENTMEMORY	Out of memory.
E_OUTOFMEMORY	Out of memory.
E_INVALIDARG	One or more of the arguments is invalid.
TYPE_E_IOERROR	The function could not write to the file.
TYPE_E_UNSUPFORMAT	The type library has an old format.
TYPE_E_INVALIDSTATE	The type library could not be opened.
TYPE_E_ELEMENTNOTFOUND	The element was not found.
TYPE_E_WRONGTYPEKIND	Type mismatch.

Comments   If the passed-in member ID is MEMBERID_NIL, then the opcode string for marshaling the fields of the structure described by the type description is returned. Otherwise, the opcode string for marshaling the function specified by the index is returned.

ITypeInfo::GetNames

HRESULT ITypeInfo::GetNames(*memid*, *rgbstrNames*, *cNameMax*, *lpcName*)
MEMBERID *memid*
BSTR FAR* *rgbstrNames*
unsigned int *cNameMax*
unsigned int FAR* *lpcName*

Retrieves the variable with the specified member ID, or the name of the function and parameter names corresponding to the specified function ID.

Parameters   *memid*
    ID of member whose name (or names) is to be returned.

. *rgbstrNames*
    Pointer to caller-allocated array. On return, each of these *lpcName* elements is filled in to point to a BSTR containing the name (or names) associated with the member.

cNameMax
    Length of the passed-in *rgbstrNames* array.

lpcName
    On return, points to number representing the number of names in *rgbstrNames* array.

Return Value

The SCODE obtained from the returned HRESULT is one of the following:

SCODE	Meaning
S_OK	Success.
STG_E_INSUFFICIENTMEMORY	Out of memory.
E_OUTOFMEMORY	Out of memory.
E_INVALIDARG	One or more of the arguments is invalid.
TYPE_E_IOERROR	The function could not write to the file.
TYPE_E_INVDATAREAD	The function could not read from the file.
TYPE_E_UNSUPFORMAT	The type library has an old format.
TYPE_E_INVALIDSTATE	The type library could not be opened.
TYPE_E_WRONGTYPEKIND	Type mismatch.
TYPE_E_ELEMENTNOTFOUND	The element was not found.

Comments

The caller must release the returned BSTR array. If the member ID identifies a property that is implemented with property functions, the property name is returned.

For property put and put reference functions, the right-hand side of the assignment is unnamed. If *cNameMax* is less than is required to return all the names of parameters of a function, then only the names of the first *cNameMax* − 1 parameters are returned. The names of the parameters are returned in the array in the same order they appear elsewhere in the interface, for example, in the same order they appear in the parameter array associated with the FUNCDESC.

ITypeInfo::GetRefTypeInfo

HRESULT ITypeInfo::GetRefTypeInfo(*hreftype*, *lplptinfo*)
HREFTYPE *hreftype*
ITypeInfo FAR* FAR* *lplptinfo*

If a type description references other type descriptions, this function retrieves the referenced type descriptions.

Parameters

hreftype
Handle to the referenced type description to be returned.

lplptinfo
Points to a pointer to the referenced type description.

Return Value

The SCODE obtained from the returned HRESULT is one of the following:

SCODE	Meaning
S_OK	Success.
STG_E_INSUFFICIENTMEMORY	Out of memory.
E_OUTOFMEMORY	Out of memory.
E_INVALIDARG	One or more of the arguments is invalid.
TYPE_E_IOERROR	The function could not write to the file.
TYPE_E_INVDATAREAD	The function could not read from the file.
TYPE_E_UNSUPFORMAT	The type library has an old format.
TYPE_E_INVALIDSTATE	The type library could not be opened.
TYPE_E_WRONGTYPEKIND	Type mismatch.
TYPE_E_ELEMENTNOTFOUND	The element was not found.
TYPE_E_REGISTRYACCESS	There was an error accessing the system registration database.
TYPE_E_LIBNOTREGISTERED	The type library was not found in the system registration database.

Comments

On return, the second parameter contains a pointer to a pointer to a type description that is referenced by this type description. A type description must have a reference to each type description which occurs as the type of any of its variables, function parameters, or function return types. For example, if the type of a data member is a record type, TypeDesc for that data member contains the *hreftype* of a referenced type description. To get a pointer to the type description, the reference is passed to **GetRefTypeInfo**.

ITypeInfo::GetTypeAttr

HRESULT ITypeInfo::GetTypeAttr(*lplptypeattr*)
TYPEATTR FAR* FAR* *lplptypeattr*

Retrieves a TYPEATTR structure containing the attributes of the type description.

Parameter

lplptypeattr
Upon return, points to a pointer to a structure that contains the attributes of this type description.

Return Value   The SCODE obtained from the returned HRESULT is one of the following:

SCODE	Meaning
S_OK	Success.
STG_E_INSUFFICIENTMEMORY	Out of memory.
E_OUTOFMEMORY	Out of memory.
E_INVALIDARG	One or more of the arguments is invalid.
TYPE_E_IOERROR	The function could not write to the file.
TYPE_E_INVDATAREAD	The function could not read from the file.
TYPE_E_UNSUPFORMAT	The type library has an old format.
TYPE_E_INVALIDSTATE	The type library could not be opened.

Comments   To free the TYPEATTR structure, use **ReleaseTypeAttr**.

Example
```
CHECKRESULT(ptypeinfoCur->GetTypeAttr(&ptypeattrCur));
```

ITypeInfo::GetTypeComp

HRESULT ITypeInfo::GetTypeComp(*lplpcomp*)
ITypeComp FAR* FAR* *lplpcomp*

Retrieves the ITypeComp interface for the type description, which enables a client compiler to bind to the type description's members.

Parameter   *lplpcomp*
        Upon return, points to a pointer to the **ITypeComp** of the containing type library.

Return Value   The SCODE obtained from the returned HRESULT is one of the following:

SCODE	Meaning
S_OK	Success.
STG_E_INSUFFICIENTMEMORY	Out of memory.
E_OUTOFMEMORY	Out of memory.
E_INVALIDARG	One or more of the arguments is invalid.
TYPE_E_IOERROR	The function could not write to the file.
TYPE_E_INVDATAREAD	The function could not read from the file.

SCODE	Meaning
TYPE_E_UNSUPFORMAT	The type library has an old format.
TYPE_E_INVALIDSTATE	The type library could not be opened.
TYPE_E_WRONGTYPEKIND	Type mismatch.

Comments   A client compiler can use the **ITypeComp** interface to bind to members of the type.

ITypeInfo::GetRefTypeOfImplType

HRESULT ITypeInfo::GetRefTypeOfImplType(*index, lphreftype*)
unsigned int *index*
HREFTYPE FAR* *lphreftype*

If this type description describes a component object class, this function retrieves the type description of the specified implemented interface types.

Parameters   *index*
Index of the implemented type whose handle is returned. The valid range is 0 to the *cImplTypes* field in the TYPLIBATTR structure.

lphreftype
Upon return, points to a handle for the implemented interface (if any). This handle can be passed to **ITypeInfo::GetRefTypeInfo** to get the type description.

Return Value   The SCODE obtained from the returned HRESULT is one of the following:

SCODE	Meaning
S_OK	Success.
TYPE_E_ELEMENTNOTFOUND	Passed index is outside the range 0 to 1 less than the number of function descriptions.
E_INVALIDARG	One or more of the arguments is invalid.
TYPE_E_ILLEGALINDEX	The *index* argument was outside the range of 0 to *cImplTypes* .
TYPE_E_IOERROR	The function could not write to the file.
TYPE_E_INVDATAREAD	The function could not read from the file.
TYPE_E_UNSUPFORMAT	The type library has an old format.
TYPE_E_INVALIDSTATE	The type library could not be opened.

Comments   For an interface, **GetRefTypeOfImplType** returns the type information for inherited interfaces, if any exist.

ITypeInfo::GetVarDesc

HRESULT ITypeInfo::GetVarDesc(*index, lplpvardesc*)
unsigned int *index*
VARDESC FAR* FAR* *lplpvardesc*

Retrieves a VARDESC structure describing the specified variable.

Parameters

index
Index of the variable whose description is to be returned. The index should be in the range of 0 to 1 less than the number of variables in this type.

lplpvardesc
Upon return, points to a pointer to a VARDESC that describes the specified variable.

Return Value

The SCODE obtained from the returned HRESULT is one of the following:

SCODE	Meaning
S_OK	Success.
STG_E_INSUFFICIENTMEMORY	Out of memory.
E_OUTOFMEMORY	Out of memory.
E_INVALIDARG	One or more of the arguments is invalid.
TYPE_E_IOERROR	The function could not write to the file.
TYPE_E_INVDATAREAD	The function could not read from the file.
TYPE_E_UNSUPFORMAT	The type library has an old format.
TYPE_E_INVALIDSTATE	The type library could not be opened.

Comments

The number of variables in the type is one of the attributes contained in the TYPEATTR structure.

To free the TYPEATTR structure, use **ReleaseVarDesc**.

Example

```
CHECKRESULT(ptypeinfo->GetVarDesc(i, &pvardesc));
idMember = pvardesc->elemdescVar.ID;
CHECKRESULT(ptypeinfo->GetDocumentation(idMember, &bstrName, NULL, NULL,
NULL));
ptypeinfo->ReleaseVarDesc(pvardesc);
pvardesc = NULL;
```

ITypeInfo::Invoke

HRESULT ITypeInfo::Invoke(*lpvInstance, dispidMember, wFlags,*
pdispparams, pvargResult, pexcepinfo, puArgErr)
VOID FAR* *lpvInstance*
MEMBERID *memid*
unsigned short *wFlags*
DISPPARAMS FAR* *pdispparams*
VARIANT FAR* *pvargResult*
EXCEPINFO FAR* *pexcepinfo*
unsigned int FAR* *puArgErr*

Invokes a method or accesses a property of an object that implements the interface
described by the type description.

Parameters

lpvInstance
Pointer to an instance of the interface described by this type description.

memid
Identifies the interface member.

wFlags
Flags describing the context of the invoke call, as follows:

Value	Description
DISPATCH_METHOD	The member was accessed as a method. If there is ambiguity, both this and the DISPATCH_PROPERTYGET flag may be set.
DISPATCH_PROPERTYGET	The member is being retrieved as a property or data member.
DISPATCH_PROPERTYPUT	The member is being changed as a property or data member.
DISPATCH_PROPERTYPUTREF	The member is being changed via a reference assignment, rather than a value assignment. This value is only valid when the property accepts a reference to an object.

pdispparams
Points to a structure containing an array of arguments, an array of DISPIDs for
named arguments, and counts for number of elements in the arrays.

pvargResult
Should be NULL if the caller expects no result; otherwise, it should be a
pointer to the location at which the result is to be stored. If *wFlags* specifies
DISPATCH_PROPERTYPUT or DISPATCH_PROPERTYPUTREF,
pvargResult is ignored.

pexcepinfo

    Points to an exception information structure, which is filled in only if DISP_E_EXCEPTION is returned. May not be NULL.

puArgErr

    If **Invoke** returns DISP_E_TYPEMISMATCH, *puArgErr* indicates the index (within *rgvarg*) of the argument with incorrect type. If more than one argument has an error, *puArgErr* indicates only the first argument with an error. Note that arguments in *pdispparams->rgvarg* appear in reverse order, so the first argument is the one having the highest index in the array. Cannot be NULL.

Return Value

The SCODE obtained from the returned HRESULT is one of the following:

SCODE	Meaning
S_OK	Success.
E_INVALIDARG	One or more of the arguments is invalid.
TYPE_E_IOERROR	The function could not write to the file.
TYPE_E_ILLEGALINDEX	The member ID is invalid.
TYPE_E_INVDATAREAD	The function could not read from the file.
TYPE_E_UNSUPFORMAT	The type library has an old format.
TYPE_E_REGISTRYACCESS	There was an error accessing the system registration database.
TYPE_E_LIBNOTREGISTERED	The type library was not found in the system registration database.
TYPE_E_INVALIDSTATE	The type library could not be opened.
TYPE_E_WRONGTYPEKIND	Type mismatch.
TYPE_E_ELEMENTNOTFOUND	The element was not found.
TYPE_E_BADMODULEKIND	The module does not support **Invoke**.
Other returns	Any of the **IDispatch::Invoke** errors may also be returned.

Comments

Use **Invoke** to access a member of an object or invoke a method that implements the interface described by this type description. For objects that support the **IDispatch** interface, **Invoke** can be used to implement **IDispatch::Invoke**. **ITypeInfo::Invoke** takes a pointer to an instance of the class. Otherwise, its parameters are the same as **IDispatch::Invoke**, except that **ITypeInfo::Invoke** omits the REFIID and LCID parameters. When called, **ITypeInfo::Invoke** performs the actions described by the **IDispatch::Invoke** parameters on the specified instance.

ITypeInfo::ReleaseFuncDesc

VOID ITypeInfo::ReleaseFuncDesc(*lpfuncdesc*)
FUNCDESC FAR* *lpfuncdesc*

Releases a FUNCDESC previously returned by **GetFuncDesc**.

Parameter

lpfuncdes
　　Pointer to the FUNCDESC to be freed.

Comments

ReleaseFuncDesc releases a FUNCDESC which was returned via
ITypeInfo::GetFuncDesc.

Example

```
ptypeinfoCur->ReleaseFuncDesc(pfuncdesc);
```

ITypeInfo::ReleaseTypeAttr

VOID ITypeInfo::ReleaseTypeAttr(*lptypeattr*)
TYPEATTR FAR* *lptypeattr*

Releases a TYPEATTR previously returned by **GetTypeAttr**.

Parameter

lptypeattr
　　Pointer to the TYPEATTR to be freed.

Comments

ReleaseTypeAttr releases a TYPEATTR which was returned via
ITypeInfo::GetTypeAttr.

ITypeInfo::ReleaseVarDesc

VOID ITypeInfo::ReleaseVarDesc(*lpvardesc*)
VARDESC FAR* *lpvardesc*

Releases a VARDESC previously returned by **GetVarDesc**.

Parameter

lpvardesc
　　Pointer to the VARDESC to be freed.

Comments

ReleaseVarDesc releases a VARDESC which was returned via
ITypeInfo::GetVarDesc.

Example
```
VARDESC    FAR *pvardesc;
CHECKRESULT(ptypeinfo->GetVarDesc(i, &pvardesc));
idMember = pvardesc->elemdescVar.id;
CHECKRESULT(ptypeinfo->GetDocumentation(idMember, &bstrName, NULL, NULL,
NULL));
ptypeinfo->ReleaseVarDesc(pvardesc);
pvardesc = NULL;
```

ITypeComp Interface

Implemented by	Used by	Header file name
TYPELIB.DLL	Tools that compile references to objects contained in type libraries	**DISPATCH.H**

Binding is the process of mapping names to types and type members. The **ITypeComp** interface provides a fast way to access information that compilers need when binding to and instantiating structures and interfaces.

Structures and Enumerations

BINDPTR

A union containing a pointer to either a FUNCDESC, VARDESC, or an **ITypeComp**:

```
typedef union tagBINDPTR {
    FUNCDESC *lpfuncdesc;
    VARDESC *lpvardesc;
    ITypeComp *lptcomp
} BINDPTR;
```

DESCKIND

Identifies the type of the type description being bound to.

```
typedef enum tagDESCKIND {
    DESCKIND_NONE,
    DESCKIND_FUNCDESC,
    DESCKIND_VARDESC,
    DESCKIND_TYPECOMP
    DESCKIND_IMPLICITAPPOBJ
} DESCKIND;
```

Comments

Value	Description
DESCKIND_NONE	Indicates that no match was found.
DESCKIND_FUNCDESC	Indicates that a FUNCDESC has been returned.
DESCKIND_VARDESC	Indicates that a VARDESC has been returned.
DESCKIND_TYPECOMP	Indicates that a TYPECOMP has been returned.
DESCKIND_IMPLICITAPPOBJ	Indicates that an IMPLICITAPPOBJ has been returned.

ITypeComp::Bind

HRESULT ITypeComp::Bind (*szName, lHashVal, wFlags, lplptinfo, lpdesckind, lpbindptr* **)**
TCHAR FAR* *szName*
unsigned long *lHashVal*
unsigned short *wFlags*
ITypeInfo FAR* FAR* *lplptinfo*
DESCKIND *lpdesckind*
BINDPTR FAR* *lpbindptr*

Maps a name to a member of a type, or binds global variables and functions contained in a type library.

Parameters

szName
Name to be bound.

lHashVal
Hash value for the name computed by **LHashValOfName**.

wFlags
Flags word containing one or more of the INVOKE flags defined in the INVOKEKIND enumeration. Specifies whether the name was referenced as a method or as a property. When binding to a variable, specify the INVOKE_PROPERTYGET flag.

lplptinfo
If a FUNCDESC or VARDESC was returned, then *lplptinfo* points to a pointer to the type description that contains the item to which it is bound.

desckind
Specifies whether the name bound to a VARDESC, a FUNCDESC, or a TYPECOMP. Points to DESCKIND_NONE if there was no match.

lpbindptr
Upon return, contains a pointer to the bound-to VARDESC, FUNCDESC, or **ITypeComp**.

Return Value

The SCODE obtained from the returned HRESULT is one of the following:

SCODE	Meaning
S_OK	Success.
STG_E_INSUFFICIENTMEMORY	Out of memory.
E_OUTOFMEMORY	Out of memory.
E_INVALIDARG	One or more of the arguments is invalid.
TYPE_E_IOERROR	The function could not write to the file.
TYPE_E_INVDATAREAD	The function could not read from the file.
TYPE_E_UNSUPFORMAT	The type library has an old format.
TYPE_E_INVALIDSTATE	The type library could not be opened.
TYPE_E_AMBIGUOUSNAME	More than one instance of this name occurs in the type library.

Comments

Used for binding to the variables and methods of a type or for binding to the global variables and methods contained within a type library. The returned BINDPTR (*lplpbindptr*) points to either a VARDESC, a FUNCDESC, or an **ITypeComp** as specified by the DESCKIND. If a data member or method is bound to, then *lplptinfo* is set to point to the containing type description. It is possible that **Bind** will bind to a nested binding context, in which case an **ITypeComp** instance and a NULL type description pointer are returned. For example, if the **ITypeComp** instance of a type library is passed the name of a type description with TYPEKIND TKIND_MODULE, TKIND_ENUM, or TKIND_COCLASS, then the **ITypeComp** instance of that type description is returned.

This provides support for compiling references to the members of a type description which are qualified by the name of the type description. For example, a module function can be referenced by *modulename.functionname*.

As with other methods of **ITypeComp**, **ITypeInfo**, and **ITypeLib**, the caller is responsible for releasing any returned object instances or structures. If a VARDESC or FUNCDESC is returned, the caller is responsible for deleting it via the returned type description and releasing the type description instance itself; otherwise, if an **ITypeComp** instance is returned, the caller must release it.

A special case for binding occurs when a client calls a type library's **Bind** method, passing it the name of a member of an Application object class (that is, a class that has the TYPEFLAG_FAPPOBJECT flag set). In this case, DESCKIND_IMPLICITAPPOBJ is returned along with a VARDESC that describes the Application object and the **ITypeInfo** of the application object class.

It is the client's responsibility to get the **ITypeComp** of the application object class and reinvoke its **Bind** method with the name initially passed to the type library's **ITypeComp**.

The **ITypeInfo** pointer (*lplptinfo*) is returned so that the caller can use it to get the address of the member.

Note that the *wflags* parameter is the same as the *wflags* parameter in **IDispatch::Invoke**.

ITypeComp::BindType

HRESULT ITypeComp::BindType(*szName, lHashVal, lplpitinfo, lplpitcomp*)
TCHAR FAR* *szName*
unsigned long *lHashVal*
ITypeInfo FAR* FAR* *lplpitinfo*
ITypeComp FAR* FAR* *lplpitcomp*

Binds to the type descriptions contained within a type library.

Parameters

szName
    Name to be bound.

lHashVal
    Hash value for the name computed by **LHashValOfName**.

lplpitinfo
    Upon return, contains a pointer to a pointer to an **ITypeInfo** of the type to which it was bound.

lplpitcomp
    Reserved for future use. Pass NULL.

Return Value

The SCODE obtained from the returned HRESULT is one of the following:

SCODE	Meaning
S_OK	Success.
STG_E_INSUFFICIENTMEMORY	Out of memory.
E_OUTOFMEMORY	Out of memory.
E_INVALIDARG	One or more of the arguments is invalid.
TYPE_E_IOERROR	The function could not write to the file.
TYPE_E_INVDATAREAD	The function could not read from the file.
TYPE_E_UNSUPFORMAT	The type library has an old format.

SCODE	Meaning
TYPE_E_INVALIDSTATE	The type library could not be opened.
TYPE_E_AMBIGUOUSNAME	More than one instance of this name occurs in the type library.

Comments
Used for binding a type name to the **ITypeInfo** which describes that type. This function is invoked on the **ITypeComp** returned by an **ITypeLib::GetTypeComp** to bind to types defined within that library. It could also be used in the future for binding to nested types.

Type Compilation Functions

LHashValOfName

unsigned long LHashValOfName(*lcid, szName*)
LCID *lcid*
TCHAR FAR* *szName*

Computes a hash value for a name that can then be passed to **ITypeComp::Bind, ITypeComp::BindType**, or **ITypeComp::IsName**.

Parameters
lcid
    The locale ID for the string.

szName
    String whose hash value is to be computed.

Return Value
32-bit hash value representing the name passed in.

Comments
LHashValOfName computes a 32-bit hash value for a name which can then be passed to **ITypeComp::Bind**, **ITypeComp::BindType**, or **ITypeLib::IsName**. The returned hash value is independent of the case of the characters in *szName* as long as the language of the name is one of the languages supported by the OLE National Language Specification API. Specifically, for any two strings, if those strings match when a case-insensitive comparison is done using any language, then they will produce the same hash value.

LHashValOfNameSys

> unsigned long **LHashValOfName**(*syskind, lcid, szName*)
> **SYSKIND** *syskind*
> **LCID** *lcid*
> **TCHAR FAR*** *szName*

Computes a hash value for a name that can then be passed to **ITypeComp::Bind, ITypeComp::BindType**, or **ITypeComp::IsName**.

Parameters

syskind
   The SYSKIND of the target operating system.

lcid
   The locale ID for the string.

szName
   String whose hash value is to be computed.

Return Value   32-bit hash value representing the name passed in.

Comments   This function is equivalent to **LHashValOfName**. The DISPATCH.H header file contains macros that define **LHashValOfName** as **LHashValOfNameSys** with the target operating system (*syskind*), based on your build preprocessor flags.

Type Library Loading and Registration Functions

LoadTypeLib

> **HRESULT LoadTypeLib**(*szFileName, lplptlib*)
> **TCHAR FAR*** *szFileName*
> **ITypeLib FAR* FAR*** *lplptlib*

Loads and registers a type library created with MkTypLib.

Parameters

szFileName
   Contains the name of the file from which **LoadTypeLib** should attempt to load a type library.

lplptlib
   Contains a pointer to the loaded type library.

Return Value

The SCODE obtained from the returned HRESULT is one of the following:

SCODE	Meaning
S_OK	Success.
STG_E_INSUFFICIENTMEMORY	Out of memory.
E_OUTOFMEMORY	Out of memory.
E_INVALIDARG	One or more of the arguments is invalid.
TYPE_E_IOERROR	The function could not write to the file.
TYPE_E_INVALIDSTATE	The type library could not be opened.
TYPE_E_INVDATAREAD	The function could not read from the file.
TYPE_E_UNSUPFORMAT	The type library has an old format.
TYPE_E_INVALIDSTATE	The type library could not be opened.
TYPE_E_UNKNOWNLCID	The passed in LCID could not be found in the OLE support DLLs.
TYPE_E_CANTLOADLIBRARY	The type library or DLL could not be loaded.
Other returns	All FACILITY_STORAGE errors may also be returned.

Comments

LoadTypeLib loads and registers a type library (usually created with MkTypLib) that is stored in the specified file. First, **LoadTypeLib** tries to load the file as a compound-document file and extract the type library from its root. If that fails, it tries to load the type library from the substream name. If both of these attempts fail, it tries to load the file as a DLL and extract the type library from the first resource of type typelib.

If the type library is already loaded, **LoadTypeLib** increments the type library's reference count and returns a pointer to the type library.

LoadTypeLib compares the requested version numbers against those found in the system registry and takes one of the following actions:

- If one of the registered libraries exactly matches both the requested major and minor version numbers, then that type library is loaded.

- If one or more registered type libraries exactly match the requested major version number and have a greater minor version number than that requested, the one with the greatest minor version number is loaded.

- If none of the register type libraries exactly match the requested major version number or if none of those which do exactly match the major version number also have a minor version number greater than or equal to the requested minor version number, then **LoadRegTypeLib** will return an error.

LoadRegTypeLib

HRESULT LoadRegTypeLib(*guid, wVerMajor, wVerMinor, lcid, lplptlib*)
REFGUID *guid*
unsigned short *wVerMajor*
unsigned short *wVerMinor*
LCID *lcid*
ITypeLib FAR* FAR* *lplptlib*

Uses registry information to load a type library.

Parameters

guid
ID of the library being loaded.

wVerMajor
Major version number of library being loaded.

wVerMinor
Minor version number of library being loaded.

lcid
National language code of library being loaded.

lplptlib
On return, points to a pointer to the loaded type library.

Return Value

The SCODE obtained from the returned HRESULT is one of the following:

SCODE	Meaning
S_OK	Success.
STG_E_INSUFFICIENTMEMORY	Out of memory.
E_OUTOFMEMORY	Out of memory.
E_INVALIDARG	One or more of the arguments is invalid.
TYPE_E_IOERROR	The function could not write to the file.
TYPE_E_INVALIDSTATE	The type library could not be opened.
TYPE_E_INVDATAREAD	The function could not read from the file.
TYPE_E_UNSUPFORMAT	The type library has an old format.
TYPE_E_INVALIDSTATE	The type library could not be opened.
TYPE_E_UNKNOWNLCID	The passed in LCID could not be found in the OLE support DLLs.
TYPE_E_CANTLOADLIBRARY	The type library or DLL could not be loaded.
Other returns	All FACILITY_STORAGE and system registry errors may also be returned.

Comments

LoadRegTypeLib defers to **LoadTypeLib** to load the file.

For information on how version numbers are used, see the Comments section for **LoadTypeLib**.

RegisterTypeLib

HRESULT RegisterTypeLib(*ptlib, szFullPath, szHelpDir*)
ITypeLib *ptlib*
TCHAR FAR** *szFullPath*
TCHAR FAR** *szHelpDir*

Adds information about a type library to the system registry.

Parameters

ptlib
Pointer to the type library being registered.

szFullPath
Fully qualified path specification for the type library being registered.

szHelpDir
Directory in which the Help file for the library being registered can be found. May be NULL.

Return Value

The SCODE obtained from the returned HRESULT is one of the following:

SCODE	Meaning
S_OK	Success.
STG_E_INSUFFICIENTMEMORY	Out of memory.
E_OUTOFMEMORY	Out of memory.
E_INVALIDARG	One or more of the arguments is invalid.
TYPE_E_IOERROR	The function could not write to the file.
TYPE_E_REGISTRYACCESS	The system registration database could not be opened.
TYPE_E_INVALIDSTATE	The type library could not be opened.

Comments

RegisterTypeLib can be used by during application initialization to correctly register the application's type library.

QueryPathOfRegTypeLib

HRESULT QueryPathOfRegTypeLib(*guid, wVerMajor, wVerMinor, lcid, lpBstrPathName*)
REFGUID *guid*
unsigned short *wVerMajor*
unsigned short *wVerMinor*
LCID *lcid*
BSTR *lpBstrPathName*

Retrieves the pathname of a registered type library.

Parameters

guid
ID of the library whose path is to be queried.

wVerMajor
Major version number of the library whose path is to be queried.

wVerMinor
Minor version number of the library whose path is to be queried.

lcid
National language code for the library whose path is to be queried.

lpBstrPathName
Caller-allocated BSTR in which the type library name is returned.

Return Value

The SCODE obtained from the returned HRESULT is one of the following:

SCODE	Meaning
S_OK	Success

Comments

Returns the fully qualified file name specified for the type library in the registry. The caller allocates the BSTR that is passed in, and must free it after use.

CHAPTER 9

Type Building Interfaces

Use the type-building interfaces, **ICreateTypeInfo** and **ICreateTypeLib** to build tools that can be used to automate the process of describing objects and types (each of which is called a type description, as described in Chapter 8, "Type Description Interfaces") and creating type libraries (collections of type descriptions). For example, the tool MkTypLib uses these interfaces to create type libraries. See Chapter 7, "Object Description Language" for more information on MkTypLib.

Normally you would not need to write custom implementations of these interfaces; MkTypLib itself uses the default implementation supplied in TYPELIB.DLL. If you want to create tools similar to MkTypLib, calling the default implementation should suffice.

Implemented by	Used by	Header file name	Import library name
TYPELIB.DLL	Applications that expose programmable objects	DISPATCH.H	TYPELIB.LIB

ICreateTypeInfo Interface

The type building interfaces include the following member functions:

Interface	Member name	Purpose
ICreateTypeInfo	**AddFuncDesc**	Adds a function description as a type description.
	AddImplType	Specifies an inherited interface.
	AddRefTypeInfo	When a type description is being created, this function adds a type description to the type information being referenced by the type description being created.
	AddVarDesc	Adds a data member description as a type description.

Interface	Member name	Purpose
	DefineFuncAsDllEntry	Associates a DLL entry point with a function that has a specified index.
	LayOut	Assigns vtable offsets for virtual functions and instance offsets for per-instance data members.
	SetAlignment	Reserved for future use.
	SetDocString	Sets brief documentation of the type description.
	SetFuncAndParamNames	Sets the function name and names of its parameters. If the function is a property function, only the function name is set.
	SetFuncDocString	Sets specified function's documentation string.
	SetFuncHelpContext	Sets specified function's Help context.
	SetHelpContext	Sets the Help context of the type description.
	SetImplTypeFlags	Reserved for future use.
	SetMops	Set the opcode string for a type description.
	SetSchema	Reserved for future use.
	SetTypeDescAlias	Sets type description for which this type description is an alias, assuming that TypeKind=TKIND_Alias.
	SetTypeFlags	Sets type flags of the type description being created.
	SetTypeIdlDesc	Reserved for future use.
	SetGuid	Sets the globally unique ID for the type library.
	SetVarDocString	Sets specified variable's documentation string.
	SetVarHelpContext	Sets specified variable's Help context.
	SetVarName	Sets the variable's name.
	SetVersion	Sets version numbers of the type description.

Interface	Member name	Purpose
ICreateTypeLib	**CreateTypeInfo**	Creates a new type description instance within the type library.
	SaveAllChanges	Saves the **ICreateTypeLib** instance.
	SetDocString	Sets the documentation string for the type library.
	SetHelpContext	Sets Help context for general information about the type library in the Help file.
	SetHelpFileName	Sets the Help file name.
	SetLcid	Sets locale code indicating the national language associated with the library.
	SetLibFlags	Sets library flags, such as LIBFLAG_FRESTRICTED.
	SetName	Sets the name of the type library.
	SetGuid	Sets the globally unique ID for the type library.
	SetVersion	Sets major and minor version numbers for the type library.
Library creation functions	**CreateTypeLib**	Gives access to a new object instance that supports the **ICreateTypeLib** interface.

Structures

LIBFLAGS

LIBFLAGS is defined as follows:

```
typedef enum tagLIBFLAGS {
    LIBFLAG_FRESTRICTED = 1
    } LIBFLAGS;
```

Value	Description
LIBFLAG_FRESTRICTED	The type library is restricted and should not be displayed to users.

SYSKIND

The **SYSKIND** identifies the target operating system platform.

```
typedef enum tagSYSKIND[
    SYS_WIN16,
    SYS_WIN32,
    SYS_MAC
] SYSKIND;
```

Value	Description
SYS_WIN16	The target operating system for the type library is Win16. Data members are packed.
SYS_WIN32	The target operating system for the type library is Win32. Data members are naturally aligned (for example, 2-byte integers are aligned on even-byte boundaries; 4-byte integers are aligned on quad-word boundaries, and so forth).
SYS_MAC	The target operating system for the type library is Macintosh. All data members are aligned on even-byte boundaries.

ICreateTypeInfo::AddFuncDesc

HRESULT ICreateTypeInfo::AddFuncDesc(*index*, *lpFuncDesc*)
unsigned int *index*
FUNCDESC FAR* *lpFuncDesc*

Parameters

index
Specifies the index of the new FUNCDESC in the type information.

lpFuncDesc
Points to a FUNCDESC structure that describes the function. The bstrIDLInfo field should be set to NULL for future compatibility.

Return Value

The SCODE value of the returned HRESULT is one of the following:

SCODE	Meaning
S_OK	Success.
STG_E_INSUFFICIENTMEMORY	Out of memory.
E_OUTOFMEMORY	Out of memory.
E_INVALIDARG	One or more of the arguments is invalid.

SCODE	Meaning
TYPE_E_READONLY	Can't write to destination.
TYPE_E_WRONGTYPEKIND	Type mismatch.

Comments

AddFuncDesc is used to add a function description to the type description. The index specifies the order of the functions within the type information. The first function has an index of zero. If an index is specified that exceeds one less than the number of functions in the type information, then an error is returned. Calling this function does not pass ownership of the FUNCDESC structure to the **ICreateTypeInfo**. Therefore, the caller must still deallocate the FUNCDESC structure.

Note that the passed-in vtable field of the FUNCDESC is ignored. This attribute will be set when **ICreateTypeInfo::LayOut** is called. Also the member ID fields within each FUNCDESC are ignored unless the typekind of the class is TKIND_DISPATCH (or the typekind is TKIND_INTERFACE and the ID is DISPID_VALUE).

All function descriptions with the same name (properties) must have the same DISPID.

ICreateTypeInfo::AddImplType

HRESULT ICreateTypeInfo::AddImplType(*index, hreftype*)
unsigned int *index*
HREFTYPE *hreftype*

Parameters

index
    Index of the implementation class to be added; specifies the order of the type relative to the other type.

hreftype
    Handle to the referenced type description obtained from **AddRefType description**.

Return Value

The SCODE value of the returned HRESULT is one of the following:

SCODE	Meaning
S_OK	Success.
STG_E_INSUFFICIENTMEMORY	Out of memory.
E_OUTOFMEMORY	Out of memory.
TYPE_E_READONLY	Can't write to destination.
TYPE_E_WRONGTYPEKIND	Type mismatch.

Comments   **AddImplType** is used only for specifying an inherited interface or an interface implemented by a component object class. It does not currently support multiple inheritance.

ICreateTypeInfo::AddRefTypeInfo

HRESULT ICreateTypeInfo::AddRefTypeInfo(*lptinfo*, *lphreftype*)
ITypeInfo FAR* *lptinfo*
HREFTYPE FAR* *lphreftype*

Parameters   *lptinfo*
    Pointer to the type description to be referenced.

lphreftype
    Output parameter which points to the handle which this type description associates with the referenced type information.

Return Value   The SCODE value of the returned HRESULT is one of the following:

SCODE	Meaning
S_OK	Success.
STG_E_INSUFFICIENTMEMORY	Out of memory.
E_OUTOFMEMORY	Out of memory.
E_INVALIDARG	One or more of the arguments is invalid.
TYPE_E_READONLY	Can't write to destination.
TYPE_E_WRONGTYPEKIND	Type mismatch.

Comments   Adds a type description to those referenced by the type description being created. The second parameter returns a pointer to the handle of the added type information. If **AddRefTypeInfo** has previously been called for the same type information, the index that was returned by that previous call is returned in *lphreftype*.

ICreateTypeInfo::AddVarDesc

HRESULT ICreateTypeInfo::AddVarDesc(*index, lpVarDesc*)
unsigned int *index*
VARDESC FAR* *lpVarDesc*

Parameters

index
Specifies the index of the variable or data member to be added to the type description.

lpVarDesc
Points to the variable or data member description to be added.

Return Value

The SCODE value of the returned HRESULT is one of the following:

SCODE	Meaning
S_OK	Success.
STG_E_INSUFFICIENTMEMORY	Out of memory.
E_OUTOFMEMORY	Out of memory.
E_INVALIDARG	One or more of the arguments is invalid.
TYPE_E_READONLY	Can't write to destination.
TYPE_E_WRONGTYPEKIND	Type mismatch.

Comments

Adds a variable or data member description to the type description. The index is used to specify the order of the variables. The first variable has an index of zero. **ICreateTypeInfo::AddVarDesc** returns an error if an index is specified that is greater than the number of variables currently in the type information. Calling this function does not pass ownership of the VARDESC structure to the **ICreateTypeInfo**. Note that the Instance field of the specified VARDESC is ignored; this attribute is set when **ICreateTypeInfo::LayOut** is called. Also, the member ID fields within the VARDESCs are ignored unless the typekind of the class is TKIND_DISPATCH.

AddVarDesc ignores the contents of the idldesc portion of the elemdesc.

ICreateTypeInfo::DefineFuncAsDllEntry

HRESULT ICreateTypeInfo::DefineFuncAsDllEntry(*index*, *szDllName*, *szProcName*)
INT *index*
TCHAR FAR* *szDllName*
TCHAR FAR* *szProcName*

Parameters

index
　　Index of the function.

szDllName
　　Name of the DLL containing the entry point.

szProcName
　　Name of the entry point or an ordinal (if the high word is zero).

Return Value

The SCODE value of the returned HRESULT is one of the following:

SCODE	Meaning
S_OK	Success.
STG_E_INSUFFICIENTMEMORY	Out of memory.
E_OUTOFMEMORY	Out of memory.
E_INVALIDARG	One or more of the arguments is invalid.
TYPE_E_ELEMENTNOTFOUND	The element was not found.
TYPE_E_WRONGTYPEKIND	Type mismatch.

Comments

Associates a DLL entry point with the function having the specified index. If the high word of *szProcName* is zero, then the low word contains the ordinal of the entry point; otherwise, *szProcName* points to the zero-terminated name of the entry point.

ICreateTypeInfo::LayOut

HRESULT ICreateTypeInfo::LayOut()

Return Value

The SCODE value of the returned HRESULT is one of the following:

SCODE	Meaning
S_OK	Success.
STG_E_INSUFFICIENTMEMORY	Out of memory.
E_OUTOFMEMORY	Out of memory.

SCODE	Meaning
TYPE_E_READONLY	Can't write to destination.
TYPE_E_UNDEFINEDTYPE	Bound to unrecognized type.
TYPE_E_INVALIDSTATE	The type library's state is not valid for this operation.
TYPE_E_WRONGTYPEKIND	Type mismatch.
TYPE_E_ELEMENTNOTFOUND	The element was not found.
TYPE_E_AMBIGUOUSNAME	More than one item exists with this name.
TYPE_E_ALREADYBEINGLAIDOUT	There is a circular dependency between type libraries and modules.
TYPE_E_SIZETOOBIG	The type information is too large to lay out.
TYPE_E_TYPEMISMATCH	Type mismatch.

Comments

LayOut assigns vtable offsets for virtual functions and instance offsets for per-instance data members. **LayOut** also assigns member ID numbers to the functions and variables unless the TYPEKIND of the class is TKIND_DISPATCH. **LayOut** should be called after all members of the type information are defined and before the type library is saved.

Use **SaveAllChanges** to save the type information after calling **LayOut**. Don't call other members of the **ICreateTypeInfo** interface after calling **LayOut**.

Note that different implementations of **ICreateTypeInfo** or other interfaces for creation of type information are free to assign any member ID numbers as long as all members, including inherited members, have unique IDs.

ICreateTypeInfo::SetDocString

HRESULT ICreateTypeInfo::SetDocString(*szDoc*)
TCHAR FAR* *szDoc*

Parameters

szDoc
Pointer to the documentation string.

Return Value

The SCODE value of the returned HRESULT is one of the following:

SCODE	Meaning
S_OK	Success.
STG_E_INSUFFICIENTMEMORY	Out of memory.
E_OUTOFMEMORY	Out of memory.
TYPE_E_READONLY	Can't write to destination.

SCODE	Meaning
TYPE_E_INVALIDSTATE	The type library's state is not valid for this operation.

Comments   Sets the documentation string displayed by type browsers. The documentation string is a brief description of the type description being created.

ICreateTypeInfo::SetFuncAndParamNames

HRESULT ICreateTypeInfo::SetFuncAndParamNames(*index*, *rgszNames,cNames*)
unsigned int *index*
TCHAR FAR* FAR* *rgszNames*
unsigned int *cNames*

Parameters

index
> Index of the function whose function name and parameter names are to be set.

rgszNames
> Array of pointers to names: first element is name of function, subsequent elements are names of parameters.

cNames
> Number of elements in the *rgszNames* array.

Return Value   The SCODE value of the returned HRESULT is one of the following:

SCODE	Meaning
S_OK	Success.
STG_E_INSUFFICIENTMEMORY	Out of memory.
E_OUTOFMEMORY	Out of memory.
E_INVALIDARG	One or more of the arguments is invalid.
TYPE_E_READONLY	Can't write to destination.
TYPE_E_ELEMENTNOTFOUND	The element was not found.

Comments   Sets the name of a function and the names of its parameters to the names in the array of pointers *rgszNames*. You only need to use **SetFuncAndParamNames** once for each property, since all property accessor functions are identified by one name. For property functions, provide names for the named parameters only; the last parameter for put and putref accessor functions is unnamed.

ICreateTypeInfo::SetFuncDocString

HRESULT ICreateTypeInfo::SetFuncDocString(*index*, *szDocString*)
unsigned int *index*
TCHAR FAR* *szDocString*

Parameters

index
    Index of the function.

szDocString
    Pointer to the documentation string.

Return Value

The SCODE value of the returned HRESULT is one of the following:

SCODE	Meaning
S_OK	Success.
STG_E_INSUFFICIENTMEMORY	Out of memory.
E_OUTOFMEMORY	Out of memory.
E_INVALIDARG	One or more of the arguments is invalid.
TYPE_E_READONLY	Can't write to destination.
TYPE_E_ELEMENTNOTFOUND	The element was not found.

Comments

Sets the documentation string for the function with the specified *index*. The documentation string is a brief description of the function for use by tools like type browsers. You only need to use **SetFuncDocString** once for each property, since all property accessor functions are identified by one name.

ICreateTypeInfo::SetFuncHelpContext

HRESULT ICreateTypeInfo::SetFuncHelpContext(*index*, *dwHelpContext*)
unsigned int *index*
unsigned long *dwHelpContext*

Parameters

index
    Index of the function.

dwHelpContext
    A Help context ID for the Help topic.

Return Value   The SCODE value of the returned HRESULT is one of the following:

SCODE	Meaning
S_OK	Success.
STG_E_INSUFFICIENTMEMORY	Out of memory.
E_OUTOFMEMORY	Out of memory.
E_INVALIDARG	One or more of the arguments is invalid.
TYPE_E_READONLY	Can't write to destination.
TYPE_E_ELEMENTNOTFOUND	The element was not found.

Comments   Sets the Help context for the function with the specified index. You only need to use **SetFuncHelpContext** once for each property, since all property accessor functions are identified by one name.

ICreateTypeInfo::SetMops

HRESULT ICreateTypeInfo::SetMops(*index, bstrMops*)
unsigned int *index*
BSTR *bstrMops*

Parameters   *index*
    If index is –1, then the opcode string for the type description is set; otherwise the opcode string for the member with the specified index is set.

bstrMops
    Specifies the opcode string.

Return Value   The SCODE value of the returned HRESULT is one of the following:

SCODE	Meaning
S_OK	Success.
STG_E_INSUFFICIENTMEMORY	Out of memory.
E_OUTOFMEMORY	Out of memory.
E_INVALIDARG	One or more of the arguments is invalid.
TYPE_E_READONLY	Can't write to destination.

Comments   SetMops sets the marshaling opcode string associated with the type description or the function.

ICreateTypeInfo::SetHelpContext

HRESULT ICreateTypeInfo::SetHelpContext(*dwHelpContext*)
unsigned long *dwHelpContex*

Parameters

dwHelpContext
    Handle to the Help context.

Return Value

The SCODE value of the returned HRESULT is one of the following:

SCODE	Meaning
S_OK	Success.
STG_E_INSUFFICIENTMEMORY	Out of memory.
E_OUTOFMEMORY	Out of memory.
E_INVALIDARG	One or more of the arguments is invalid.
TYPE_E_READONLY	Can't write to destination.

Comments

Sets the Help context of the type information having *index*.

ICreateTypeInfo::SetTypeDescAlias

HRESULT ICreateTypeInfo::SetTypeDescAlias(*lptDescAlias*)
TYPEDESC* *lptDescAlias*

Parameters

lptDescAlias
    Pointer to a type description that describes the type for which this is an alias.

Return Value

The SCODE value of the returned HRESULT is one of the following:

SCODE	Meaning
S_OK	Success.
STG_E_INSUFFICIENTMEMORY	Out of memory.
E_OUTOFMEMORY	Out of memory.
E_INVALIDARG	One or more of the arguments is invalid.
TYPE_E_READONLY	Can't write to destination.
TYPE_E_WRONGTYPEKIND	Type mismatch.

Comments

Call **SetTypeDescAlias** for a type description whose TYPEKIND is
TKIND_ALIAS to set the type for which it is an alias.

ICreateTypeInfo::SetTypeFlags

HRESULT ICreateTypeInfo::SetTypeFlags(*uTypeFlags*)
unsigned int *uTypeFlags*

Parameter

uTypeFlags
   Settings for the type flags.

Return Value

The SCODE value of the returned HRESULT is one of the following:

SCODE	Meaning
S_OK	Success.
STG_E_INSUFFICIENTMEMORY	Out of memory.
E_OUTOFMEMORY	Out of memory.
E_INVALIDARG	One or more of the arguments is invalid.
TYPE_E_READONLY	Can't write to destination.
TYPE_E_WRONGTYPEKIND	Type mismatch.

Comments

Use **SetTypeFlags** to set the flags for the type description (as described in the section "TYPEFLAGS," in Chapter 8, "Type Description Interfaces").

ICreateTypeInfo::SetGuid

HRESULT ICreateTypeInfo::SetGuid(*guid*)
REFGUID *guid*

Parameters

guid
   Globally unique ID to be associated with the type description.

Return Value

The SCODE value of the returned HRESULT is one of the following:

SCODE	Meaning
S_OK	Success.
STG_E_INSUFFICIENTMEMORY	Out of memory.
E_OUTOFMEMORY	Out of memory.
TYPE_E_READONLY	Can't write to destination.

Comments

Sets the globally unique ID (GUID) associated with the type description; for an interface, this is an interface ID. For a coclass, it is a Class ID. See Chapter 7, "Object Description Language" for information on GUIDs.

ICreateTypeInfo::SetVarDocString

HRESULT ICreateTypeInfo::SetVarDocString(*index*, *szDocString*)
unsigned int *index*
TCHAR FAR* *szDocString*

Parameters

index
    Index of the variable being documented.

szDocString
    The documentation string to be set.

Return Value

The SCODE value of the returned HRESULT is one of the following:

SCODE	Meaning
S_OK	Success.
STG_E_INSUFFICIENTMEMORY	Out of memory.
E_OUTOFMEMORY	Out of memory.
TYPE_E_READONLY	Can't write to destination.
TYPE_E_ELEMENTNOTFOUND	The element was not found.

Comments

Sets the documentation string for the variable with the specified *index*.

ICreateTypeInfo::SetVarHelpContext

HRESULT ICreateTypeInfo::SetVarHelpContext(*index*, *dwHelpContext*)
unsigned int *index*
unsigned long *dwHelpContext*

Parameters

index
    Index of the variable described by the type description.

dwHelpContext
    Handle to the Help context for the Help topic on the variable.

Return Value

The SCODE value of the returned HRESULT is one of the following:

SCODE	Meaning
S_OK	Success.
STG_E_INSUFFICIENTMEMORY	Out of memory.
E_OUTOFMEMORY	Out of memory.

SCODE	Meaning
TYPE_E_READONLY	Can't write to destination.
TYPE_E_ELEMENTNOTFOUND	The element was not found.

Comments   Sets the Help context for the variable with the specified *index*.

ICreateTypeInfo::SetVarName

HRESULT ICreateTypeInfo::SetVarName(*index*, *szName*)
unsigned int *index*
TCHAR FAR* *szName*

Parameters   *index*
Index of the variable whose name is being set.

szName
Name for the variable whose name is to be set.

Return Value   The SCODE value of the returned HRESULT is one of the following:

SCODE	Meaning
S_OK	Success.
STG_E_INSUFFICIENTMEMORY	Out of memory.
E_OUTOFMEMORY	Out of memory.
TYPE_E_READONLY	Can't write to destination.
TYPE_E_ELEMENTNOTFOUND	The element was not found.

Comments   Sets the name of a variable.

ICreateTypeInfo::SetVersion

HRESULT ICreateTypeInfo::SetVersion(*wMajorVerNum*, *wMinorVerNum*)
unsigned short *wMajorVerNum*
unsigned short *wMinorVerNum*

Parameters   *wMajorVerNum*
Major version number for the type.

wMinorVerNum
Minor version number for the type.

Return Value   The SCODE value of the returned HRESULT is one of the following:

SCODE	Meaning
S_OK	Success.
TYPE_E_READONLY	Can't write to destination.
TYPE_E_INVALIDSTATE	The type library's state is not valid for this operation.

Comments   Sets the major and minor version number of the type information.

ICreateTypeLib Interface

ICreateTypeLib::CreateTypeInfo

HRESULT ICreateTypeLib::CreateTypeInfo(*szName*, *tkind*, *lplpctinfo*)
TCHAR FAR* *szName*
TYPEKIND *tkind*
ICreateTypeInfo** *lplpctinfo*

Parameters   *szName*
    Name of the new type.

tkind
    Kind of the type description to be created.

lplpctinfo
    Contains a pointer to the type description when **CreateTypeInfo** returns.

Return Value   The SCODE value of the returned HRESULT is one of the following:

SCODE	Meaning
S_OK	Success.
STG_E_INSUFFICIENTMEMORY	Out of memory.
E_OUTOFMEMORY	Out of memory.
E_INVALIDARG	One or more of the arguments is invalid.
TYPE_E_INVALIDSTATE	The type library's state is not valid for this operation.
TYPE_E_NAMECONFLICT	The provided name is not unique.
TYPE_E_WRONGTYPEKIND	Type mismatch.

Comments   Use **CreateTypeInfo** to create a new type description instance within the library. An error is returned if the specified name already appears in the library.

ICreateTypeLib::SaveAllChanges

HRESULT ICreateTypeLib::SaveAllChanges()

Return Value The SCODE value of the returned HRESULT is one of the following:

SCODE	Meaning
S_OK	Success.
STG_E_INSUFFICIENTMEMORY	Out of memory.
E_OUTOFMEMORY	Out of memory.
E_INVALIDARG	One or more of the arguments is invalid.
TYPE_E_IOERROR	The function could not write to the file.
TYPE_E_INVALIDSTATE	The type library's state is not valid for this operation.
Other returns	All FACILITY_STORAGE errors.

Comments Saves the **ICreateTypeLib** instance following the layout of the type information.

Do not call any other **ICreateTypeLib** methods after calling **SaveAllChanges**.

ICreateTypeLib::SetDocString

HRESULT ICreateTypeLib::SetDocString(*szDoc***)**
TCHAR FAR* *szDoc*

Parameters *szDoc*
A documentation string briefly describing the type library.

Return Value The SCODE value of the returned HRESULT is one of the following:

SCODE	Meaning
S_OK	Success.
STG_E_INSUFFICIENTMEMORY	Out of memory.
E_OUTOFMEMORY	Out of memory.
E_INVALIDARG	One or more of the arguments is invalid.

Comments Sets the documentation string associated with the library. This is a brief description of the library intended for use by type information browsing tools.

ICreateTypeLib::SetHelpContext

HRESULT ICreateTypeLib::SetHelpContext(*dwHelpContext*)
unsigned long *dwHelpContext*

Parameters

dwHelpContext
Help context to be assigned to the library.

Return Value

The SCODE value of the returned HRESULT is one of the following:

SCODE	Meaning
S_OK	Success.
STG_E_INSUFFICIENTMEMORY	Out of memory.
E_OUTOFMEMORY	Out of memory.
E_INVALIDARG	One or more of the arguments is invalid.
TYPE_E_INVALIDSTATE	The type library's state is not valid for this operation.

Comments

Sets the Help context for retrieving general Help information for the type library. Note that calling **SetHelpContext** with a Help context of zero is equivalent to not calling it at all, since zero is used to indicate a NULL Help context.

ICreateTypeLib::SetHelpFileName

HRESULT ICreateTypeLib::SetHelpFileName(*szFileName*)
TCHAR FAR* *szFileName*

Parameters

szFileName
The name of the Help file for the library.

Return Value

The SCODE value of the returned HRESULT is one of the following:

SCODE	Meaning
S_OK	Success.
STG_E_INSUFFICIENTMEMORY	Out of memory.
E_OUTOFMEMORY	Out of memory.
E_INVALIDARG	One or more of the arguments is invalid.
TYPE_E_INVALIDSTATE	The type library's state is not valid for this operation.

Comments   Sets the name of the Help file. The **GetDocumentation** method of the created **ITypeLib** returns a fully qualified path for the Help file, which is formed by appending the name passed into *szFileName* to the registered Help directory for the type library. The Help directory is registered under: \TYPELIB\<*guid of library*>\<*Major.Minor version* >\HELPDIR.

ICreateTypeLib::SetLibFlags

HRESULT ICreateTypeLib::SetLibFlags(*uLibFlags*)
UNIT *uLibFlags*

Parameters   *uLibFlags*
The flags to set for the library. Flags are as follows:

Flag	Description
LIBFLAG_FRESTRICTED	Indicates that the type library is restricted and should not be displayed to users.

Return Value   The SCODE value of the returned HRESULT is one of the following:

SCODE	Meaning
S_OK	Success.
STG_E_INSUFFICIENTMEMORY	Out of memory.
E_OUTOFMEMORY	Out of memory.
E_INVALIDARG	One or more of the arguments is invalid.
TYPE_E_INVALIDSTATE	The type library's state is not valid for this operation.

Comments   Sets the binary Microsoft national language ID associated with the library. For more information on national language IDs, see Chapter 10, "National Language Support Functions."

ICreateTypeLib::SetLcid

> **HRESULT ICreateTypeLib::SetLcid**(*lcid*)
> **LCID** *lcid*

Parameters

lcid
   An LCID representing the locale ID for the type library.

Return Value

The SCODE value of the returned HRESULT is one of the following:

SCODE	Meaning
S_OK	Success.
STG_E_INSUFFICIENTMEMORY	Out of memory.
E_OUTOFMEMORY	Out of memory.
E_INVALIDARG	One or more of the arguments is invalid.
TYPE_E_INVALIDSTATE	The type library's state is not valid for this operation.

Comments

Sets the binary Microsoft national language ID associated with the library. For more information on national language IDs, see Chapter 10, "National Language Support Functions."

ICreateTypeLib::SetName

> **HRESULT ICreateTypeLib::SetName**(*szName*)
> **TCHAR FAR*** *szName*

Parameters

szName
   Name to be assigned to the library.

Return Value

The SCODE value of the returned HRESULT is one of the following:

SCODE	Meaning
S_OK	Success.
STG_E_INSUFFICIENTMEMORY	Out of memory.
E_OUTOFMEMORY	Out of memory.
E_INVALIDARG	One or more of the arguments is invalid.
TYPE_E_INVALIDSTATE	The type library's state is not valid for this operation.

Comments

Sets the name of the type library.

ICreateTypeLib::SetGuid

HRESULT ICreateTypeLib::SetGuid(*guid*)
REFGUID *guid*

Parameters

guid
    The universal unique ID to be assigned to the library.

Return Value

The SCODE value of the returned HRESULT is one of the following:

SCODE	Meaning
S_OK	Success.
STG_E_INSUFFICIENTMEMORY	Out of memory.
E_OUTOFMEMORY	Out of memory.
E_INVALIDARG	One or more of the arguments is invalid.
TYPE_E_INVALIDSTATE	The type library's state is not valid for this operation.

Comments

Sets the universal unique ID (UUID) associated with the type library. UUIDs are described in Chapter 7, "Object Description Language."

ICreateTypeLib::SetVersion

HRESULT ICreateTypeLib::SetVersion(*wMajorVerNum, wMinorVerNum*)
unsigned short *wMajorVerNum*
unsigned short *wMinorVerNum*

Parameters

wMajorVerNum
    Major version number for the library.

wMinorVerNum
    Minor version number for the library.

Return Value

The SCODE value of the returned HRESULT is one of the following:

SCODE	Meaning
S_OK	Success.
TYPE_E_INVALIDSTATE	The type library's state is not valid for this operation.

Comments

Sets the major and minor version numbers of the type library.

CreateTypeLib

HRESULT CreateTypeLib(*syskind, szFile, lplpctlib*)
SYSKIND *syskind*
CHAR FAR* *szFile*
ICreateTypeLib FAR* FAR* *lplpctlib*

Parameters

syskind
Specifies the target operating system.

szFile
The name of the file to create.

lplpctlib
Gives access to a pointer to an instance supporting the **ICreateTypeLib** interface.

Return Value

The SCODE value of the returned HRESULT is one of the following:

SCODE	Meaning
S_OK	Success.
STG_E_INSUFFICIENTMEMORY	Out of memory.
E_OUTOFMEMORY	Out of memory.
E_INVALIDARG	One or more of the arguments is invalid.
TYPE_E_IOERROR	The function could not create the file.
Other returns	All FACILITY_STORAGE errors.

Comments

CreateTypeLib sets its output parameter (*lplpctlib*) to point to a newly created object which supports the **ICreateTypeLib** interface.

C H A P T E R   1 0

National Language Support Functions

Implemented by	Used by	Header file name	Import library name
OLE2NLS.DLL	Applications that support multiple national languages	OLE2NLS.H	OLE2NLS.LIB

This API provides support for applications dealing with multiple locales at once, especially for applications supporting OLE Automation. Locale information is passed to allow the application to interpret both the member names and the argument data in the proper locale context.

The primary functionality needed for OLE Automation is getting pieces of locale information and case-mapping/case-insensitive comparison of strings.

Locales are simply user preference information that's related to the user's language and sublanguage, represented as a list of values. At a high level, national language support incorporates several disparate definitions of a locale into one coherent model. It is designed to be general enough at a low level to support multiple distinct high-level functions, such as the ANSI C locale functions.

A *code page* is the mapping between character glyphs (shapes) and the 1-byte numeric values which are used to represent them. Windows version 3.1 has several code pages that it uses, depending on the localized version of Windows installed. For example, the Russian version uses code page 1251 (Cyrillic), while the U.S. and Western European versions use code page 1252 (Multilingual). For historical reasons, the Windows code page in effect is referred to as the ANSI code page.

Since only one code page is in effect at a time, it is impossible for a computer running U.S. Windows version 3.1 to correctly display or print data from the Cyrillic code page; the fonts do not contain those characters. However, it can still manipulate the characters internally, and they will display correctly again if moved back to a machine running Russian Windows.

All of the National Language Support (NLS) functions use the locale ID as a means of identifying which code page a piece of text is assumed to lie in; for example, when returning locale information (like month names) for Russian, the returned string can only be meaningfully displayed in the Cyrillic code page, since other code pages don't contain the appropriate characters. Similarly, when asking to case map a string with the Russian locale, the case mapping rules assume the characters are in the Cyrillic code page.

These functions can be broken down into two areas:

- String transformation. The supported types of string transformation are uppercasing, lowercasing, sort key generation (all locale-dependent), and getting string type information.
- Locale manipulation. This includes getting information about installed locales for use in string transformations.

Overview of Functions

Function	Purpose
CompareStringA	Compares two strings of the same locale.
LCMapStringA	Transforms the case or sort order of a string.
GetLocaleInfoA	Retrieves locale information from the user's system.
GetStringTypeA	Retrieves locale type information about each character in a string.
GetSystemDefaultLangID	Retrieves the default LangID from a user's system.[1]
GetSystemDefaultLCID	Retrieves the default LCID from a user's system.
GetUserDefaultLangID	Retrieves the default LangID from a user's system.
GetUserDefaultLCID	Retrieves the default LCID from a user's system.[1]

[1] Since Microsoft Windows is a single-user system, **GetUserDefaultLangID** and **GetUserDefaultLCID** return the same information as **GetSystemDefaultLangID** and **GetSystemDefaultLCID**.

Localized Member Names

An application may expose a set of objects whose members have names that differ across localized versions of the product. This poses a problem for programming languages that want to access such objects because it means that late binding will be sensitive to the locale of the application. The **IDispatch** interface has been designed to allow the class implementor a range of solutions which vary in cost of implementation and quality of national language support. All methods of the **IDispatch** interface that are potentially sensitive to language are passed a local ID (LCID).

Following are some of the possible approaches a class implementation may take:

- Accept any LCID and use the same member names in all locales. This is acceptable if the interface will typically be accessed only by advanced users. For example, the member names for OLE interfaces will never be localized.

- Simply return an error (DISP_E_UNKNOWNLCID) if the caller's LCID doesn't match the localized version of the class. This would prevent users from being able to write late-bound code which runs on machines with different localized implementations of the class.

- Recognize the particular version's localized names, as well as one language which is recognized in all versions. For example, a French version might accept French and English names, where English is the language supported in all versions. This would constrain users, who want to write code which runs in all countries, to use English.

- Accept all LCIDs supported by all versions of the product. This means that the implementation of **GetIDsOfNames** would need to interpret the passed array of names based on the given LCID. This is the preferred solution because users would be able to write code in their national language and run the code on any localized version of the application.

At the very least, the application must check the LCID before interpreting member names. Also note that the meaning of parameters passed to a member function may depend on the caller's national language. For example, a spreadsheet application might interpret the arguments to a SetFormula method differently, depending on the LCID.

Locale ID (LCID)

The **IDispatch** interface uses the Win32 definition of a Locale ID (LCID) to identify locales. An LCID is a DWORD value which contains the language ID in the lower word and a reserved value in the upper word. The bits are as follows:

Reserved	LANGID
31 16	15 0	Bits

This LCID has the components necessary to uniquely identify one of the installed system-defined locales.

```
/*
 * LCID creation/extraction macros:
 *
 *     MAKELCID - construct locale ID from language ID and
 *                country code.
 */
#define MAKELCID(l) ((DWORD)(((WORD)(l)) | (((DWORD)((WORD)(0))) <<
16)))
```

There are two predefined LCID values: LOCALE_SYSTEM_DEFAULT is the system default locale, and LOCALE_USER_DEFAULT is the current user's locale. However, when querying the NLS APIs for many pieces of information, it is more efficient to query once for the current locale with **GetSystemDefaultLCID** or **GetUserDefaultLCID**, rather than using these constants.

Language ID (LANGID)

A LANGID is a 16-bit value which is the combination of a primary and sublanguage ID. The bits are as follows:

Sublanguage ID	Primary Language ID
15	14	13	12	11	10	9	8	7	6	5	4	3	2	1	0	Bits

Macros are provided for constructing a language ID and extracting the fields:

```
/*
 * Language ID creation/extraction macros:
 *
 *     MAKELANGID - construct language ID from primary language ID and
 *                  sublanguage ID.
 *     PRIMARYLANGID - extract primary language ID from a language ID.
 *     SUBLANGID - extract sublanguage ID from a language ID.
 *     LANGIDFROMLCID - get the language ID from a locale ID.
 */
#define MAKELANGID(p, s)            (((((USHORT)(s)) << 10) | (USHORT)(p))
```

```
#define PRIMARYLANGID(lgid)      ((USHORT)(lgid) & 0x3ff)
#define SUBLANGID(lgid)          ((USHORT)(lgid) >> 10)
#define LANGIDFROMLCID(lcid)     ((WORD)(lcid))
```

The following three combinations of primary language ID and sublanguage ID have special semantics:

PRIMARYLANGID	SUBLANGID	Result
LANG_NEUTRAL	SUBLANG_NEUTRAL	User default language
LANG_NEUTRAL	SUBLANG_SYS_DEFAULT	System default language
LANG_NEUTRAL	SUBLANG_DEFAULT	User default language

For primary language IDs, the range 0x200 to 0x3ff is user definable. The range 0x000 to 0x1ff is reserved for system use. For sublanguage IDs, the range 0x20 to 0x3f is user definable. The range 0x00 to 0x1f is reserved for system use.

Table 10.1   Primary Language IDs

Language	PRIMARYLANGID
Neutral	0x00
Czech	0x05
Danish	0x06
Dutch	0x13
English	0x09
Finnish	0x0b
French	0x0c
German	0x07
Hungarian	0x0e
Italian	0x10
Norwegian	0x14
Polish	0x15
Portuguese	0x16
Russian	0x19
Serbo Croatian	0x1a
Slovak	0x1b
Spanish	0x0a
Swedish	0x1d

Table 10.2   Sublanguage IDs

Sublanguage	SUBLANGID
Neutral	0x00
Default	0x01
System Default	0x02
Dutch	0x01
Dutch (Belgian)	0x02
English (US)	0x01
English (UK)	0x02
English (Australian)	0x03
English (Canadian)	0x04
English (New Zealand)	0x05
French	0x01
French (Belgian)	0x02
French (Canadian)	0x03
French (Swiss)	0x04
German	0x01
German (Swiss)	0x02
German (Austrian)	0x03
Italian	0x01
Italian (Swiss)	0x02
Norwegian (Bokmal)	0x01
Portuguese	0x02
Portuguese (Brazilian)	0x01
Serbo Croatian (Latin)	0x01
Spanish (Castilian)[1]	0x01
Spanish (Mexican)	0x02
Spanish (Modern)[1]	0x03

[1] The only difference between Spanish (Castilian) and Spanish (Modern) is the sort ordering. All of the LCType values are identical between the two.

Locale Constants (LCTYPE)

An LCTYPE is a constant which specifies a particular piece of locale information.

```
typedef  DWORD  LCTYPE;
```

The list of supported LCTYPES follows. All values are null-terminated, variable length strings. Numeric values are expressed as strings of decimal digits unless otherwise noted. The values in the brackets indicate a maximum number of characters allowed for the string (including the null-termination). If no maximum is indicated, then the string may be of variable length.

Table 10.3   Locale Constants

Constant name	Description
LOCALE_ILANGUAGE	A language ID represented in hexadecimal digits; see previous sections. [5]
LOCALE_SLANGUAGE	The full localized name of the language.
LOCALE_SENGLANGUAGE	The full English name of the language from the ISO Standard 639. This will always be restricted to characters mappable into the ASCII 127 character subset.
LOCALE_SABBREVLANGNAME	The abbreviated name of the language, created by taking the two-letter language abbreviation, as found in ISO Standard 639, and adding a third letter as appropriate to indicate the sublanguage.
LOCALE_SNATIVELANGNAME	The native name of the language.
LOCALE_ICOUNTRY	The country code, based on international phone codes, also referred to as IBM country codes. [6]
LOCALE_SCOUNTRY	The full localized name of the country.
LOCALE_SENGCOUNTRY	The full English name of the country. This will always be restricted to characters mappable into the ASCII 127 character subset.
LOCALE_SABBREVCTRYNAME	The abbreviated name of the country as found in ISO Standard 3166.
LOCALE_SNATIVECTRYNAME	The native name of the country.
LOCALE_IDEFAULTLANGUAGE	Language ID for the principal language which is spoken in this locale. This is provided so that partially specified locales can be completed with default values. [5]
LOCALE_IDEFAULTCOUNTRY	Country code for the principal country in this locale. This is provided so that partially specified locales can be completed with default values. [6]

Table 10.3   Locale Constants *(continued)*

Constant name	Description
LOCALE_IDEFAULTCODEPAGE	OEM code page associated with the country. [6]
LOCALE_SLIST	Character(s) used to separate list items, for example, comma is used in many locales.
LOCALE_IMEASURE	This value is "0" for the metric system (S.I.) and "1" for the U.S. system of measurements. [2]
LOCALE_SDECIMAL	Character(s) for the decimal separator.
LOCALE_STHOUSAND	Character(s) used as the separator between groups of digits left of the decimal.
LOCALE_SGROUPING	Sizes for each group of digits to the left of the decimal. An explicit size is needed for each group; sizes are separated by semicolons. If the last value is 0, the preceding value is repeated. To group thousands, specify "3;0".
LOCALE_IDIGITS	The number of fractional digits. [3]
LOCALE_ILZERO	Whether to use leading zeros in decimal fields. [2] A setting of 0 means use no leading zeros; 1 means use leading zeros.
LOCALE_SNATIVEDIGITS	The ten characters that are the native equivalent to the ASCII '0-9'.
LOCALE_SCURRENCY	The string used as the local monetary symbol.
LOCALE_SINTLSYMBOL	Three characters of the International monetary symbol specified in ISO 4217 *Codes for the Representation of Currencies and Funds,* followed by the character separating this string from the amount.
LOCALE_SMONDECIMALSEP	Character(s) for the monetary decimal separators.
LOCALE_SMONTHOUSANDSEP	The character(s) used as monetary separator between groups of digits left of the decimal.
LOCALE_SMONGROUPING	Sizes for each group of monetary digits to the left of the decimal. An explicit size is needed for each group; sizes are separated by semicolons. If the last value is 0, the preceding value is repeated. To group thousands, specify "3;0".

Table 10.3   Locale Constants *(continued)*

Constant name	Description
LOCALE_ICURRDIGITS	Number of fractional digits for the local monetary format. [3]
LOCALE_IINTLCURRDIGITS	Number of fractional digits for the international monetary format. [3]
LOCALE_ICURRENCY	Positive currency mode. [2]
	"0" Prefix, No Separation "1" Suffix, No Separation "2" Prefix, 1 Char Separation "3" Suffix, 1 Char Separation
LOCALE_INEGCURR	Negative currency mode. [2]

	"0"Sample: ($1.1)
	"1" Sample: -$1.1
	"2" Sample: $-1.1
	"3" Sample: $1.1-
	"4" Sample: $(1.1$)
	"5" Sample: -1.1$
	"6" Sample: 1.1-$
	"7" Sample: 1.1$-
	"8" Sample: -1.1 $
	         (space before $)
	"9" Sample: -$ 1.1
	         (space after $)
	"10" Sample: 1.1 $-
	         (space before $)

LOCALE_SDATE	Character(s) for the date separator.
LOCALE_STIME	Character(s) for the time separator.
LOCALE_SSHORTDATE	Short Date_Time formatting strings for this locale.
LOCALE_SLONGDATE	Long Date_Time formatting strings for this locale.
LOCALE_IDATE	Short Date format ordering specifier. [2]
	"0" Month-Day-Year "1" Day-Month-Year "2" Year-Month-Day

Table 10.3   Locale Constants *(continued)*

Constant name	Description
LOCALE_ILDATE	Long Date format ordering specifier. [2]
	"0" Month-Day-Year "1" Day-Month-Year "2" Year-Month-Day
LOCALE_ITIME	Time format specifier. [2]
	"0" Use AM/PM 12-hour format "1" Use 24-hour format
LOCALE_ICENTURY	Specifies whether to use full 4-digit century. [2]
	"0" Two digit "1" Full century
LOCALE_ITLZERO	Whether to use leading zeros in time fields. [2]
	"0" Use no leading zeros "1" Use leading zeros for hours
LOCALE_IDAYLZERO	Whether to use leading zeros in day fields. [2]
	"0" Use no leading zeros "1" Use leading zeros
LOCALE_IMONLZERO	Whether to use leading zeros in month fields. [2]
	"0" Use no leading zeros "1" Use leading zeros
LOCALE_S1159	String for the AM designator.
LOCALE_S2359	String for the PM designator.
LOCALE_SDAYNAME1	Long name for Monday.
LOCALE_SDAYNAME2	Long name for Tuesday.
LOCALE_SDAYNAME2	Long name for Tuesday.
LOCALE_SDAYNAME3	Long name for Wednesday.
LOCALE_SDAYNAME4	Long name for Thursday.
LOCALE_SDAYNAME5	Long name for Friday.
LOCALE_SDAYNAME6	Long name for Saturday.
LOCALE_SDAYNAME7	Long name for Sunday.
LOCALE_SABBREVDAYNAME1	Abbreviated name for Monday.

Table 10.3   Locale Constants *(continued)*

Constant name	Description
LOCALE_SABBREVDAYNAME2	Abbreviated name for Tuesday.
LOCALE_SABBREVDAYNAME3	Abbreviated name for Wednesday.
LOCALE_SABBREVDAYNAME4	Abbreviated name for Thursday.
LOCALE_SABBREVDAYNAME5	Abbreviated name for Friday.
LOCALE_SABBREVDAYNAME6	Abbreviated name for Saturday.
LOCALE_SABBREVDAYNAME7	Abbreviated name for Sunday.
LOCALE_SMONTHNAME1	Long name for January.
LOCALE_SMONTHNAME2	Long name for February.
LOCALE_SMONTHNAME3	Long name for March.
LOCALE_SMONTHNAME4	Long name for April.
LOCALE_SMONTHNAME5	Long name for May.
LOCALE_SMONTHNAME6	Long name for June.
LOCALE_SMONTHNAME7	Long name for July.
LOCALE_SMONTHNAME8	Long name for August.
LOCALE_SMONTHNAME9	Long name for September.
LOCALE_SMONTHNAME10	Long name for October.
LOCALE_SMONTHNAME11	Long name for November.
LOCALE_SMONTHNAME12	Long name for December.
LOCALE_SABBREVMONTHNAME	Abbreviated name for January.
LOCALE_SABBREVMONTHNAME	Abbreviated name for February.
LOCALE_SABBREVMONTHNAME	Abbreviated name for March.
LOCALE_SABBREVMONTHNAME	Abbreviated name for April.
LOCALE_SABBREVMONTHNAME	Abbreviated name for May.
LOCALE_SABBREVMONTHNAME	Abbreviated name for June.
LOCALE_SABBREVMONTHNAME	Abbreviated name for July.
LOCALE_SABBREVMONTHNAME	Abbreviated name for August.
LOCALE_SABBREVMONTHNAME	Abbreviated name for September.
LOCALE_SABBREVMONTHNAME	Abbreviated name for October.

Table 10.3   **Locale Constants** (*continued*)

Constant name	Description
LOCALE_SABBREVMONTHNAME	Abbreviated name for November.
LOCALE_SABBREVMONTHNAME	Abbreviated name for December.
LOCALE_SPOSITIVESIGN	String value for the positive sign.
LOCALE_SNEGATIVESIGN	String value for the negative sign.
LOCALE_IPOSSIGNPOSN	A formatting index for positive values. [2]
	"0" Parenthesis surround the amount and the monetary symbol.
	"1" The sign string precedes the amount and the monetary symbol.
	"2" The sign string precedes the amount and the monetary symbol.
	"3" The sign string precedes the amount and the monetary symbol.
	"4" The sign string precedes the amount and the monetary symbol.
LOCALE_INEGSIGNPOSN	A formatting index for negative values, same values as for PosSignPosn. [2]
LOCALE_IPOSSYMPRECEDES	"1" if the monetary symbol precedes; "0" if it succeeds a positive amount. [2]
LOCALE_IPOSSEPBYSPACE	"1" if the monetary symbol is separated by a space from a positive amount; "0" otherwise. [2]
LOCALE_INEGSYMPRECEDES	"1" if the monetary symbol precedes; "0" if it succeeds a negative amount. [2]
LOCALE_INEGSEPBYSPACE	"1" if the monetary symbol is separated by a space from a negative amount; "0" otherwise. [2]

The following table shows the equivalence between LCTYPE values and the information stored in the [intl] section of WIN.INI. These values will be retrieved from WIN.INI if information for the current system locale is queried. Values for LCTYPEs not in the following table do not depend on information stored in WIN.INI.

Table 10.4   WIN.INI settings and LCTYPE equivalents

WIN.INI settings	LCTYPE
sLanguage[1]	LOCALE_SABBREVLANGNAME
iCountry	LOCALE_ICOUNTRY
sCountry	LOCALE_SCOUNTRY
sList	LOCALE_SLIST
iMeasure	LOCALE_IMEASURE
sDecimal	LOCALE_SDECIMAL
sThousand	LOCALE_STHOUSAND
iDigits	LOCALE_IDIGITS
iLZero	LOCALE_ILZERO
sCurrency	LOCALE_SCURRENCY
iCurrDigits	LOCALE_ICURRDIGITS
iCurrency	LOCALE_ICURRENCY
iNegCurr	LOCALE_INEGCURR
sDate	LOCALE_SDATE
sTime	LOCALE_STIME
sShortDate	LOCALE_SSHORTDATE
sLongDate	LOCALE_SLONGDATE
iDate	LOCALE_IDATE
iTime	LOCALE_ITIME
iTLZero	LOCALE_ITLZERO
s1159	LOCALE_S1159
s2359	LOCALE_S2359

1 Unlike in WIN.INI, values returned by LOCALE_SABBREVLANGNAME are always in uppercase.

CompareStringA

> **int CompareStringA**(*LCID*, *dwCmpFlags*, *lpString1*, *cchCount1*, *lpString2*, *cchCount2*)
> **LCID** *LCID*
> **DWORD** *dwCmpFlags*
> **LPCSTR** *lpString1*
> **int** *cchCount1*
> **LPCSTR** *lpString2*
> **int** *cchCount2*

Compares two character strings of the same locale according to the supplied LCID.

Parameters

LCID

Locale context for the comparison. The strings are assumed to be represented in the default ANSI code page for this locale.

dwCmpFlags

Indicates what character traits to use or ignore when comparing the two strings. Several flags can be combined (in the case of this function, there are no illegal combinations of flags), or none can be used at all. Compare flags include the following.

Value	Meaning
NORM_IGNORECASE	Ignore case; default is OFF.
NORM_IGNORENONSPACE	Ignore nonspacing marks (accents, diacritics and vowel marks); default is OFF.
NORM_IGNORESYMBOLS	Ignore symbols; default is OFF.

lpString1 and *lpString2*

The two strings to be compared.

cchCount1 and *cchCount2*

The character counts of the two strings. The count does *not* include the null-terminator (if any). If either *cchCount1* or *cchCount2* is −1, the corresponding string is assumed to be null-terminated and the length will be calculated automatically.

Return Value

Value	Meaning
0	Failure.
1	*lpString1* is less than *lpString2*.
2	*lpString1* is equal to *lpString2*.
3	*lpString1* is greater than *lpString2*.

Comments   When used without any flags, this function uses the same sorting algorithm as **lstrcmp** in the given locale. When used with NORM_IGNORECASE, the same algorithm as **lstrcmpi** is used.

The NORM_IGNORENONSPACE flag only has an effect for the locales in which accented characters are sorted in a second pass from main characters (that is, all characters in the string are first compared without regard to accents and, if the strings are equal, a second pass over the strings to compare accents is done). In this case, this flag causes the second pass not to be done. Some locales sort accented characters in the first pass, in which case this flag will have no effect.

Note that if the return value is 2, the two strings are "equal" in the collation sense, though not necessarily identical (case might be ignored, and so on).

If the two strings are of different lengths, they are compared up to the length of the shortest one. If they are equal to that point, the return value will indicate that the longer string is greater.

To maintain the C run-time convention of comparing strings, the value 2 can be subtracted from a nonzero return value. The meaning of < 0, == 0, and > 0 is then consistent with the C run-times.

LCMapStringA

int LCMapStringA(*LCID, dwMapFlags, lpSrcStr, cchSrc, lpDestStr, cchDest*)
LCID *LCID*
DWORD *dwMapFlags*
LPCSTR *lpSrcStr*
int *cchSrc*
LPSTR *lpDestStr*
int *cchDest*

Parameters   *LCID*
    Locale context for the mapping. The strings are assumed to be represented in the default ANSI code page for this locale.

dwMapFlags
    Indicates what type of transformation is to occur during mapping. Several flags can be combined on a single transformation (though some combinations are illegal). Mapping options include the following.

Name	Meaning
LCMAP_LOWERCASE	Lowercase.
LCMAP_UPPERCASE	Uppercase.
LCMAP_SORTKEY	Character sort key.
NORM_IGNORECASE	Ignore case; default is OFF.
NORM_IGNORENONSPACE	Ignore nonspacing; default is OFF.
NORM_IGNORESYMBOLS	Ignore symbols; default is OFF.

The latter three options (NORM_IGNORECASE, NORM_IGNORENONSPACE, and NORM_IGNORESYMBOLS) are normalization options, and cannot be specified in conjunction with the casing options (LCMAP_LOWERCASE and LCMAP_UPPERCASE).

The casing options (LCMAP_LOWERCASE and LCMAP_UPPERCASE) and the sortkey option (LCMAP_SORTKEY) are all mutually exclusive, and one of them must specified.

lpSrcStr
Pointer to the supplied string to be mapped.

cchSrc
Character count of the input string buffer. If –1, *lpSrcStr* is assumed to be null-terminated and the length will be calculated automatically.

lpDestStr
Pointer to the memory buffer to store the resulting mapped string.

cchDest
The character count of the memory buffer pointed to by *lpDestStr*. If *cchDest* is 0, then the return value of this function is the number of characters required to hold the mapped string. The *lpDestStr* pointer is not referenced in this case.

Return Value

Value	Meaning
0	Failure
The number of characters written to *lpDestSt*	Success

Comments

LCMapStringA maps one character string to another, performing the specified locale-dependent translation.

The flag LCMAP_UPPER produces the same result as **AnsiUpper** in the given locale; the flag LCMAP_LOWER produces the same result as **AnsiLower**. In particular, like these functions, this function always maps a single character to a single character.

The mapped string will be null-terminated if the source string is null-terminated.

When used with LCMAP_UPPER and LCMAP_LOWER, the *lpSrcStr* and *lpDestStr* may be the same to produce an in-place mapping. When LCMAP_SORTKEY is used, the *lpSrcStr* and *lpDestStr* pointers may *not* be the same; an error will result in this case.

The LCMAP_SORTKEY transformation transforms two strings such that when compared with the standard C library function **strcmp** (by strict numerical valuation of their characters), the same order would result as if the original strings were compared with **CompareStringA**. When LCMAP_SORTKEY is specified, the output string will be a string (without NULLs, except for the terminator), but the "character" values will not be meaningful display values. This is similar behavior to the ANSI C function **strxfrm**.

GetLocaleInfoA

> int **GetLocaleInfoA**(*LCID*, *LCType*, *lpLCData*, *cchData*)
> **LCID** *LCID*
> **LCTYPE** *LCType*
> **LPSTR** *lpLCData*
> **int** *cchData*

Parameters

LCID
> ID for a locale. The returned string will be represented in the default ANSI code page for this locale.

LCType
> Indicates the type of information to be returned by the call. See the listing of constant values in this chapter. *LOCALE_NOUSEROVERRIDE* | LCTYPE indicates that the desired information will always be retrieved from the locale database, even if the LCID is the current one, and the user has changed some of the values with the control panel. If this flag is not specified, values in WIN.INI take precedence over the WIN.INI settings when getting values for the current system default locale.

lpLCData
> Pointer to the memory where **GetLocaleInfoA** will return the requested data. This pointer is not referenced if *cchData* is 0.

cchData
> The character count of the supplied *lpLCData* memory buffer. If *cchData* is 0, the return value is the number of characters required to hold the string, including the terminating NULL character. *lpLCData* is not referenced in this case.

Return Value

Value	Meaning
0	Failure
The number of characters copied, including the terminating NULL character	Success

Comments

GetLocaleInfoA returns one of the various pieces of information about a locale, by querying the stored locale database, or WIN.INI. The call also indicates how much memory is necessary to contain the desired information.

The information returned is always a null-terminated string. No integers are returned by this function—any numeric values are returned as text (see format descriptions under LCTYPE).

GetStringTypeA

BOOL GetStringTypeA(*LCID*, *dwInfoType*, *lpSrcStr*, *cchSrc*, *lpCharType*)
LCID *LCID*
DWORD *dwInfoType*
LPCSTR *lpSrcStr*
int *cchSrc*
LPWORD *lpCharType*

Parameters

LCID

Locale context for the mapping. The string is assumed to be represented in the default ANSI code page for this locale.

dwInfoType

Specifies the type of character information the user wants to retrieve. The various types are divided into different levels (see the comments at the end of this call description for a list of what information is included in each type). The options are mutually exclusive. The following types are supported:

CT_CTYPE1
CT_CTYPE2
CT_CTYPE3

lpSrcStr

The string for which character types are requested. If *cchSrc* is −1, *lpSrcStr* is assumed to be null-terminated.

cchSrc

The character count of *lpSrcStr*. If *cchSrc* is −1, *lpSrcStr* is assumed to be null-terminated. Note that this must also be the character count of *lpCharType*.

lpCharType

An array of the same length as *lpSrcStr* (*cchSrc*) which, on output, contains one word corresponding to each character in *lpSrcStr*.

Return Value

Value	Meaning
0	Failure
1	Success

Comments

The *lpSrcStr* and *lpCharType* pointers may *not* be the same; in this case the error ERROR_INVALID_PARAMETER results.

The character type bits are divided up into several levels. One level's information can be retrieved by a single call.

The various character types supported by this function include these three types:

- Ctype 1
- Ctype 2
- Ctype 3

Ctype 1 types support ANSI C and POSIX character typing functions. A bitwise OR of these values is returned when *dwInfoType* is set to CT_CTYPE1. The following table lists the Ctype 1 character types.

Name	Value	Meaning
C1_UPPER	0x0001	Uppercase[1]
C1_LOWER	0x0002	Lowercase[1]
C1_DIGIT	0x0004	Decimal digits
C1_SPACE	0x0008	Space characters
C1_PUNCT	0x0010	Punctuation
C1_CNTRL	0x0020	Control characters
C1_BLANK	0x0040	Blank characters
C1_XDIGIT	0x0080	Hexadecimal digits
C1_ALPHA	0x0100	Any letter

[1] The Windows version 3.1 functions **IsCharUpper** and **IsCharLower** do not always produce correct results for characters in the range 0x80-0x9f, so they may produce different results than this function for characters in that range. (For example, the German Windows version 3.1 language driver incorrectly reports 0x9a, lowercase s hacek, as uppercase).

Ctype 2 types support the proper layout of text. The directional attributes are assigned so that the BiDi layout algorithm standardized by Unicode produces the correct results. See *The Unicode Standard: Worldwide Character Encoding* from Addison-Wesley for more information on the use of these attributes.

	Name	Value	Meaning
Strong	C2_LEFTTORIGHT	0x1	Left to right
	C2_RIGHTTOLEFT	0x2	Right to left
Weak	C2_EUROPENUMBER	0x3	European number, European digit
	C2_EUROPESEPARATOR	0x4	European numeric separator
	C2_EUROPETERMINATOR	0x5	European numeric terminator
	C2_ARABICNUMBER	0x6	Arabic number
	C2_COMMONSEPARATOR	0x7	Common numeric separator
Neutral	C2_BLOCKSEPARATOR	0x8	Block separator
	C2_SEGMENTSEPARATOR	0x9	Segment separator
	C2_WHITESPACE	0xA	White space
	C2_OTHERNEUTRAL	0xB	Other neutrals
Not applicable	C2_NOTAPPLICABLE	0x0	No implicit direction, for example, control codes

Ctype 3 types are general text-processing information. A bitwise OR of these values is returned when *dwInfoType* is set to CT_CTYPE3.

Name	Value	Meaning
C3_NONSPACING	0x1	Nonspacing mark
C3_DIACRITIC	0x2	Diacritic nonspacing mark
C3_VOWELMARK	0x4	Vowel nonspacing mark
C3_SYMBOL	0x8	Symbol
C3_NOTAPPLICABLE	0x0	Not applicable

GetSystemDefaultLangID

LANGID GetSystemDefaultLangID(void);

Return Value

Value	Meaning
0	Failure
The system default language ID	Success

Comments   See **GetSystemDefaultLCID** for information on how this value is determined.

GetSystemDefaultLCID

LCID GetSystemDefaultLCID(void)

Return Value

Value	Meaning
0	Failure
System default locale ID	Success

Comments   The return value is determined by examining the values of *sLanguage* and *iCountry* in WIN.INI, and comparing the values to those in the stored locale database. If no matching values are found, the required values cannot be read from WIN.INI, or if the stored locale database cannot be loaded, the value 0 is returned.

GetUserDefaultLangID

LANGID GetUserDefaultLangID(void)

Return Value

Value	Meaning
0	Failure
The user default language ID	Success

Comments   Since Windows version 3.1 is a single-user system, the value returned from this function is always the same as that returned from **GetSystemDefaultLangID**.

GetUserDefaultLCID

LCID GetUserDefaultLCID(void)

Return Value

Value	Meaning
0	Failure
The user default locale ID	Success

Comments   Since Windows version 3.1 is a single-user system, the value returned from this function is always the same as that returned from **GetSystemDefaultLCID**.

C H A P T E R   1 1

DispTest

DispTest tests applications that expose objects by allowing you to program against them using Visual Basic language constructs. DispTest also lets you test an OLE object by means of an OLE container control.

DispTest provides two functions to access programmable objects:

- **CreateObject**—creates a new instance of an object.
- **GetObject**—gets the current active object.

In addition, DispTest provides an OLE container control you can use to test your implementation of OLE objects. DispTest uses the same language constructs provided in Microsoft Visual Basic version 3.0. For your convenience, a copy of the Help file is provided with DispTest and is accessible from the Program Manager.

CreateObject Function

Creates an OLE Automation object.

Syntax   **CreateObject**(*class*)

Remarks   The *class* argument is a string indicating the name of the application used to create the object and the type of object. To specify an object's class, use the following syntax:

"*appname.objecttype*"

The *class* argument has these parts:

Part	Description
appname	The name of the application that provides the object.
objecttype	The type or class of object to create.

Each application that supports OLE Automation provides at least one type of object. For example, a word processing application may provide an Application object, a document object, and a toolbar object.

Note To get a list of the OLE Automation objects that an application supports, consult your application's documentation.

Use this function to create an OLE Automation object and assign the object to an object variable. To do this, first dimension a variable of type object. Then use the **Set** statement to assign the object returned by **CreateObect** to the object variable. For example:

```
Dim MyObject As Object
Set MyObject = CreateObject("WordProc.Document")
```

When this code executes, the application creating the object is started, if it is not already running (WORDPROC.EXE in this example), and an object of the specified type is created. Unlike creating a linked or embedded object using the OLE control, the object's image is not displayed anywhere in DispTest, nor is the object's data maintained by DispTest.

Note To create an object, the application providing the object must either be active or on the system's path.

Once an object is created, you reference it in DispTest code using the object variable you defined. In the previous example you access properties and methods of the new object using the object variable, MyObject. For example:

```
MyObject.Bold
MyObject.Insert "Hello, world."
MyObject.Print
MyObject.SaveAs "C:\WordProc\Docs\Test.Doc"
```

GetObject Function

Retrieves an OLE Automation object from a file.

Syntax

GetObject(*filename*[, *class*])

Remarks

The **GetObject** function has these parts:

Part	Description
filename	The full path and name of the file containing the object to retrieve. If *filename* is an empty string (""), then *class* is required.
class	A string representing the class of the object to retrieve.

The *class* argument is optional. It uses the following syntax:

"*appname.objecttype*"

The *class* argument has these parts:

Part	Description
appname	The name of the application that provides the object.
objecttype	The type, or class of object to create.

Use the **GetObject** function to access an OLE Automation object from a file and assign the object to an object variable. To do this, first dimension a variable of type object. Then use the **Set** statement to assign the object returned by **GetObject** to the object variable. For example:

```
Dim MyObject As Object
Set MyObject = GetObject("C:\WORDPROC\DOCS\OLETEST.DOC")
```

When this code executes, the application associated with the specified file name is started (WORDPROC.EXE in this example) and the object in the specified file is activated.

If the *filename* argument is set to an empty string (""), this function returns the currently active object of the specified type. If there is no object of that type active, an error occurs.

The previous example shows how to activate an entire file. However, some applications let you activate part of an object. To specify that you want to activate part of a file, add an exclamation point (!) to the end of the file name followed by a string that identifies the part of the file you want to activate. For information on how to create this string, see the documentation for the application that created the object.

For example, in many spreadsheet applications you specify the rows and columns of a range of cells using an R1C1 syntax. The following code could be used to activate a range of cells within a spreadsheet called REVENUE.SPD:

```
Set Sheet = GetObject("C:\ACCOUNTS\REVENUE.SPD!R1C1:R10C20")
```

If you do not specify the object's *class*, the OLE DLLs determine the application to invoke and the object to activate based on the file name you provide. Some files, however, may support more than one class of object. For example, a spreadsheet might support three different types of objects: an Application object, a worksheet object, and a toolbar object, all of which are part of the same file. To specify which object in a file you want to activate, use the optional *Class* argument. For example:

```
Set Sheet = GetObject("C:\ACCOUNTS\REVENUE.SPD", "SPDSHEET.WORKSHEET")
```

Once an object is activated, you reference it in DispTest code using the object variable you defined. In the above example you access properties and methods of the new object using the object variable, MyObject. For example:

```
Sheet.Row      = 4
Sheet.Column= 2
Sheet.Insert    = "Hello, world."
Sheet.SaveAs "C:\WordProc\Docs\Test.Doc"
Sheet.Print
```

Using the OLE Container Control

You can use the OLE control to display an OLE object on a form. You can create the object either at design time by using standard OLE dialogs or at run time by setting the appropriate properties.

Creating Objects—Design Time vs. Run Time

There are advantages and disadvantages to creating objects at design time and to creating them at run time. You must decide which technique is best for your application.

It can take several seconds to create an object, regardless of when the object is created. If you create an object at run time, the only logical place to put this code may be in the Form_Load event of the form containing the OLE control. Remember that when you create an object in code, the system suspends all other processing until the object is created. Therefore, if you create an object in a Form_Load event, the form will not be displayed until the object is created.

CoCreateGuid

CoCreateGuid(*pguid*)
GUID FAR* *pguid*

CoCreateGuid is used to create a GUID, which is a 128-bit integer used to represent CLSIDs and interface IDs.

Parameters

pguid
Points to where to return the GUID.

Return Values

Value	Meaning/Occurrence
S_OK	The GUID was successfully created.
E_FAIL	The GUID was not created.
REGDB_E_WRITEREGDB	Unable to write necessary state information to registration database.
E_OUTOFMEMORY	Out of memory.
E_INVALIDARG	*pguid* is invalid.
E_UNEXPECTED	An unexpected error occurred.

The implementation of **CoCreateGuid** does not require a network card. If no card is present, a machine identifier is created from varible machine state and stored persistently.

IsEqualGUID

BOOL IsEqualGUID(*rguid1*, *rguid2*)
REFGUID *rguid1*
REFGUID *rguid2*

IsEqualGUID compares two GUIDs to see whether they are equal.

Parameters

rguid1
Specifies the GUID to compare with *rguid2*.

rguid2
Specifies the GUID that is to be compared with *rguid1*.

Return Values

Value	Meaning/Occurrence
TRUE	The GUIDs are equal.
FALSE	The GUIDs are not equal.

If you allow the user to make changes to the linked data, you do not need to write any code to maintain these changes. The user can save the linked data using the application that created the object. For example, if you create an object linked to a Microsoft Excel spreadsheet, the user can activate Microsoft Excel at run time by double-clicking the object. When the spreadsheet is opened, the user makes any desired changes and saves the spreadsheet using the Microsoft Excel File Save command. When the user closes Microsoft Excel, the new data is displayed in the OLE control.

Linking to Data Within a File

When creating a linked object, you may not want to link an entire file. For example, you may want to link a range of cells in a spreadsheet or a paragraph in a word processor.

One way to do this is to use the SourceItem property to specify the data within the source document you want to link. The exact syntax used to set this property varies depending on the application supplying the object. For example, when linking to a Microsoft Excel spreadsheet, you specify SourceItem using an R1C1 syntax. This type of syntax is commonly used by spreadsheet applications to indicate the rows and columns in a range of cells. Here's how to specify the range A1:D5 in a Microsoft Excel spreadsheet using R1C1 syntax:

```
R1C1:R5C4
```

Alternately, you specify a range of cells using a named range.

An easier way to link to data within a file is to copy the desired data to the Clipboard and choose Paste Special from the OLE control's pop-up menu (click the OLE control with the right mouse button). Pop-up menus are explained later in this chapter.

Creating Embedded Objects

When you create an embedded object, you can either create an object from a file or create a new object. When you create an object from a file, a copy of the specified file's data is displayed in the OLE control. When you create a new object, the application that created the object is invoked and the user is allowed to enter any desired data. New embedded objects are usually created at run time to allow the user to enter data in the object.

Typically, you create embedded objects that display existing data at design time. This allows you to view the object's data as it will appear to the user. You can then move and size the OLE control and the other controls on the form and create your application's user interface accordingly.

You display existing data in an embedded object by creating the object using an existing file as a template. The OLE control then contains an image of the file along with a copy of the embedded file's data.

Since the OLE control contains the embedded data, an application that displays data using an embedded object will be larger than an application that displays the same data using a linked object.

▶ **To create an embedded object using an existing file**

1. Display the Insert Object dialog.

2. In the Insert Object dialog, choose the Insert File option button.

3. Choose the Browse button.

   A Browse dialog is displayed.

4. Use the Browse dialog to select the file you want to embed.

5. Click OK to return to the Insert File dialog.

6. In the Insert File dialog, click OK to create the object.

Data in an embedded object is not persistent. If the user modifies the object's data, you must write code to save the data if you want the changed data to appear the next time your application is run. Saving embedded data to a file is discussed in the section "Working with Files" later in this chapter.

Using the OLE Control's Pop-up Menus

At design time, you click the OLE control with the right mouse button to display a pop-up menu. The commands displayed on the pop-up menu depend on the state of the OLE control. If the control contains an embedded object, the pop-up menu shown below is displayed.

```
┌──────────────────────────────┐
│ Insert Object...             │
│ Paste Special...             │
│ Delete Embedded Object       │
├──────────────────────────────┤
│ Edit                         │
└──────────────────────────────┘
```

You use the Insert Object command to delete an existing object and create a new one. The Paste Special command allows you to paste an object from the Clipboard into the OLE control. The commands displayed below the separator bar are determined by the application that created the object. These commands reflect the *verbs* that the object supports. A verb is an action, such as play or edit, that the user can perform on an object.

When the OLE control is empty (that is, when it does not contain an object), the menu shown below is displayed.

```
┌──────────────────────────────┐
│ Insert Object...             │
│ Paste Special...             │
│ Create Link                  │
│ Create Embedded Object       │
└──────────────────────────────┘
```

In this figure, the Create Link and Create Embedded Object commands are grayed (disabled). The Paste Special command is grayed unless there is an OLE object on the Clipboard.

To activate the Create Link and Create Embedded Object commands, enter a valid class name in the Properties window. In addition, to activate the Create Link command, you must enter a value for the SourceDoc property. If the OleTypeAllowed property is set to a value other than 2 (Either), only the appropriate menu item is activated. When OleTypeAllowed is 0, Create Embedded Object is omitted from the menu. When OleTypeAllowed is 1, Create Link is omitted.

Tip To choose from a list of valid class names, select the Class property in the Properties window and click the three dots (...) in the Settings box.

Creating Objects Using Paste Special

The Paste Special dialog shown below allows you to create linked and embedded objects from data that has been copied to the Clipboard. To display the Paste Special dialog at design time, click the OLE control with the right mouse button and select Paste Special from the pop-up menu.

▶ **To create an object using the Paste Special dialog**

1. Run the application containing the data you want to link or embed.

2. Select the data you want to link or embed.

3. From the Edit menu, choose Copy.

    The data is copied to the Clipboard.

4. In DispTest, right click the OLE control and choose the Paste Special command.

5. Choose the Paste option to create an embedded object.
    –or–
    Choose the Paste Link option to create a linked object.

6. Click OK to create the object.

Creating Objects at Run Time

To create objects at design time, you use the Insert Object and Paste Special dialogs. To create an OLE object at run time, however, you set properties in code.

Setting Properties

To create an OLE object at run time, set the following properties.

Property	Description
Class	Identifies the application that created the object.
OleTypeAllowed	Determines if the object you can create is linked, embedded, or either.
SourceDoc	When creating a linked object, this property determines the file to link to.
	When creating an embedded object, this property determines the file to use as a template.
SourceItem	Specifies data within a file to link to (linked objects only).
Action	Specifies the operation to perform on an OLE control.

Class Property

The Class property determines the *type* of data that the object contains and the *name* of the application that supplied the object. For example, to create an object that contains data from a Microsoft Excel spreadsheet, you set the Class property to "ExcelWorksheet."

You can get a list of the class names available to your application by highlighting the Class property in the Properties window and clicking the three dots (...) in the Settings box.

Important When you create an object, the executable file associated with the object's class must be either active or on the system's path.

OleTypeAllowed Property

The OleTypeAllowed property determines the type of object you can create. You set the OleType property to OLE_LINKED, OLE_EMBEDDED, or OLE_EITHER.

SourceDoc and SourceItem Properties

To create a linked object or display existing data in an embedded object, you must also set the SourceDoc property.

The SourceDoc property specifies the name of the document you want to link to (or the name of the file you want copied to an embedded object). When you set the SourceDoc property, you must include the path and the name of the file you want to link. For example:

```
Ole1.SourceDoc = "C:\REVENUES\QUARTER1.XLS"
```

Tip   You can display a dialog at design time that allows you to browse your disk for files by highlighting the SourceDoc property in the Properties window and clicking the three dots (...) in the Settings box.

For linked objects, you can optionally specify data within the source document to link. You do this using the SourceItem property.

Action Property

The Action property specifies the operation to perform on an OLE control. Setting this property serves the same function as a Visual Basic method—it performs an action on an object. For example, you can use the Action property to create, activate, or delete an object.

Creating a Linked Object at Run Time

Before creating a linked object, you must first specify the document you want to link to by setting the SourceDoc property. Optionally, you can specify the data within the document that you want to link by setting the SourceItem property. The document specified in the SourceDoc property must already exist.

The following code fragment creates a linked object at run time:

```
' Define the constant.
Const OLE_CREATE_LINK = 1
' Specify the application that will supply the object.
Ole1.Class = "ExcelWorksheet"
' Specify the file to link to.
Ole1.SourceDoc = "C:\EXCEL\TEST.XLS"
' Link to a range of cells within TEST.XLS.
Ole1.SourceItem = "R1C1:R3C3"
' Create the linked object (OLE_CREATE_LINK = 1).
Ole1.Action = OLE_CREATE_LINK
```

When you create a linked object, the data specified by the SourceDoc and SourceItem properties is displayed in the OLE control.

If the AutoActivate property is set to 2 (Double-Click), the default, double-clicking an object at run time automatically activates the object. Exactly how an object behaves when it is activated depends on the object's default verb.

Note When AutoActivate is **True**, the DblClick event does not occur when the user double-clicks an OLE control.

Creating an Embedded Object at Run Time

When creating an embedded object at run time, you display existing data by creating the object from a file template, or you create a new object and let the user enter new data.

When you create an embedded object from a file, the specified file's data is displayed in the OLE control. This is typically done in a front-end application in which you want to display, and provide access to, data in another application.

▶ **To create an embedded object from a file at run time**

1. Set the Class property to determine the object's type.

2. Set the SourceDoc property to specify the file to use as a template.

3. Set Action = OLE_CREATE_EMBED.

The following code fragment creates an embedded object using an existing file as a template for the object.

```
' Define the constant.
Const OLE_CREATE_EMBED = 0
' Specify the type of object.
Ole1.Class = "ExcelWorksheet"
' Specify the file to be embedded.
Ole1.SourceDoc = "Q1PROFIT.XLS"
' Specify data within the SourceDoc.
Ole1.SourceItem = "R1C1:R23C7"
' Create embedded object using the data specified in the
' SourceDoc and SourceItem properties (OLE_CREATE_EMBED = 0).
Ole1.Action = OLE_CREATE_EMBED
```

When you create an empty embedded object, the application providing the object is activated and displayed to the user. The user can then enter any desired data into the application. The user then displays this newly entered data by choosing the Update command on the File menu (this menu command should appear on the application providing the object, not in your DispTest application).

▶ **To create an empty embedded object at run time**

1. Set the Class property to determine the object's type.

2. Set Action = OLE_CREATE_EMBED.

The following code fragment creates an empty embedded object.

```
' Specify the type of object.
Ole1.Class = "ExcelWorksheet"
' Create an embedded object (OLE_CREATE_EMBED = 0).
Ole1.Action = OLE_CREATE_EMBED
```

This technique is useful when creating a document-centered application in which you allow the user to embed different types of data in a single document. This is discussed in more detail in the section "Displaying the OLE Dialogs" later in this chapter.

Activating an Object

When you activate an object, you perform an action on the object using the object's default verb (or the verb you specify using the Verb property). You activate an object either programmatically or by setting the AutoActivate property.

At run time you activate an object in code by setting Action = 7. By activating an object in this way, you maintain control over when an object is activated. Use the AutoActivate property to allow users to activate an object at their convenience.

In-Place Activation

Some objects can be activated from within the OLE control. When such an object is activated, the user can edit the object (or perform some other action) from inside the boundaries of the OLE control. This feature is called *In-Place Activation*. If an object supports In-Place Activation, you set AutoActivate to 1 (GetFocus) to activate an object when the OLE control gets the focus.

You typically activate objects that don't support In-Place Activation when the user double-clicks an object. To do this automatically, set AutoActivate to 2. When AutoActivate is set to 2 (Double-Click) at run time, the object is activated (using its default verb) whenever the user double-clicks the OLE control or presses ENTER when the object has the focus.

Displaying an Object's Verbs

When the AutoVerbMenu property is set to **True**, a pop-up menu showing all the object's available verbs is displayed when the user clicks the OLE control with the right mouse button.

Note When the AutoVerbMenu property is set to **True**, Click events and MouseDown events do not occur when the user clicks the OLE control with the right mouse button.

The list of verbs an object supports may vary, depending on the state of the object. For example, it may make sense for an object to allow the user to *play* data, *edit* data, or both *play* or *edit* data. To update the list of verbs that an object supports, set Action = 17 (Fetch Verbs). Be sure to update the list of verbs before presenting the list of available verbs to the user.

When AutoVerbMenu is set to **True**, the verb list is updated automatically before the pop-up menu is displayed.

Displaying the OLE Dialogs

At run time, you use the Action property to display the Insert Object or Paste Special dialog to the user. The Insert Object dialog presents a list of available objects and creates an object based on user selection. The Paste Special dialog allows the user to paste an object from the Clipboard to an OLE control.

Using these dialogs, you allow the user to decide what type of object to create. You may do this, for example, when creating a document-centered application. In such an application, the user combines data from different applications to create a single document. This type of application is easy to visualize in terms of a word processor in which the user might enter some text and then embed a spreadsheet and a chart.

To create such an application in DispTest, you need to provide some sort of document into which the user can embed objects. For example, you could write a calendar application in which each month is maintained as a separate document. You allow the user to embed an object in the calendar by displaying the Insert Object or Paste Special dialog.

You display the Insert Object or Paste Special dialog at run time by setting the Action property. For example:

```
Sub InsObjectDlg_Click ()
    ' Display Insert Object dialog (OLE_INSERT_OBJ_DLG = 14).
    Ole1.Action = OLE_INSERT_OBJ_DLG
    ' Check to make sure object was created (OLE_NONE = 3).
    If Ole1.OleType = OLE_NONE Then
        MsgBox "Object Not Created."
    End If
End Sub

Sub PstSpecialDlg_Click ()
    ' Determine if Clipboard contents can be pasted into the
    ' OLE control.
    If Ole1.PasteOK Then
        ' Display Paste Special dialog (OLE_PASTE_SPECIAL_DLG = 15)
        Ole1.Action = OLE_PASTE_SPECIAL_DLG
        ' Check to make sure object was created.
        If Ole1.OleType = OLE_NONE Then
```

```
            MsgBox "Object Not Created."
        End If
    End If
End Sub
```

Once the dialog is displayed, you do not need to write any more code to create the object. The user makes choices in the dialogs and clicks OK to create an object. If the user cancels a dialog, an object is not created.

As shown in the previous examples, you may want to query the value of the OleType property to check the state of the OLE control.

If OleType is	Then
OLE_LINKED	The OLE control contains a linked object.
OLE_EMBEDDED	The OLE control contains an embedded object.
OLE_NONE	The OLE control does not contain an object.

Working with Files

Data associated with an OLE object is not persistent; that is, when a form containing an OLE control is closed, any data associated with that control is lost. To save the data from an OLE object to a file, you use the Action property. Once this data has been saved to a file, you can open the file and restore the OLE object.

Objects in the OLE control can be saved only to open, binary files.

▶ **To save the data from an OLE object**

1. Open a file in binary mode.

2. Set the FileNumber property to the file number used in step 1.

3. Set the Action property to OLE_SAVE_TO_FILE (11).

The SaveObject_Click event procedure illustrates these steps:

```
Sub SaveObject_Click ()
    ' Get file number.
    FileNum = FreeFile
    ' Open file to be saved.
    Open "FOOD.OLE" For Binary As #FileNum
    ' Set the file number.
    Ole1.FileNumber = FileNum
    ' Save the file (OLE_SAVE_TO_FILE = 11).
    Ole1.Action = OLE_SAVE_TO_FILE
    ' Close the file.
    Close #FileNum
End Sub
```

Once an OLE object has been saved to a file, it can be opened and displayed in an OLE control.

Note   When you set Action = 11 (Save To File) or 12 (Read From File), the file position is located immediately following the object.

▶ **To read data from a file into an OLE control**

1. Open the file in binary mode.

2. Set the FileNumber property to the file number used in step 1.

3. Set the Action property to OLE_READ_FROM_FILE (12).

The OpenObject_Click event procedure illustrates these steps:

```
Sub OpenObject_Click ()
    ' Get file number.
    FileNum = FreeFile
    ' Open the file.
    Open "FOOD.OLE" For Binary As #FileNum
    ' Set the file number.
    Ole1.FileNumber = FileNum
    ' Open the file (OLE_READ_FROM_FILE = 12).
    Ole1.Action = OLE_READ_FROM_FILE
    ' Close the binary file.
    Close #FileNum
End Sub
```

OLE Container Control Reference

This section lists and describes the events and properties of the OLE container control.

Properties

Action	Object
AppRunning	Parent
AutoActivate	PasteOK
AutoVerbMenu	Picture
BackColor	ObjectAcceptFormats
BorderStyle	ObjectAcceptFormatsCount
Class	ObjectGetFormats
Data	ObjectGetFormatsCount
DataText	OleType
DisplayType	OleTypeAllowed

Properties

DragI	ObjectVerbs
DragMode	ObjectVerbFlags
FileNumber	ObjectVerbsCount
Format	SizeMode
Height	SourceDoc
HelpContextID	SourceItem
HostName	Tag
hWnd	Top
Index	UpdateOptions
Left	Visible
lpOleObject	Width
Name	

Events

Click	KeyDown
MouseMove	DblClick
KeyPress	MouseUp
DragDrop	KeyUp
Resize	DragOver
LostFocus	Updated
GotFocus	MouseDown

Methods

Drag	**SetFocus**
Move	**ZOrder**
Refresh	

The Updated event is useful for determining if an object's data has been changed since it was last saved. To do this, set a global variable in the Updated event indicating that the object needs to be saved. When you save the OLE object, reset the variable. The constants are defined in the file CONSTANT.TXT.

Action Property

Description   Determines an action to take; not available at design time; write-only at run time.

Usage   [*form.*]*ole*.**Action** = *setting*

Setting   By setting the Action property at run time, these operations can be performed:

Setting	Description
0	CreateEmbed creates an embedded object.

To use this action, you must first set the Class and OleTypeAllowed properties. You must set the OleTypeAllowed property to 1 (Embedded), or 2 (Either). The Class property determines the type of OLE object to create. To view a list of valid class names on your system, select the Class property in the Properties window and click the three dots (...) in the Settings box.

When you create a new OLE object, the executable file associated with the class name (for example, EXCEL.EXE) must either be active or on the system's path.

Setting	Description
1	CreateLink creates a linked OLE object from the contents of a file. To use this action, you must first set the OleTypeAllowed and SourceDoc properties. You must set OleTypeAllowed to 0 (Linked), or 2 (Either). The SourceDoc property specifies the file from which the OLE object is created. You can also set the SourceItem property (for example a row/column range specification if the application creating the object is a Microsoft Excel worksheet). When an OLE object is created with this action, the OLE control simply displays an image of the SourceDoc. If the OLE object is saved, only the link references are saved, since the OLE control contains only a metafile image of the data and no source data.

When creating a new OLE object, the executable file associated with the class name (for example, EXCEL.EXE) must either be active or on the system's path. |
| 2 | This number is reserved for future use. |
| 3 | This number is reserved for future use. |

Setting	Description
4	Copy copies the object to the clipboard. When an OLE object is copied to the Clipboard, all the data and link information associated with the object is placed on the Clipboard. You can copy both linked and embedded objects to the Clipboard. You can use this action to support an Edit Copy command.
5	Paste copies data from the Clipboard to an OLE control. To use this action, set the OleTypeAllowed property, and then check the value of the PasteOK property. You cannot paste successfully unless PasteOK returns a value of **True**. If the Paste was successful, the OleType property will be set to 0 (Link) or 1 (Embed). If the Paste was not successful, the OleType property will be set to 2 (None). You can use this action to support an Edit Paste command. See the PasteOK property topic for more information and an example.
6	Update retrieves the current data from the application that supplied the object and displays that data as a picture in the OLE control.
7	Activate opens an OLE object for an operation, such as editing. To use this action, first set the Verb property. The Verb property specifies the operation to perform when the OLE object is activated. If you set the AutoActivate property to 2 (Double-Click), the OLE control will automatically activate the current object when the user double clicks the control.
8	This number is reserved for future use.
9	Close closes an OLE object and terminates the connection with the application that provided the object. This action is equivalent to the user selecting Close from the object's Control-menu box.
10	Delete deletes the specified OLE object and frees the memory associated with it. This action allows the programmer to explicitly delete an OLE object. Objects are automatically deleted when a form is closed or when the object is updated to a new object.

Setting	Description
11	SaveToFile saves an OLE object to a data file. To use this action, first set the FileNumber property. The FileNumber property must correspond to an open, binary file. If the OLE object is linked (OleType = 0, Linked), then only the link information and an image of the data is saved to the specified file. The object's data is maintained by the application that created the object. If the OLE object is embedded (OleType = 1, Embedded), the object's data is maintained by the OLE control and can be saved by your DispTest application. See the FileNumber property topic for an example.
12	ReadFromFile loads an OLE object from a data file created using the SaveToFile action. To use this action, first set the FileNumber property. The FileNumber property must correspond to an open, binary file. See the FileNumber property topic for an example.
13	This number is reserved for future use.
14	InsertObjDialog displays the Insert Object dialog. At run time, you display this dialog to allow the user to create a linked or embedded object. Using this dialog, the user chooses the type of object (link or embed) and the application that is to provide the object.
15	PasteSpecialDlg displays the Paste Special dialog. At run time, you display this dialog to allow the user to paste an object from the clipboard. This dialog displays several options to the user, including the choice of pasting either a linked or embedded object.
16	This number is reserved for future use.
17	FetchVerbs updates the list of verbs an object supports.
18	Save object to the Ole1 file format.

DataType   Integer (Enumerated)

AppRunning Property

Description   Indicates whether the application that created the object in the OLE control is currently activated and running. Not available at design time; read-only at run time.

Usage   [*form.*]*ole*.**AppRunning**

Remarks   The AppRunning property settings are:

Setting	Description
True	The application that produced the object in the OLE control is currently running.
False	The application that produced the object in the OLE control is not currently running.

Data Type   Integer (Boolean)

AutoActivate Property

Description   Allows the user to activate an object by double-clicking the OLE control, or by giving the OLE control the focus.

Usage   [*form.*]*ole*.**AutoActivate** = [*setting*]

Remarks   The AutoActivate property settings are:

Setting		Description
0	Manual	The OLE object is not automatically activated. You can activate an object programmatically by setting Action = 0 (create embed), or 1 (create link).
1	Focus	If the OLE control contains an object, the application that provided the object will be activated when the OLE control gets the focus.
2 (Default)	Double-Click	If the OLE control contains an object, the application that provided the object will be activated when the user double-clicks the OLE control or presses Enter when the control has the focus.

Remarks   You can determine if the OLE control contains an object by querying the OleType property.

Some objects have the ability to be activated from within the OLE control. When such an object is activated, the user can edit the object (or perform some other action) from inside the boundaries of the OLE control. This feature is called *In-Place Activation*. If an object supports In-Place Activation, you can set AutoActivate to 1 (GetFocus) to activate an object when the OLE control gets the focus.

Note When AutoActivate is set to 2 (Double-Click), the double click event does not occur when the user double-clicks an OLE control.

Data Type   Integer (Enumerated)

AutoVerbMenu Property

Description   Determines if a pop-up menu containing the object's verbs is displayed when the user clicks the OLE control with the right mouse button.

Usage   [*form.*]*ole*.**AutoVerbMenu**[= *boolean*]

Setting   The AutoVerbMenu property settings are:

Setting	Description
True	(Default) When the user clicks the OLE control with the right mouse button, a pop-up menu is displayed showing the commands the object supports.
False	No pop-up menu is displayed.

Remarks   When this property is set to **True**, click events and MouseDown events do not occur when the OLE control is clicked with the right mouse button.

Data Type   Integer (Boolean)

Class Property

Description   Determines the class name of an embedded OLE object.

Usage   [*form.*]*ole*.**Class** [= *classname*]

Remarks   A class name defines the type of an OLE object. For example, Microsoft Excel supports three types of OLE objects spreadsheets, charts, and macro sheets. Their class names are "ExcelWorksheet," "ExcelChart," and "ExcelMacrosheet" respectively.

When you create an object at design time using the Insert Object or Paste Special dialogs, the Class of the new object is automatically entered in the Properties window.

To view a list of Class names available on your system, select the Class property in the Properties window and click the three dots (...) in the Settings box.

This property is updated when an object is copied from the Clipboard. For example, if a Microsoft Excel chart is pasted from the Clipboard to an OLE object that previously contained a Microsoft Excel worksheet, the Class property changes from "ExcelGraph" to "ExcelWorksheet." You can paste an object from the Clipboard by setting Action = 5 (Paste), or Action = 15 (Paste Special Dialog).

Note With the advent of OLE 2 and OLE Automation, the syntax for the Class property will change. Applications that are updated to support OLE 2 or OLE Automation will define their objects using the following syntax:

ApplicationName.ObjectType

ApplicationName specifies the name of the application supplying the object. *ObjectType* specifies the object's type (for example, worksheet, chart, macro sheet).

Data Type   String

Data Property

Description   Determines a handle to a memory or graphical device interface (GDI) object containing data in a specified format; not available at design time.

Usage   [*form.*]*ole*.**Data** [= *data*]

Remarks   You send data to an application that created an object by setting this property. Before using the Data property, set the Format property to determine the type of data contained in the memory or GDI object.

You can get a list of acceptable formats for an OLE object using the ObjectAcceptFormats and ObjectGetFormats properties.

Setting this property to 0 frees the memory associated with the handle.

OLE Automation provides an easier and more reliable solution for sending data and commands to and from an object. If an object supports OLE Automation, you can access the object through the Object property, or using the **CreateObject** and **GetObject** functions.

Data Type   Long

DataText Property

Description   Sends or retrieves a string from the specified OLE object; not available at design time.

Usage   [*form.*]*ole.***DataText** [= *data*]

Remarks   To send a string to an object, first set the Format property to a format the object supports. Use the ObjectGetFormats and ObjectAcceptFormats properties to get a list of formats supported by an object.

When getting data from an object, the DataText property returns the string sent from the object, ending at the first null character.

The DataText string must be less than 64K.

OLE Automation provides an easier and more reliable solution for sending data and commands to and from an object. If an object supports OLE Automation, you can access the object through the Object property, or using the **CreateObject** and **GetObject** functions.

Data Type   String

Example   The example sends data to the Microsoft Graph application, so you must have Graph to run the example. Create a form about half the size of the screen with an OLE control named Ole1 in the top four-fifths of the form and a command button Command1 in the bottom one-fifth. When the Insert Object dialog is displayed, select Cancel. Start the DispTest application.

The DispTest application will transfer focus to the Microsoft Graph application with the Microsoft Graph default data showing. Choose Update from the Microsoft Graph File menu, then click the DispTest application. The default graph data appears in Ole1. Press the command button, and then click Microsoft Graph to see that the data from the DispTest application has been transmitted to Microsoft Graph. Choose Exit and Return from the Microsoft Graph File menu to see the data displayed in Ole1.

```
Sub Form_Load ()
    Ole1.Format = "CF_TEXT" ' Set up link to Graph.
    Ole1.Class = "MSGRAPH"
    Ole1.Action = 0      ' Show default graph in
End Sub                              ' Graph application.

Sub Command1_Click ()
    Dim Msg, NL, TB ' Declare variables.
    TB = Chr(9)         ' Tab character.
    NL = Chr(10)       ' Newline character.
    ' Create data to replace default Graph data.
    Msg = TB + "Drew" & TB & "Lorin" & TB & "Bob"
```

```
                    Msg = Msg + NL & "Eric" & TB & "1" & TB & "2" & TB & "3"
                    Msg = Msg + NL & "Ted" & TB & "11" & tb & "22" & TB & "33"
                    Msg = Msg + NL & "Arthur" & TB & "21" & TB & "32" & TB & "23"
                    ' Send the data through the DataText property.
                    Ole1.DataText = Msg
                End Sub
```

DisplayType Property

Description   Determines if an object displays its contents or an icon.

Usage   [*form.*]*ole*.**DisplayType** [= *setting*]

Remarks   The DisplayType property settings are:

Setting		Description
0 (Default)	Content	When the OLE control contains an object, the object's data is displayed in the control.
1	Icon	When the OLE control contains an object, the object's icon is displayed in the control. This property determines the default setting of the Icon checkbox in the Insert Object and Paste Special dialogs. When you display these dialogs either at run time (set Action to 14 or 15) or design time, the Icon checkbox is automatically selected if this property is set to 1 (Icon). Once an object is created, you cannot change its display type.

Data Type   Integer

FileNumber Property

Description   Determines the file number to be used when saving or loading an OLE object, or reflects the last file number used. Not available at design time.

Usage   [*form.*]*ole*.**FileNumber** [= *filenumber*]

Remarks   The FileNumber must correspond to an open, binary file.

Use this property to specify the number of the file to be opened or saved when setting Action = 11 (Save) or Action = 12 (Read).

Data Type   Integer

Example   The example shows how to save and open the data associated with Ole1 in a file named MYOB.OLE. To run the example you need Microsoft Excel running or on your path. Create a form with an OLE control named Ole1. When the Insert Object dialog is displayed, press Cancel. Place a command button (Command1) on the form. Place a menu named File on the form with two menu items: mnuOpenObject and the other named mnuSaveObject.

Press F5, then press the command button to set the Class and Action properties. Microsoft Excel starts if it is not already running. Enter data in a spreadsheet, then choose Update from the Microsoft Excel File menu to show the data in the OLE control. Choose Save from the example form's File menu. This creates the file in which the OLE object is saved. You can end the example application, start it again and choose Open Object from its File menu to display the object independent of Microsoft Excel. Note that when you do so, the command button is disabled.

```
Sub Command1_Click ()
    Ole1.Class = "ExcelWorksheet"    ' Set class.
    Ole1.Action = 0                  ' Create OLE object.
    Show                             ' Show form with object,
    Command1.Enabled = False         ' then disable button...
End Sub

Sub mnuSaveObject_Click ()
    Dim FileNum                      ' Declare variable.
    FileNum = FreeFile               ' Get a valid file number.
    Open "MYOB.OLE" For Binary As FileNum ' Open file to be saved
    Ole1.FileNumber = FileNum            ' Set the filenumber.
    Ole1.Action = 11                 ' Save the file.
    Close #FileNum                       ' Close the file.    End Sub

Sub mnuOpenObject_Click ()
    Dim FileNum                      ' Declare variable.
    FileNum = FreeFile               ' Get a valid file number.
    Open "MYOB.OLE" For Binary As FileNum ' Open the file.
    Ole1.FileNumber = FileNum            ' Set the filenumber.
    Ole1.Action = 12                 ' Get data from file.
    Close #FileNum                        ' Close the binary file.
    ' Since you've opened the file, disable button that initiates the
        object
    Command1.Enabled = False
End Sub
```

Format Property

Description   Determines the format when setting and getting data from an application that created an object. Not available at design time.

Usage   [*form.*]*ole.***Format** [= *format*]

Remarks   This property determines the format used with the Data and DataText properties.

Use the ObjectAcceptFormats, ObjectAcceptFormatsCount, ObjectGetFormats, and ObjectGetFormatsCount properties to get a list of the acceptable data formats for a specific class of OLE object.

Many applications that provide objects support only one or two formats. For example, Microsoft Draw accepts only the CF_METAFILEPICT format. CF_METAFILEPICT is a string literal and would be assigned as:

```
Ole1.Format = "CF_METAFILEPICT"
```

In many cases the list of formats an object can accept (ObjectAcceptFormats) is different from the list of formats that a object can provide (ObjectGetFormats).

Data Type   String

HostName Property

Description   Determines the friendly host name of your DispTest application.

Usage   [*form.*]*ole.***HostName** [= *name*]

Remarks   When editing an OLE object, the HostName may be displayed in the object's window title. Some applications that provide objects do not display the host name.

Data Type   String

---

lpOLEObject Property

Description   Specifies the address of the OLE object. Not available at design time; read-only at run time.

Usage   [*form.*]*ole.***lpOleObject**

Remarks   Many function calls in the OLE 2 DLLs require the address of an object as an argument. Pass the value specified in the lpOleObject property when making API calls to the OLE 2 DLLs. The value is 0 if no object is currently displayed. If a call is made to an API that makes a callback to the OLE control, the result is unpredictable.

The address returned by this property is a far pointer to the IOleObject interface for the current object.

Data Type   Long

Object Property

Description   Represents the object in an OLE control. Not available at design time; read-only at run time.

Usage   [*form.*]*ole*.**Object**[*.property* | *.method*] [= *setting*]

Remarks   Use this property to specify an OLE object when performing OLE Automation tasks.

You perform OLE Automation tasks on the object using properties and methods the object supports. For information on the properties and methods an object supports, see the documentation for the application that created the object.

Data Type   Long

PasteOK Property

Description   Specifies whether the contents of the Clipboard can be pasted into the OLE control. Not available at design time; read-only at run time.

Usage   [*form.*]*ole*.**PasteOK**

Remarks   When this property returns **True**, the contents of the Clipboard can be pasted into the OLE control.

Use the OleTypeAllowed property to specify the type of object (linked or embedded) that can be pasted into the OLE control. Once an object has been successfully pasted into the OLE control, you can query the OleType property to determine the type of object that was created.

This property can be useful if your application supports an Edit Paste command. If PasteOK is **False**, then the Edit Paste command should be disabled; otherwise it can be enabled. Enable and disable menu commands by setting their Enabled property to **True** and **False**, respectively.

You paste an object into the OLE control by setting Action = 5 (paste).

To provide more flexibility to the user, display a Paste Special dialog (set Action = 15) when the user selects the Edit Paste command. When this dialog is displayed, an object is pasted to the Clipboard based on the user's selections in the dialog.

Data Type   Integer (Boolean)

Example   The example code cannot run by itself, but illustrates how to paste the contents of the Clipboard into the OLE control when the user chooses the appropriate menu item. To see how this works in an application, load the sample program OLE2DEMO.MAK, and place a breakpoint in the mnuEditClick procedure, then press F5 and choose Paste from the Edit menu.

```
Sub mnuEditPaste_Click ()
    ' Check value of PasteOK.
    If Ole1.PasteOK Then
        Ole1.Action = 5              ' Do the Paste if OK.
    Else                             ' Otherwise disable Paste
        mnuEditPaste.Enabled = False ' menu item and give
        MsgBox "Cannot Paste"            ' appropriate message.
    End If
End Sub
```

ObjectAcceptFormats Property

Description   Specifies the list of formats an object can accept. Not available at design time; read-only at run time.

Usage   [*form.*]*ole.***ObjectAcceptFormats** (*index*)

Remarks   ObjectAcceptFormats is a zero-based array of strings describing the valid formats that can be used in the Format property when exchanging data with an object using the Data and DataText properties. ObjectAcceptFormatsCount specifies the number of elements in the ObjectAcceptFormats array.

The list of acceptable formats is obtained from an object. If the OLE control does not contain an object, an error will occur when you attempt to access this property.

Data Type   String

To run this example, place an OLE control and three list boxes on a form. When the Insert Object dialog is displayed, select an application in the New Object list box and click OK to create an object. Then paste the example code into the declarations section of the form.

```
Sub Form_Click ()
    Dim I    ' Declare variable.
    ' Update the list of available verbs
    Ole1.Action = 17     ' Fetch verbs
    ' Fill the Verbs list box.
    For I = 0 To Ole1.ObjectVerbsCount - 1
        List1.AddItem Ole1.ObjectVerbs(I)
    Next I

    'Fill the Accept Formats list box.
    For I = 0 To Ole1.ObjectAcceptFormatsCount - 1
        List2.AddItem Ole1.ObjectAcceptFormats(I)
    Next I

    ' Fill the Get Formats list box.
    For I = 0 To Ole1.ObjectGetFormatsCount - 1
        GetFmtsList3.AddItem Ole1.ObjectGetFormats(I)
    Next I
End Sub
```

ObjectAcceptFormatsCount Property

Description   Specifies the number of formats that can be accepted by an object. Not available at design time; read-only at run time.

Usage   [*form.*]*ole*.**ObjectAcceptFormatsCount**

Remarks   Use this property to get the number of elements in the ObjectAcceptFormats property array.

Data Type   Integer

ObjectGetFormats Property

Description   Specifies the list of formats an object can return. Not available at design time; read-only at run time.

Usage   [*form.*]*ole*.**ObjectGetFormats** (*index*)

Remarks   The list is a zero-based string array. Elements of the array can be used to set the Format property when getting data from an object using the Data and DataText properties.

Data Type   String

ObjectGetFormatsCount Property

Description   Specifies the number of formats an object can provide. Not available at design time; read-only at run time.

Usage   [*form.*]*ole*.**ObjectGetFormatsCount**

Remarks   Use this property to determine the number of elements in the ObjectGetFormats property array.

Data Type   Integer

OleType Property

Description   Specifies the status of an object.

Usage   [*form.*]*ole*.**OleType**

Remarks   The OleType property settings are:

Setting	Description
0 - Linked	The OLE control contains a linked object. All the object's data is managed by the application that created it. When the object is saved (set Action = 11), only link information such as SourceDoc, SourceItem, and so on, is saved in the specified file by your DispTest application.
1 - Embedded	The OLE control contains an embedded object. All the OLE object's data is managed with the DispTest application. When the object is saved (set Action = 11), all data associated with the object is saved in the specified file.

Setting	Description
3 - None	The OLE control does not contain an object. Use this property to determine if the OLE control contains an object, or to determine the type of object the OLE control contains. Use the AppRunning property to determine if the application that created the object is running. When creating an object, use the OleTypeAllowed property to determine the type of object that can be created.

Data Type   Integer

OleTypeAllowed Property

Description   Determines the type of object that can be created.

Usage   [*form.*]*ole*.**OleTypeAllowed** [= *setting*]

Remarks   The OleTypeAllowed property settings are:

Setting	Description
0 - Linked	The OLE control can only contain a linked object.
1 - Embedded	The OLE control can only contain an embedded object.
2 (Default) - Either	The OLE control can contain either a linked or an embedded object.

When you allow the user to create an object by displaying the Insert Object dialog (set Action = 14) or the Paste Special dialog (set Action = 15), use this property to determine the type of object the user is allowed to create.

Use the OleType property to determine an object's type (linked, embedded, or none).

Data Type   Integer

ObjectVerbs Property

Description   Returns a list of verbs an object supports. Not available at design time; read-only at run time.

Usage   [*form.*]*ole*.**ObjectVerbs** (*index*)

Remarks   ObjectVerbs is a zero-based string array. Use this property along with the ObjectVerbsCount property to get the verbs supported by an object. These verbs are used by the Verb property to determine an action to perform when an OLE object is activated (set Action = 7).

The first verb in the ObjectVerbs array—ObjectVerbs(0) is the default verb. If the Verb property has not been set, this is the action performed when the object is activated.

The remaining verbs in the array are suitable for display in a menu. If it is appropriate to display the default verb in a menu (in most cases this is true), then the default verb will have two entries in the ObjectVerbs array.

Applications that display OLE objects typically include an Object command on the Edit menu. When the user selects Edit Object, a cascading menu displays the object's verbs. Use the ObjectVerbs, ObjectVerbsCount, and ObjectVerbFlags properties to create such a menu at run time.

The list of verbs an object supports may vary, depending on the state of the object. To update the list of verbs an object supports, set Action = 17 (Fetch Verbs). Be sure to update the list of verbs before presenting it to the user.

To automatically display the verbs in the ObjectVerbs array in a pop-up menu when the user clicks an object with the right mouse button, set the AutoVerbMenu property to **True**.

Note Each object supports three special verbs which may or may not be listed in the ObjectVerbs property. These verbs are represented by the values 0, −1, −2, and −3. They are used by the Verb property to show, open, or hide an object.

Data Type   String

ObjectVerbsCount Property

Description   Specifies the number of verbs supported by an object. Not available at design time; read-only at run time.

Usage   [*form.*]*ole*.**ObjectVerbsCount**

Remarks   Use this property to determine the number of elements in the ObjectVerbs property array.

The list of verbs an object supports may vary, depending on the state of the object. To update the list of verbs an object supports, set Action = 17 (Fetch Verbs).

Data Type   Integer

ObjectVerbFlags Property

Description   Specifies the menu state for each verb in the ObjectVerbs array. Not available at design time; read-only at run time.

Usage   [*form.*]*ole*.**ObjectVerbFlags** (*index*)

Remarks   The first verb in the ObjectVerbs array is the default verb. The remaining verbs in this array are suitable for being displayed on a menu. The ObjectVerbFlags array contains information about the menu state (such as grayed, checked, and so on) for each verb in the ObjectVerbs array.

When displaying a menu containing an object's verbs, check the value of this property to see how the item should be displayed.

The following table describes the possible ObjectVerbFlags.

Constant	Value	Description
MF_CHECKED	&H0008	The menu item should be checked.
MF_DISABLED	&H0002	The menu item should be disabled (but not grayed).
MF_ENABLED	&H0000	The menu item should be enabled.
MF_GRAYED	&H0001	The menu item should be grayed.
MF_SEPARATOR	&H0800	The menu item is a separator bar.

Data Type   String

SizeMode Property

Description   Determines how the OLE control is sized or how its image is displayed when it contains an object.

Usage   [*form.*]*ole*.**SizeMode** [= *setting*]

Setting	The SizeMode property settings are:

Setting	Description
0 - Clip (Default)	The object is displayed in actual size. If the object is larger than the OLE control, its image is clipped by the control's borders.
1 - Stretch	The object's image is sized to fill the OLE control.
2 - Autosize	The OLE control is resized to display the entire object.

Data Type	Integer

SourceDoc Property

Description	Determines the file name to use when you create an OLE object.
Usage	[*form.*]*ole*.**SourceDoc** [= *filename*]
Remarks	You use the SourceDoc property to specify the file to be linked when creating a linked object (set Action = 1). You use the SourceItem property to specify data within the file to be linked.

When creating an embedded object (set Action = 0), if the SourceDoc property is set to a valid file name, an embedded object is created using the specified file as a template.

When a linked object is created, the SourceItem property is concatenated to the SourceDoc property. The SourceDoc property then returns the entire path to the linked file along with any SourceItem information. For example:

```
"C:\WORK\QTR1\REVENUE.XLS!R1C1:R30C15"
```

When the SourceItem is concatenated to the SourceDoc property, the SourceItem property returns an empty string.

Data Type	String

The example creates a linked OLE object when the user clicks the command button. First, use Microsoft Excel to create a spreadsheet named OLETEST.XLS. Then create a form with an OLE control named Ole1. When the Insert Object dialog is displayed, choose Cancel. Place a command button on the form and copy the following code into the form's declarations section, then press F5.

The file OLETEST.XLS must exist in the specified path.

```
Sub Command1_Click
    ' Set class.
    Ole1.Class = "ExcelWorksheet"
    ' Specify source file.
    Ole1.SourceDoc = "C:\EXCEL\OLETEST.XLS"
    ' Specify the data within the file to be linked.
    Ole1.SourceItem = "R1C1:R5C5"
    ' Create a linked object using OleTest.xls.
    Ole1.Action = 1
    Ole1.Refresh' Show the worksheet.
End Sub
```

SourceItem Property

Description   Determines the data within the file to be linked when you create a linked object.

Usage   [*form.*]ole.**SourceItem** [= *stringexpression*]

Remarks   OleTypeAllowed must be set to 0 (Linked) or 2 (Either) when using this property. Use the SourceDoc property to specify the file to link.

Each object uses its own syntax to describe units of data. To set this property, specify a unit of data recognized by the object. For example, when you link to Microsoft Excel, you specify the SourceItem using a cell or cell-range reference such as "R1C1" or "R3C4:R9C22."

To determine the syntax to describe a unit of data for an object, see the documentation for the application that created the object.

Tip   You may be able to determine this syntax by creating a linked object at design time using the Paste Special command (click the OLE control with the right mouse button). Once the object is created, select the SourceDoc property in the Properties window and look at the string in the Settings box. For most objects, this string will contain a path to the linked file, followed by an exclamation mark (!), or a backslash (\) and the syntax for the linked data.

When a linked object is created, the SourceItem property is concatenated to the SourceDoc property. At run time, the SourceItem property returns an empty string ("") and the SourceDoc property returns the entire path to the linked file, followed by an exclamation mark (!) or a backslash (\), followed by the SourceItem. For example:

```
"C:\WORK\QTR1\REVENUE.XLS!R1C1:R30C15"
```

StringUpdateOptions Property

Description   Determines how an object is updated when linked data is modified. Not available at design time.

Usage   [*form.*]*ole*.**UpdateOptions** [= *option*]

Remarks   The UpdateOptions property settings are:

Setting	Description
0 - Automatic (Default)	The object is updated each time the linked data changes.
1 - Frozen	The object is updated whenever the user saves the linked document from within the application in which it was created.
2 - Manual	The object is updated only when the Action property is set to 6 (Update). This property is useful for linked objects where other users or applications can access and modify the linked data.

When an object's data is changed, the Updated event is invoked.

Data Type   Integer (Enumerated)

Verb Property

Description   Specifies an operation to perform when an OLE object is activated (Action = 7).

Usage   [*form.*]*ole*.**Verb** [= *verbnumber*]

Remarks   Each object can support its own set of verbs. For example, many objects support the verbs "edit" and "play". Use the ObjectVerbs and ObjectVerbsCount properties to access the list of verbs supported by an object. Set Verb = 1 to specify the first verb in the list, set Verb = 2 to specify the second verb in the list, and so on.

These standard verbs are supported by every object:

Value	Action
0	The default action for the object.
-1	Activates the object for editing. If the application that created the object supports in-place editing, the object is activated within the OLE control.
-2	Opens the object in a separate application window. If the application that created the object supports in-place editing, the object is activated in its own window.
-3	For embedded objects, this verb hides the application that created the object.

Note These verbs may not be listed in the ObjectVerbs property array.

Set AutoActivate = 2 (Double-Click) to automatically activate an object when it is double-clicked by the user.

Set AutoVerbMenu = **True** to display a pop-up menu containing the object's verbs when the user clicks the object with the right mouse button.

Data Type   Integer

Updated Event

Description   Occurs when an object's data has been modified.

Syntax   **Sub** *OLE*_**Updated** (*Code* **As Integer**)

Remarks   *Code* indicates how the OLE object was updated. Its possible values are:

Value	Constant	Description
0	OLE_CHANGED	The object's data has changed.
1	OLE_SAVED	The object's data has been saved by the application that created the object.
2	OLE_CLOSED	The file containing the linked object's data has been closed by the application that created the object.
3	OLE_RENAMED	The file containing the linked object's data has been renamed by the application that created the object.

A P P E N D I X   A

Questions and Answers

This appendix includes answers to many common questions asked by developers implementing OLE Automation objects and controllers.

Questions about GUIDs

Globally unique identifiers (GUIDs) appear in multiple places in a typical OLE Automation application. GUID errors make for pernicious bugs. This document is meant to save you time and effort. It describes all the places GUIDs appear in a typical OLE Automation application and some common GUID bug characteristics. Finally, it offers some GUID management techniques.

The Basics

GUID: a globally unique identifier. Same as a UUID.

UUID: a universally unique identifier. Same as a GUID.

CLSID: a class identifier—an identifier (UUID/GUID) used to refer to a class.

Registry

The system registry is a central repository containing information about objects. GUIDs are used to index that information. You can view the registration information on your machine by running "RegEdit /v". Usually a name is connected to a GUID (that is, "hello.hello" maps to a GUID) and then the GUID is connected to all the other relevant aspects (that is, the GUID maps to "hello.exe").

A GUID/UUID/CLSID is created by the tool GUIDGEN.EXE. Running GUIDGEN.EXE produces a huge hex number which uniquely identifies your object, whether it be a class, an interface, a library, or some other kind of object.

Where GUIDs live

.REG files

> When you create an application, you'll usually create one or more .REG files. Your .REG files contain the GUIDs for the classes that your application exposes. These GUIDs are added to the registry when you run RegEdit.Exe to register your classes.

The system registry

> The system registry contains the GUIDs for your classes in multiple places. This is where OLE and applications get information about your classes.

.ODL files

> When you describe objects in an Object Description Language (ODL) file, you provide a GUID for each object. Compiling the .ODL file with MkTypLib.Exe places the GUIDs in a type library, which usually exists as a .TLB file. If you change a GUID in an .ODL file, make sure that you run MkTypLib again.

.TLB files

> Type libraries describe your classes, and this information includes the GUIDs for the classes. You can browse .TLB files using the TiBrowse sample application supplied with OLE.

.h files

> Most application developers will declare CLSIDs for their classes in a header file using the DEFINE_GUID macro.

GUID and Registry Troubleshooting

"DispTest's GetObject can't seem to create an instance of my application."

▶ **DispTest uses OLE calls to find out where to get the .EXE file that creates your application instance. To do this, DispTest does the following steps:**

1. A call is generated to look up the GUID for your object. For the hello application, this means changing "hello.hello" into a GUID.

2. A call is generated to find the "LocalServer" for the object. This is "hello.exe" for the hello application.

3. A call is generated to launch the application.

There is a lot of room for error in this area. Ask yourself the following questions, and you'll probably find the root of the problem:

- Did I remember to run the .REG file?

- Are the entries in the registry correct? Do all the GUIDs match?

- Can my application be launched? The executable for the application, listed in the LocalServer entry, should be on the path **or** it should be fully specified, as in "c:\hello\hello.exe."

"When I use DispTest's GetObject, the application launches and then the GetObject call fails."

Normally, a class factory is registered using CoRegisterClassObject when your application is started. Some applications only register their class factories when launched with the /Automation switch. If you inherited someone else's code, or copied a sample, you should find out whether or not you are testing for this switch. The /Automation option could appear in the .REG file, the registry, and in your development environment.

"GetTypeInfoOfGuid() is failing to get the type information from my type library."

This behavior can occur if the GUID in your code is not the same as the GUID in your .TLB file. When you call GetTypeInfoOfGuid, you provide a GUID. If this GUID doesn't match the GUID in your .TLB file, no type information will be returned. Check that the GUID in your code matches the GUID in your .TLB file. The GUID in your code is likely to be declared in a header file. You can check the GUID in your .TLB file by using TiBrowse, which is provided with OLE.

GUID Management Techniques

The problem is not that managing GUIDs is difficult, but that they are pervasive, and their length prohibits a simple comparison.. This section describes some GUID management techniques which will take you a few minutes, but could save you hours.

Recommendation

Keep a central list of all the GUIDs you have ever consumed. An easy way to do this is to run GUIDGEN.EXE several times, and place the resulting strings in the first column of a spreadsheet. As you consume GUIDs, use the second column to enter a description of what the GUID was used for.

Benefits

- Putting all the GUIDs in one location may prevent you from accidentally reusing a GUID. This often happens when you clone an application in order to create another one.

- You can use the spreadsheet to compare GUIDs. You can check that a GUID is correct by copying it from the place it is being used (a .REG file, for example), pasting it into the spreadsheet, and then comparing the two cells with the "="operator.

- You'll have a record of your GUID use in case of future problems, and you'll only need to look in one place to find out what the GUID is for your object.

How OLE Automation Compares Strings

This section describes how the OLE Automation implementations compare strings. Understanding these comparisons is useful when creating applications that support national languages that use accents and diagraphs. The information in this section affects these components:

- **CreateStdDispatch** (OLE2DISP.DLL)
- **DispGetIDsOfNames** (OLE2DISP.DLL)
- **ITypeLib::FindName** (TYPELIB.DLL)
- **ITypeLib::GetIDsOfNames** (TYPELIB.DLL)
- MkTypLib (MKTYPLIB.EXE)

When comparing strings, OLE Automation components use the following rules:

- Comparisons are sensitive to locale based on the string's LCID. A string must have an LCID that is supported by the application or type library. Locales and LCIDs are described in Chapter 10, "National Language Support Functions."
- Accent characters are ignored. For example, the string "à" compares as the same as "a."
- Case is ignored. For example, the string "A" compares as the same as "a."
- Comparisons are sensitive to digraphs. For example, the string "Æ" is not the same as "AE."

Glossary

A

Application object An object that identifies the application to the system. This object is specified by the appobj attribute in the type library. Typically, the Application object becomes active when the application starts.

C

Collection object A grouping of exposed objects. You create collection objects when you want to address multiple occurrences of an object as a unit, such as when you want to draw a set of points.

E

Exposed object See OLE Automation object.

I

Interface One or more well-defined base classes providing member functions that, when implemented in an application, provide a specific service. Interfaces may include compiled support functions to simplify their implementation.

M

Methods Member functions of an exposed object that perform some action on the object, such as saving it to disk.

O

OLE Automation controller An application or scripting language that accesses OLE Automation objects. DispTest and Visual Basic are OLE Automation controllers.

OLE Automation object An instance of a class defined within your application that is exposed for access by other applications or programming tools by means of OLE Automation interfaces.

Object Description Language (ODL) The language used to describe an application's interface. ODL scripts are compiled into type libraries using the MkTypLib tool included with the OLE 2 SDK.

P

Programmable object See OLE Automation object.

Property A data member of an exposed object. Properties are set or returned by means of get and put accessor functions.

T

Type description The information used to build the type information for one or more aspects of an application's interface. Type descriptions are written in Object Description Language (ODL). Note that this includes programmable and nonprogrammable interfaces.

Type information Information that describes the interfaces of an application. Type information is created from type descriptions using OLE Automation tools, such as MkTypLib or the **CreateDispTypeInfo** function. Type information may be accessed through the **ITypeInfo** interface.

Type information element A unit of information identified by one of these statements in a type description: typedef, enum, struct, module, interface, dispinterface, or coclass.

Type library A file or component within another file that contains type information. Type libraries are created from type descriptions using MkTypLib, and may be accessed through the **ITypeLib** interface.

V

Value property The property that defines the default behavior of an object when no other methods or properties are specified. You indicate the Value property by specifying the [default] attribute in ODL.

Index

Symbols

A

Microsoft® Windows NT™ Resource Kit

Microsoft Corporation

This exclusive three-volume Microsoft collection is a comprehensive source of technical information and tools necessary to support Windows NT installations. The *Microsoft Windows NT Resource Kit* includes *Windows NT Resource Guide* (with four 3.5-inch disks), *Windows NT Messages* (with three 3.5-inch disks), and *Optimizing Windows NT* (with one 3.5-inch disk). The three volumes are also available separately.

BONUS! The three-volume set also includes a CD-ROM containing all the disk-based utilities PLUS tools and utilities for RISC-based computers.

Three-volume set boxed with eight 3.5-inch disks and one CD-ROM
$109.95 ($148.95 Canada)   ISBN 1-55615-602-2

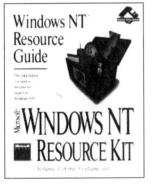

Volume 1:
Windows NT Resource Guide

This complete technical guide to Windows NT features information about installing, configuring, customizing, and troubleshooting Windows NT. It also includes information on applications compatibility and migration from Windows 3.1, MS-DOS, OS/2, and LAN Manager, and using database services with Windows NT. The four disks include more than 50 tools, utilities, and value-added software, including tools to manage users and groups of servers, a computer profile setup to easily set up large groups of workstations, an adapter card Help file, an online registry Help file, and utilities for the POSIX subsystem.

1024 pages, with four 3.5-inch disks
$49.95 ($67.95 Canada)
ISBN 1-55615-598-0

Volume 2:
Windows NT Messages

An alphabetic reference and online database that provides in-depth, accessible information about Windows NT and Windows NT Advanced Server error and system-information messages. Also includes detailed discussions about Windows NT executive messages and an extensive glossary of common message terms and user actions. The messages have been loaded into a Microsoft Access database with a simple user interface, which enables the user to search the database, add personal notes under a message, back up the database, and print a selected group of messages. The three disks contain a runtime version of Microsoft Access and the Messages database.

624 pages with three 3.5-inch disks
$39.95 ($53.95 Canada)
ISBN 1-55615-600-6

Volume 3:
Optimizing Windows NT

The one resource that provides all the information needed to maximize the capacity and speed of Windows NT, including information on bottleneck detection and capacity planning for the desktop and network. Also includes information on designing and tuning your Windows NT applications for high performance. Included with the book is one disk full of software accessories and utilities for performance monitoring, troubleshooting, fine-tuning, and optimizing PC performance.

608 pages with one 3.5-inch disk
$34.95 ($46.95 Canada)
ISBN 1-55615-619-7

Microsoft Press books are available wherever quality books are sold and through CompuServe's Electronic Mall—GO MSP.
Call 1-800-MSPRESS for direct ordering information or for placing credit card orders.*
Please refer to BBK when placing your order. Prices subject to change.

*In Canada, contact Macmillan Canada, Attn: Microsoft Press Dept., 164 Commander Blvd., Agincourt, Ontario, Canada M1S 3C7, or call (416) 293-8464, ext. 340. Outside the U.S. and Canada, write to International Coordinator, Microsoft Press, One Microsoft Way, Redmond, WA 98052-6399.